Charleston Conference Proceedings 2003

Charleston Conference Proceedings 2003

Edited by Rosann Bazirjian and Vicky Speck

Katina Strauch, Series Editor

LIBRARIES

UNLIMITED

A Member of the Greenwood Publishing Group

Westport, Connecticut • London

Library of Congress Cataloging-in-Publication Data

Charleston Conference (23rd : 2003 : Charleston, S.C.)
    Charleston Conference proceedings, 2003 / Katina Strauch, series editor ; edited by
Rosann Bazirjian and Vicky Speck.
        p. cm.
    Includes bibliographical references and index.
    ISBN 1-59158-217-2 (pbk. : alk. paper)
    1. Libraries—United States—Congresses. 2. Library users—Effect of technological
innovations on—United States—Congresses. 3. Communication in learning and
scholarship—United States—Congresses. 4. Collection management (Libraries)—United
States—Congresses. 5. Library materials—Storage—United States—Congresses. 6. Digital
preservation—United States—Congresses. 7. Libraries and electronic publishing—United
States—Congresses. 8. Collection development (Libraries)—United States—Congresses. 9.
Publishers and publishing—Forecasting—United States—Congresses. 10.
Libraries—Information technology—United States—Congresses. I. Strauch, Katina P.,
1946- II. Bazirjian, Rosann. III. Speck, Vicky H. IV. Title.
Z731.C46   2004
027.073—dc22   2004048735

British Library Cataloguing in Publication Data is available.

Library of Congress Catalog Number: 2004048735
ISBN: 1–59158–217–2

First published in 2004

Libraries Unlimited, 88 Post Road West, Westport, CT 06881
A Member of the Greenwood Publishing Group, Inc.
www.lu.com

Printed in the United States of America

The paper used in this book complies with the
Permanent Paper Standard issued by the National
Information Standards Organization (Z39.48-1984).

10 9 8 7 6 5 4 3 2 1

Table of Contents

Electronic Publishing

Collection Development

Future of the Book

Technology

Users

Preface and Acknowledgments

I was recently at a committee meeting of acquisitions and collection development librarians who were discussing potential additions to the state's digital library. In the course of the meeting, one of the committee members commented on the 2003 Charleston Conference and one of the Lively Lunches that had taken place there. She wanted to make sure that the person who had run the lively lunch returned to Charleston and praised the presentation, saying that she didn't know whether to eat or write. Now many of the papers presented at the 2003 Conference are preserved for us all to read in this volume containing many of the presentations and papers presented there.

The theme of the 2003 Charleston Conference was "The Games People Play." Chapters have been grouped into seven distinct parts dealing with scholarly communication, archiving, electronic publishing, collection development, future of the book, technology, and end users. Our editors for the 2003 conference proceedings are the dedicated professionals Rosann Bazirjian and Vicky Speck.

The 2003 Charleston Conference is over, but the issues, discussions, panels, and papers are preserved here. And in reading over them, you will see some of the energy and changes that come out of the Conference every year. And, referring to the woman's comments above, you can now eat instead of taking notes!

For more information about the Charleston Conference, please visit our Web site: http://www.katina.info/conference.

These papers are the outgrowth of a meeting of professional—librarians, publishers, vendors, aggregators, consultants—who work every day in the scholarly communication chain. We would like to acknowledge the hard work, energy, and invaluable professional expertise of Rosann Bazirjian and Vicky Speck, who have worked tirelessly to collect these papers, edit them, and place them into meaningful categories. These proceedings would not have seen the light of day without Vicky and Rosann.

We would also like to thank Martin Dillon, Julia Warner, Margaret Maybury, and Sharon DeJohn of Libraries Unlimited for their assistance in seeing this book through to completion.

We look forward to seeing you in Charleston November 3-6, 2004!

Katina Strauch

The Charleston Conference is still a major highlight in the conference year for many librarians, publishers, vendors, and other interested parties. The talk is stimulating and provocative, and the topics are either those that everyone has an opinion on or those that are cutting edge that everyone wants to learn about. Almost everyone who has ever attended the Charleston Conference is eager to return because of the exchange among interested parties and the hospitable city of Charleston, South Carolina. Every year more people tell us how much of a learning experience the conference has been for them. This is the fourth year that we've put together the proceedings from the Conference, and we are pleased to share some of the learning experience that we, and other attendees, had at the Conference.

The theme of the 2003 Charleston Conference was "Games People Play." While not all presenters prepared written versions of their remarks, enough did so that we are able to include an overview of such subjects as scholarly communications, usage statistics, digital archiving, acquisitions and collection development, electronic publishing in general, the future of the book, and the user experience. All of these topics are of high interest and can be viewed from multiple perspectives.

Katina Strauch, founder of the conference, continues to serve as an inspiration for us. Her enthusiasm for the conference and the proceedings was infectious. We hope you, the reader, find the chapters as thought-provoking as we did and that they encourage the ongoing dialogue among librarian, publisher, and vendor that can only make the learning and research experience for the ultimate user better.

Signed,

Co-Editors of the 23rd Charleston Conference proceedings

Rosann Bazirjian, Assistant Dean for Technical and Access Services, Pennsylvania State University

Vicky H. Speck, Editorial Director, Serials, ABC-CLIO

Introduction

Our keynote speaker, Stephen Abram, treated conference attendees to a provoking presentation on library users, their needs, and our ability to fulfill them. Mr. Abram presented us with an overview of current technologies and suggestions on how to prosper so that libraries remain viable in this age of electronic change and uncertainty.

Keynote Speech

GROWING UP PAST YOUR GOOGLE™ YEARS: LIBRARIES AND THE NEXT GENERATION OF LEARNERS

Stephen Abram, Micromedia ProQuest

(The PowerPoint slides from the original presentation of this chapter are available at http://www.micromedia.ca/presentations/Charleston.pdf)

Are they—Gen X Y & Z—*really* different?

Were the baby boomers different for having been the first generation to grow up with TV?

Were the baby boomers' parents different for having grown up during a world war?

Were the baby boomers' grandparents different for having grown up during a depression?

Are they—Gen X Y & Z—really different?

Of course they are! And why not?

Gen X is the first generation to have had personal computing for their entire lives.

Gen Y is the first generation to have the WWW for every high school year.

Gen Z is the first generation that will live wirelessly on the Web for most of their lives.

As a child spawned in the fifties, I still wait for the robot that will clean my house and cook my food, the jetpack that will lift my earthbound body to the skies, and the teleporter that will make my travel independent of vehicles, space, and time. But wait, there's hope.

- In 1999, Lene Hau, a Harvard physicist, rode a bicycle at the speed of light. She's not a racer; she's a physicist at Harvard University. Her trick was that she accomplished this by slowing light down—to an incredible 60 kilometers (37 miles) an hour. And in 2002, she stopped light dead in its tracks—from 300 million meters (186,000 miles) per second to a dead stop.

- On June 17, 2002, a team of physicists at the Australian National successfully teleported a laser beam of light from one spot to another—yes, actually taking a laser beam in one location and rebuilding it in a different spot about one meter away—just like *Star Trek*!

- Indeed, in August 2001, researchers at the Max Planck Institute for Biochemistry performed an experiment in which a living organism's biological neurons were directly linked and communicated bidirectionally to a silicon chip for the first time. Scary and exciting at the same time, it opens the door for those advanced bionics we imagined on TV shows and links between real and artificial intelligence.

My goodness! Who are we to say what's possible or impossible anymore? The line between imagination and reality blurs further every day. Our challenge as the strategic leaders of libraries in this new millennium is to build the libraries that will meet the needs of the next generation—a generation that is significantly different from most of us. This generation will likely live past the year 2070, and their ultimate journey will see changes greater than those who traveled the last century up to now. We cannot let the limits of our own thinking and experience stop us from creating the information universe that will lift this generation up to new plateaus of innovation, discovery, and insight.

As a profession we've nailed a few things—print, text, word-based content. We're still challenged by a few others like pictures, sound, and video. Nonprint content is emerging as a *hot* issue because sounds have left the world of physical objects like tapes and CDs and become pretty virtual as MP3s; static pictures have stopped being primarily on paper and have mutated into a variety of formats like JPEG and TIFF and GIF; while movies, slide shows, DVDs, and videotape have escaped their physical chains into a multitude of MPEG and other digital streaming media formats. This is just so exciting and such a challenge for information professionals whose stock in trade is being able to find and deliver the best of everything, from the past and in the present. What tools are emerging for us to handle this onslaught of opportunity? It certainly feels like tracking, indexing, searching for, and finding this stuff is like holding water in our hands.

A new and comprehensive report from the Canadian Coalition for School Libraries shows that students who attend schools with well-funded, well-stocked libraries managed by qualified teacher-librarians have higher achievement, improved literacy, and greater success at the postsecondary level. The study, "The Crisis in Canada's School Libraries: The Case for Reform and Reinvestment," was written by Dr. Ken Haycock, professor and former director at the Graduate School of Library, Archival and Information Studies at the University of British Columbia. "The evidence is there for all to see," says Dr. Haycock. "That's why governments in the U.S., Europe and Asia are aggressively investing in their school libraries." (Free copies of this excellent report can be downloaded at http://www.peopleforeducation.com/librarycoalition/Report03.pdf).

What's disturbing is that policy makers are ignoring the findings of literally decades of research internationally that shows why libraries and qualified information professionals and teacher-librarians are essential components in academic achievement. Sadly this both neglects the opportunity to lift up the learner and ignores the essential impact that librarians have on the learner's experience and learning success.

What do we do? It's time to take the proverbial bull by the horns and, as library and learning specialists, anticipate future student and school needs and future (and current) technologies in the service of learning. In this chapter I explore a few key trends in the technology arena that will have a major impact on libraries, our user populations, our students' futures, and therefore our services.

Many of these trends will have a greater impact than the Web has had in the past decade! The Web stuff was a mere acorn compared to the oak of change coming down the pipeline. As a futurist I have developed a keen eye for identifying those trends that will make a difference. As librarians, we can make a difference by understanding what's coming, learning how it works, seeking key benefits for our learners, and becoming that resource that lifts our users up to their full potential.

For the purposes of this chapter, I see five key groups of trends coming down the pipe in the next few years:

- What will search and find look like in the next three to five years?

- What will the Web look like?

- What end-user devices will be popular?

- What will our learning and work environments be?

- What are our school libraries' micro-trends?

Search, Find, and Display

We're about to see the greatest mutation of the search paradigm ever. Until now, the Web search engines have been pretty much word searchers that searched inverted indexes and, more recently, applied relevancy algorithms to their results instead of the less-than-satisfying alphabetical or chronological results lists of olden times. These were just ranked lists and pointers to resources.

Take a look at some of these recent newcomers and how they've changed the face of "search." Do end-users need training anymore? Do they need intermediaries or search coaches? Yes, they surely do—but we need to understand the changed technology, too.

These search engines have different ways of adding value to search. Some do it through insights into the nature of "discovery," and some just display the results better for quicker access. The focus of the search engine designer has moved from the search box and algorithms to making results display more usefully on a basic learning level.

So, one major trend in search is to create a visual display that looks like a map or folders or a solar system or some other metaphor that shows the relationships and dimensionality of the information in the content—derived from the internal taxonomies, thesauri, or proprietary algorithms. This is very interesting and has a great deal of potential. Some of the most interesting are KartOO.com, WebBrain.com from TheBrain.com, InXight, iLOR, Antarcti.ca, and Vivisimo. Playing with these new-style search and display services will provide insights into where and how our user populations will be exploring the Web next.

The other major trend is to not just visually map a search result but to organize the hits—not just public Web hits. These tools can be licensed and tuned to our intranets, OPACs, and invisible Web resources. Sometimes these look like folders that mirror the metadata in the source, sometimes they create metadata on the fly through sources they choose—as minor as a *Roget*'s or as proprietary and high value as MESH or LCSH headings and metadata trees. Some look like editorially (human) organized links, but they're not. You can see how some of this works using the tools from Applied Semantics and WiseNut.

We are also feeling growing pressure, as librarians, to be more timely and to predict content that users want before they know it exists or that they need it. We need to keep our eyes on the tools for proactive and personal alerting—tools like the Google Alerts, Mind-it, and Spy-on-it—and use specialized bots to create customer seek and find searches while we sleep.

The beloved Google had better evolve and adapt, too. In the search engine world, survival of the fittest rules. We're already seeing Google offering a multitude of new services (and ads) that index and serve up many information formats besides the traditional HTML and loads of new additions including some media and beyond PDF options. Indeed, Google has already announced that it will be offering search-inside-the-book features as well as links to library records and locations through OCLC. Some of these formats aren't just text—they're a peek into the multimedia future. As librarians who train searchers we have a critical responsibility to teach budding searchers how to choose the right resource to search. If search results are manipulated by advertisers or search engine optimization specialists with other priorities than "clean" results, our learners could enter a world in which they may have their "answers" manipulated in nefarious ways.

Are we ready for multimedia searching? As more and more valuable, but nontext, information is stored and accessible via the Web, we'd better be. We're starting to see picture search go on steroids—lots o' muscle. Take a gander at what Google Images, AltaVista, BayTSP.com, and MS Corbis are doing. In the new music search engines—some pretty amazing stuff here, too—we see the potential to tap into words buried in streaming sound. Are you ready to search full motion streaming digital video? Take a look at such neat stuff as the new video search engines like those from LTU Technologies that allow for the very easy searching, indexing, filtering, monitoring, and segmenting of streaming media. The days of the slide and tape shows of my youth are definitely dead!

Are we ready for multilingual searching? How about being able to easily search other languages when they are buried and wrapped in a picture or graphic? A lot is happening in this space. WiseNut has Korean and Japanese options, among others, for its visual search. The majority of fairly decent but not perfect Web-based language translations can be handled at AltaVista's Babel Fish and Babylon.com. Babylon also offers thousands of multilingual thesauri along with a new feature that offers male and female voices giving English word pronunciation. KartOO has French, Italian, Spanish, German, and Portuguese visual thesaural implementation for search. My children, who get their education in French immersion schools, can search the Web and find French native-language-based sites displayed in a French taxonomy. Imagine the power of a French or Portuguese controlled vocabulary being displayed as a constellation, and you can see how cool KartOO is.

What's Next for the Web?

First we're entering an era in which the databases are going to get even more massive. Simple original source materials, like historical newspapers, are huge databases. The Pages of the Past product, which covers all editions of the *Toronto Star* since 1894, is two terabytes of images and two million broadsheet pages of searchable text and images alone. ProQuest's *New York Times* searchable historical newspaper image database is even bigger. Learners can now view, easily, the original news report of topics like the Civil War, slavery, civil rights, and more. These tools bring history to life but require new and different, albeit easily learned, searching and database skills. The role of information literacy training will grow, not diminish, with the coming generations of learners. Being computer literate is not information literacy. The issues of finding (not just searching) both the visible and the invisible Web will challenge our schools, our learners, and our society in coming years.

It's becoming clearer that the search "problem" on the Web may end up being solved by some solutions that resemble PC games more than what we see today: navigating a three-dimensional space using such currently crude tools as joysticks, and gloves and eyeball goggles! Imagine a situation in which the result of your search is reached by a very complex path: The research result is the "princess" you're saving at the end of the game. You have to pick up clues by going through many doors as you seek to solve the issue at hand. Search and find will happen like this, and we've trained an entire generation, the video gamers, to explore information/problem space this way. It may be that kids who aren't allowed to be "gamers" will be somewhat information disabled in the future.

The next-generation, but by no means final, architecture of the Internet and Web is already here. You can see this in the file sharing (so called P2P or peer-to-peer) protocols that don't require Web pages or HTML to share information or any digital objects (images, documents, whole Web sites, records, learning nuggets, etc.). Combine this trend with our emerging "why" generation, who so easily share and retrieve files through Napster clones like

Gnutella, KaZaA, and Morpheus, and we can see that the future is more than sharing MP3s and DVDs: It's likely to extend to any digitizable object.

Peer architecture is closely related to things that are near and dear to our library hearts—full text, full image, and full article delivery. We are seeing the emergence of industry standard advanced intelligent linking services that allow us to combine our abstract and indexing services—those services that we know are necessary for accurate and productive search and find—with access to our Web-based periodical subscriptions and collections. The standard is called OpenURL, and you can see this as standard fare in the products and strategic plans from Ingenta, Catchword, Ovid, Infotrieve, OCLC, and ProQuest. It allows us to create Webliographies and pathfinders that access the rich resources of our Web and licensed collections.

What Devices Are Coming Down the Pipe?

First, I think it's pretty clear that soon the PC will not be the dominant electronic tool or even access device—it mightn't be now. Clearly laptops outsell desktops now, and handheld devices outsell both. Several things are happening that we need to watch and adapt to. We must try to explore and understand how this will play out in our students' future, not just in the present. First of all, we are seeing increasing use of flat screens. This isn't just about saving space on desktops—it's about moving products, services, and information to where the users are—so we are seeing screens appearing on our freezer doors, refrigerators, microwaves, walls, countertops, and desks. These appliances are already in the high-end stores and are common overseas. Imagine what it will mean to libraries when screens are paper-thin and can be applied anywhere—even on our book stacks! Now imagine them being wireless . . . .

Yes—wireless is another obvious trend that many libraries are adapting to very quickly. Some schools and campuses are trapped in buildings that limit their technological flexibility. It's just too expensive to wire through poured concrete, asbestos, urea formaldehyde, or historically important buildings. Many institutions have already discovered that such technological solutions as wireless SkyPort drops, WiFi, and Bluetooth can work around these limits cost-effectively and strongly enhance service and access.

Alongside the current penetration of the kid market with cell phones and pagers, we see the proliferation of Palm Pilots, RIM Blackberries, WorldPhones, and DoCoMo devices worldwide. Indeed, it's a rare new PCS digital phone that doesn't come with, or have options for, MP3 players, radio, browsers, e-mail, streaming media TV, or voice recognition. It will be this generation that uses these devices as a primary access and communication tool. Indeed, their adoption of instant messaging is already clear. Text messaging is increasing in popularity worldwide. Google is already beta-testing voice-based searching through the phone.

Some libraries are supporting nomadic computing in recognition that this is where their users are heading, and it's a strong opportunity to improve service. Mount Sinai Hospital library in Toronto has made the wireless plunge and offers many key databases available through doctors' and other health professionals' Palm Pilots at the bedside. Information now truly needs to be where the users' decisions are, not where they have to go. Doctors can check a drug's contradictions as they prescribe it. Our learners will enter a world as adults that will be more in motion than ever—our users are moving targets.

Finally, we can't forecast what's next without tipping our hats to *2001: A Space Odyssey*—"Talk to me Hal." Voice recognition (VR) is almost ready for prime time. Many of us use it when we call 411 and give our answer to the computer's query, "What city please?" We're seeing ever more amazing things from Dragon NaturallySpeaking, IBM ViaVoice Pro, RocketTalk.com, and Philips Speech Processing FreeSpeech. Microsoft XP was released with VR built right in. It doesn't take a genius to see this turning any telephone into a speak-search-and-read-it-to-me device, especially since no rational person wants to use the telephone button pad as an interface.

The Federated Search Opportunity

Federated search is a major innovation. It leaps and bridges the gap between information need and searching. Knowing how to search is a far cry from knowing where to search. Familiar OPAC vendors and shared cataloging utilities are joined by specialized software providers including MuseGlobal, Serials Solutions, WebFeat, ENCompass, OCLC Site Search, Auto-Graphics Agent, SIRSI Single Search, and Innovative's MetaFind. We are already seeing early evidence that usage statistics go up astronomically (possibly 400%+) when libraries provide a federated search tool.

Key Strategic Moves with OpenURL

OpenURL is a major new international standard that allows for content and metadata to find and connect with each other. Sometimes called link resolver technology, it's easier to understand when we know that when it is implemented on an enterprise or institutional level, all licensed and publicly available content can find, for example, your legal copy of a full text article from any index, citation, Webliography, or abstract service your users are searching and, like magic, pull up the needed content instantly. Most major aggregators, including ProQuest, have adopted this standard. It provides probably one of the best opportunities in many years for libraries to increase their relevance to the core mission of their host institutions. Examples of strategies that might be worth considering include the following:

- *The DNA Play:* Work with your course developers using Blackboard or other e-learning tools to integrate library-accessible content at the lesson level or directly into course-support Web sites. Professors, university departments, and course developers will love the access and ease of use, and copyright compliance is made easy. Increased value is derived from all library assets and subscriptions. E-learning support at the point of need is a valuable tactic that makes the library relevant in a direct way to the user and professor.

- *The Student Play:* Assist students by adopting their preferred mode of Web access. Create "Smart Pathfinders" that are more than bibliographies and pointers but actually link directly to the actual full text of articles, Web site digital content, and digital objects.

- *The OPAC Play:* Let's remember what an OPAC is in the first place: services, access, selection, and collection development aimed at a special need and driven by your organization's reason for being. OPACs can come alive when OpenURL-enabled content is loaded and directly accessible by all permissioned users, often without the need to be located in the library.

- *The Lawsuit Play:* Make it legal—cheaply and easily. Libraries license legal copies of articles for their authorized users. We have learned from the challenges brought by Tasini, Texaco, and others that we can provide the tools that ensure our institutions can reduce their risk of noncompliance. With ever more creativity and innovation in the electronic use of copyrighted materials, the OpenURL standard can be used to easily mitigate financial risk.

- *The Community Play:* Look at IP authentication differently—it actually clearly defines a *community*. It's not just about compliance with license terms. When you create an IP-authenticated community you create a market or community of users that can be seamlessly matched to the collections, services, and tools provided by the library. OpenURL allows you to reduce the distance between your users and their ultimate need for direct access to information.

- *The Partner Play:* Using OpenURL public libraries can create alliances with other players in their community. For example, the public library could ally with the city's department of parks and recreation and create Webliographies and tools using articles and tools about, for example, sports or coaching, and providing these right where citizens with library cards are using the parks and recreation Web site. Cool!

- *The Vanity Play:* Vanity sites can be a powerful tool for flattery of key users. You have databases that may contain articles written by your professors, or news about your brand or institution, or articles about your company. You can quickly and easily create a hyperlinked Webliography that flatters the professor or creates that orientation site for new employees or partners. It is useful and good public relations.

I'll bet you can think of other federated searching and OpenURL innovations that will increase the worth and value of your services to your communities and users.

Work and Learning Environments

This is probably the biggest change that's happening. For years we've been following the technological advance we've termed "convergence." That's pretty well over ("It's so last century!"), and now the challenge will be to converge the content, technology, and librarian services into our learners' context (bricks, clicks, and tricks!): moving library services to where they need it, not just when.

We can call this new environment a "collaboratory." This can be envisioned as a blended and overlapping thinking, decision-making, and learning environment. Adding librarian tricks to the bricks and clicks will be the goal. We use lots of terms that show us that this trend is emerging strongly, such as *virtual teams, collaborative digital reference, virtual reference libraries,* and *shared blogs.* This goes beyond virtual classrooms, chat rooms, and videoconferences. It's about communities of interest and communities of practice, and it's also about e-neighborhoods. We're moving to a world in which sharing and integrated, cooperative partnerships will be the norm. These partnerships are developing between teachers, teacher-librarians, boards, parents, vendors, professors, and curriculum professionals. Libraries have been on the edge of some of these trends as we have developed state- and provincewide consortial licensing and services. We have seen the trends toward teaching information literacy for the information- and knowledge-based economy.

There are newer ICQ and Internet Messenger (IM) applications, beyond chat—take a look at things like Groove, PlaceWare, WebEx, Centra, Flypaper, Raindance, or Intranets.com.

We're looking at a new way of working and a new environment in which to offer the services of librarians and researchers.

Another key trend is e-learning or Internet-enabled learning. And, to be honest, we need to acknowledge that learning is the actual human process by which learners and users adapt and absorb information. A blended learning environment is one in which classroom instruction (virtual and live) and distance education courses are combined with e-learning that combines live interactions and learning nuggets delivered in appropriate time frames—asynchronously and asymmetrically to the right work and study environment. If libraries are not integrated into the new blended learning environment, then we will lose relevance to the mainstream of society and education. Our teaching, selection, collection, and service development skills will serve us well in this new environment of buying, supporting, and introducing electronic courseware at the enterprise level.

Some sites to consult for information about this e-learning trend are the Web sites of some of the major providers: Saba, Click2Learn, SkillSoft, Docent, Isopia, and NewMindsets. Many of these e-learning companies are targeting the workspace where our learners will be heading. Many e-learning support tools and courses are also being introduced to the market by the traditional textbook publishers such as Thomson, Pearson, and McGraw-Hill. Some are being developed by the school and academic sector on their own. To be ready for this world of e-learning, we will have to prepare our students not only with the information literacy competencies they need but also with meta-learning skills: knowing how to learn. Librarians and others are well positioned to do this.

If you're interested in actually developing courses or implementing a learning management system, there are wonderful tools and templates to help you. Many librarians have already migrated many of their products, services, and information literacy training to these Web-based environments. This opportunity exists in course management systems like Blackboard, eCollege, WebCT, or Lotus Learning Space.

Another easy-to-adapt opportunity is Web-based presentation management tools. These tools allow you to place voice, video, or objects like PowerPoint™ presentations with voiceover on the Web. We see these types of applications in BrainShark, Presenter, or DoTell.

Library Micro-Trends

There are loads of opportunities in the library sector. One of the biggest is virtual reference or collaborative digital reference services. This is the ability to provide online remote service. This can be as simple as an "Ask a librarian . . . live!" button on your OPAC or library site, Web-based Q&A cafés, or a real-time live-chat, homework helper service. Some interesting things to look at are LSSI's (Library Systems and Services LLC) Virtual Reference Desk or some of the specialized software in customer relationship management or call center applications. We certainly see the day when school libraries will, of necessity, have to keep online "homework helper" hours, through instant messaging, virtual reference tools, or (sadly) e-mail.

So—what about books? We are definitely seeing cool developments in e-book management systems. We're seeing large collections that are actually tied to MARC records, allowing seamless integration into our OPACs. Some of the more interesting ones are MeansBusiness (combines books with abstracted alerts), OCLC/NetLibrary, Element K (combines books with e-learning), ProQuest Safari, and Books24x7.com (now part of the e-learning company SkillSoft), which cover the best of the IT e-books. Note that there are services emerging from Chapters/Indigo, Bordersb and Amazon in the e-books arena. Cliff's Notes can also be easily purchased online and delivered to your e-mail box 24/7.

Finally, fear and loathing are with us to stay. When we talk around the library water cooler these days, hot topics are the threats to our new digital infrastructure. Words that cut to our quick are spam, worms, viruses, denial of service (DoS) attacks, personal information, privacy, PATRIOT Act, patron records, CIPA, DMCA, FBI, Mounties, CIA, and porn filters; need I say more? We are all reminded of our professional role as library workers to protect freedom of expression, patron rights to equity of access, and privacy and intellectual freedom. Keep your armor on, folks! We're suddenly "important" and "informed" on issues that the power brokers and money folks care about.

The strategic window for opportunity for librarians is huge, but keep in mind that it won't be open long. We're about to enter the boomer retirement era. This will be the largest flight of knowledge capital from the open market in history. Knowledge—tacit, explicit, and cultural—will need to be transferred, not just information. The gauntlet has been thrown down for librarianship; use the technology, use our professional skills, learn from others, and we will be so stupendously successful that the world will beat a path to our—virtual—door.

So—if you need a short list of the top 10 trends to watch, here you go:

1. *It's an information ocean, not a highway.* Information literacy skills are about avoiding drowning, and succeeding—not following some predefined path.

2. *It's an "exploration space," not a collection space.* We collect to let learners explore and discover quality learner- and curriculum-appropriate resources and to engage in their own lifelong experience.

3. *It's about learning impact, not information delivery.* It's nice to get the right resource to the right learner at the right time and to keep those stats. It's better to measure the impact of our resources and services on their learning performance.

4. *Entertainment is a solid drive of change, and it's not about paperbacks and Hogwarts' wizards.* Denying the skills kids learn in PC games, MP3s, Web chat, and through interactive TV is foolish and shortsighted.

5. *Lifelong learning is the prime directive.* The days are long gone when you can learn a skill and apply it for a lifetime.

6. *Virtual space is service space.* Using the new tools, we are well positioned to focus on the learner's space and balance that with our partnerships in the classroom space.

7. *Culture trumps everything.* National, ethnic, and local cultures are stupendously important. The differences among us drive changes and unique insight, creativity, innovation, and success in an increasingly global world. Libraries are paths to your own and others' cultural stories and experiences

8. *Information moves.* Static content is the lowest form since primeval data! While text on a page is still critical, libraries will more and more serve up streaming media, sound beyond music and pictures. This supports the real nature of the whole earth as well as the diversity of learning styles among our diverse learning populations.

9. *Fear and loathing are with us to stay*. Learning about electronic safety is a critical skill for the future.

10. And I'll give you one final insight: *Context is king, not content*. If we understand the ecology and culture of our learners we can empower them to ever-higher levels. If we understand our institutions' real mission—creating learners, not the learned—we will succeed wonderfully.

And, this, my friends and colleagues, is our greatest gift. While our foundation is in content of every sort, our essence, our value, and our vision have always been about context. We lift our eyes up and look to see how we take our building blocks—bricks, clicks, and tricks—and apply them in the context of our society, clients, and institutions. We build better learners. We underpin a better, freer democracy. We ensure the long-term success of our institutions. We help inventors, artists, writers, and researchers create the future. Let's never forget that as we step forward to meet the challenges we encounter in this adventure we call librarianship.

The Kids Are All Right!

Many of us adults haven't played an electronic game since the days of Super Mario and Tetris. My, how things have changed! Ten years ago, I recall watching my son, Zachary, and his cousins with their Game Boys. They had their X-wire; all four boys' gaming devices were connected as one network and they were playing a cooperative game in teams. At the time I was challenged at work to get a specialized sector of libraries to network CD-ROMs, and here were 8- to 10-year-old lads seamlessly networking, playing, and collaborating—without assistance—and all under the adult radar.

A July 2003 Pew Internet & American Life report (http://www.pewinternet.org/reports/index.asp) on gaming technology and entertainment among college students showed that 90% of U.S. households had access to gaming technology. Apparently 70% of college students used games regularly and, interestingly; this study showed that more girls than boys in college used electronic games. Electronic games are mainstream, so mainstream, in fact, that many military pilots start their training with a version of Microsoft Flight Simulator that is very close to the military's real training version.

The world that we are preparing students for today is far different than anything we experienced and perhaps than we can imagine. I recall being prepared for the business world of today by taking writing lessons with fountain pens since, according to my teachers, no respectable business "man" would ever use ballpoint or felt pens!

Electronic games are one of the canaries in the mine of this coming shift. We see the almost imperceptible changes happening now. Can we learn from them, or will we just get in their way? Two things—nomadic devices and video gaming—are where we can seek some insight.

First, we can now be pretty sure that the dominant devices that students of all ages will be using for most of their adult lives will be palm-sized. These devices will be wireless, GPS enabled, and offer streaming video, Web search, short messaging and IM, e-mail, beepers, time and calendar management, MP3 players, pocket PC features, voice mail, voice recognition, and more, and all in full color. Oh wait; most phones have nearly all of these already—outside of North America. For the present, though, it is not a trivial fact that you can download new free ring tones for your phone. This easy task is intended to train you how to download to a handheld device—preparing you for the world of downloading MP3s, streaming video, IM, short messaging services, Web sites, business applications, and games—like the rest of the world does.

Electronic gaming is more complex now than we can imagine. It has grown up far beyond the days of Pong, PacMan, and Super Mario. The early days were, in retrospect, simple steps to using controllers and training our eyes and brains to work with a dynamic screen. Super Mario was a great leap forward. You learned a simple skill at level one and practiced it on level two. You learned a new skill on level three, practiced again, and then combined your two new skills at ever higher levels of difficulty and problem solving. We can easily see that games are developed on classic learning scaffold models. What does this have to do with today's kids? Everything.

It is estimated that in the world of the future the corpus of information will double every 11 minutes. Searching this ocean of information will be incredibly difficult. Searching will more closely resemble exploration, navigation, and discovery. Gee—those sound just like the names of popular Web browsers!

Suppose you're a scientist trying to solve the riddle of cancer in 2010. You have access to massive databases containing everything about everyone who has had cancer in the past 20 years. These super-databases are being built now. They will hold everything about each patient and be enhanced with each patient's individual detailed human genome; maps of where patients lived; life, family, and medical histories; and incredibly rich data waiting to be turned into discoveries. One of the ways in which scientists will explore these super-databases is by using the video game interface—*Legend of Zelda*-style—as a model. They will be able to navigate these large and rich resources in self-defined levels, just like the visual maps at the start of the standard quest-style game. Instead of saving the princess at the end of the game, they will find the cure for leukemia.

So, in my opinion, when we deter our kids from ever playing electronic games we are disabling them from acquiring the skills that they will need for their future. After all, the average grade two students today will be living well beyond the year 2075. Consider the changes society has undergone since the Roaring Twenties and we can see that we need to look more closely at the things kids learn from electronic games and discover what we can build on.

Types of Electronic Games

First, electronic games come in a wide variety of formats. These fall roughly into a few types: console games, CD-ROM games, PC-based games, video games, Web-based games, Internet games, digital phone games, and PDA games. Some are proprietary to one format or another, and some can be played in multiple ways and formats. It's a rare device nowadays that doesn't have one game or another on it. Most of our PCs and laptops come equipped with Solitaire. Of course you already know that it's not there for its gaming features. It's there to teach you mouse and cursor control. Then again, it's fun, so it doesn't look like skill acquisition and education.

A Taxonomy of Gaming and What Can Be Learned

Let's start with one of the most popular games on the Internet today—EverQuest (http://everquest.station.sony.com/)—billed as the world's number 1 massively multi-player online game. Hugely popular, this game is a global phenomenon. One of the largest Web sites about the war in Iraq was built inside this game by its gaming community. It plays on multiple devices and requires players to collaborate. Players must develop excellent skills at information handling, creativity, strategy, and collaboration to be successful within this gaming community. It certainly appears that they're modeling behaviors for the real world, too! It is so engaging that there are groups for EverQuest addicts.

Let's look at the basic types of electronic games. The following is not an exhaustive list in any sense, but it shows some key learning supports that can be used by savvy teacher-librarians and educators:

- Adventure and quest-style games

- Collaboration, multi-player games

- Trivia, word games

- Riddles, puzzles, and codes

- Skill games

- Simulation games

- Entertainment

- Action, war, fight, beat-'em and shoot-'em-up games

What useful learning can kids get from these games? Here are just a few examples:

1. *Avatar creation*: Getting some kids to do creative writing can be like pulling teeth. Many electronic games allow, indeed encourage, players to create their own avatar, which is the "body" the player "wears" in a virtual community—an animated, articulated representation of a human that represents the user in any virtual environment. Kids really get into this activity—researching myths and legends, religions, and literary and historical characters. This can engage many reluctant but bright learners in a research-driven, self-paced, creative writing project that supports their specific learning style while developing creativity, composition, and research skills along the way.

2. *Strategy*: Most quest- and adventure-style gaming is built around solving a seemingly unsolvable problem. Players gain confidence as they learn skills, gather evidence and information, and apply it to move through the complex game. Most games are difficult enough that they cannot be easily solved alone. It is somewhat of a myth that these games are the solitary and lonely purview of geeks. These games come in many levels, from the easy to the extremely difficult. Just as we try to teach critical thinking and strategic thinking skills in history and social studies, we will likely find most kids can find a metaphor for any historical event in their gaming environments.

3. *Team skills and collaboration*: Many games require cooperation to succeed. Interestingly, that's often the goal to be learned within the game. Collaborative sharing of information, tale telling of where the player has been and how he or she got there, and learning from others all play well in the gaming world. It's no coincidence that many of these games find their roots in the military and scenario planning software.

4. *Simulation games*: You've seen the names—SimCity, SimFarm, SimWorld, Roller Coaster Sim, or SimGolf. The player builds his or her own city, world, roller coaster, golf course, etc. Everything is dependent on everything else. Kids cannot be successful at the game without learning the basic rules of ecology, urban planning, physics,

and/or human behavior, among other things! It also requires long-term attention to build and create a working community that survives. Each game provides feedback along the way. Players can test their theories and make adjustments. They learn by doing and creating. It is fun and it can be gratifying to accomplish the development of a working prototype. It can be done in group work situations.

5. *Testing, math, logic, riddle, card games, chess, and solitaire*: Classic games taught things in the past and serve the same purpose in their electronic mode. Counting, memory, strategy, and logic all play a role in choosing tactics and playing the game. *Jeopardy* as learning model?

6. *Social skills*: Ha! Surprised that this is here? Most games are supported by Web clubs, blogs, chat rooms, opinion boards, and instant messaging groups. Even Yahoo has developed a few IMvironments to support players. Players learn the unique communication styles and community rules of each group. Bad behavior is disciplined, good behavior rewarded.

A Strategy for Learning?

As outlined above, we can see a few opportunities for bridging the gap between some users' play world and their learning world. In some aspects this can be a magical moment for some kids when they find their gaming skills are useful and applicable to their school and work environments and not an island of fun outside their daily life.

Here are two strategies for teacher-librarians to start drawing upon these opportunities:

1. Get your users or kids to teach you a favorite game or two. You can choose what you'd like to learn—you can outlaw shoot-'em-up games if you like and choose an adventure or quest game. What are you looking for? You're looking to see evidence of the things we are trying to support and build on that professional educators have known make a difference for years: respect for learning styles, understanding of the multiple intelligences, and active learning and engagement.

2. Buy a Sim game. Learn the basics yourself. Project it on the screen and play it as a group, sharing the (wireless?) keyboard. This can be a reward activity—you don't need to let the kids know that you're reinforcing loads of learning exercises across the curricula! You can even play as a group of information pros.

And, oh yeah, early research shows some tantalizing results: that video games are valid learning tools; learning effectiveness is increased in the visual environment; and games stimulated learning, strategic thinking, and planning skills, and focused the attention of ADD learners. Hmmm, maybe there is something to this.

Tying It All Together

The Kids Have Changed

There have been key changes in NextGen behaviors with regard to information searching and exploration:

- They learn differently, and their education was designed with major changes to ensure that their thinking and information exploration styles are more diverse than the generations that preceded them.

- They're nomadic. They have the tools to avoid being tied down to stationary information appliances, and this changes their behavior and expectations.

- They converse online with IM and use letter-style communications like e-mail less often. In this manner they can multitask, with multiple conversations occurring simultaneously.

- They're visual learners and can adapt information in many ways other than traditional text-based lists and links.

- They are format agnostic and use all formats, including streaming media and sound. Text-based information is but one format to them in a plethora of useful information presentation styles.

- Games are a model for them, and the decision making and exploration spaces of video gaming metaphors are a very comfortable mode for them.

They're going to be all right! They will use most of the tools and adapt to many of the trends I've outlined in this paper. And libraries will be all right too, but only if we understand them and understand this next generation's differences and strengths as information users. The new technological tools provide us with a great opportunity. We have the skills and competencies; let's just do it!

Stephen Abram was named by Library Journal *in March 2002 as one of the top 50 people who are shaping the future of libraries and librarianship. He received his MLS from the University of Toronto in 1980. He is the immediate past president of the Ontario Library Association, where he planned and hosted two summits, on the crisis in school libraries and on the vision for a provincewide digital library. In June 2003 he was awarded the highest award of the Special Libraries Association, the John Cotton Dana Award. Also in June 2003 he assumed the role of president-elect of the Canadian Library Association. Stephen's day job is vice president of corporate development for Micromedia ProQuest (Canada), where he influences online, print, Web, and microfilm products such as eLibrary Canada, ProQuest Newsstand, Canadian Business & Current Affairs, CanCorp, and the Canadian Almanac and Directory.*

Selected Free Studies about Trends and NextGen Behaviors

Five Personality Dimensions and Their Influence on Information Behaviour—
   http://informationr.net/ir/9-1/paper165.html
   This article emphasizes the importance of considering psychological mechanisms for a thorough understanding of users of information services. The focal point is the relationship between personality and information seeking, which is explored through a quantitative analysis of 305 university students' personality traits and information habits. It is shown that information behavior could be connected to all the personality dimensions tested in the study: neuroticism, extraversion, openness to experience, competitiveness, and conscientiousness.

Possible explanations for these relationships are discussed. It is concluded that inner traits interact with contextual factors in their final impact on information behavior.

Betraying the College Dream: How Disconnected K–12 and Post-secondary Education Systems Undermine Student Aspirations (Stanford University Bridge Project), March 2003—http://www.stanford.edu/group/bridgeproject/betrayingthecollegedream.pdf

OCLC—www.oclc.org

White Paper on the Information Habits of College Students, http://www2.oclc.org/oclc/pdf/printondemand/informationhabits.pdf

E-Learning Task Force: Full-Text White Paper: Libraries and the Enhancement of E-learning, http://www.oclc.org/index/elearning/default.htm

Dimensions and Use of the Scholarly Information Environment—(CLIR/DLF/Outsell —www.clir.org), http://www.clir.org/pubs/abstract/pub110abst.html

Pew Internet and American Life studies—www.pewinternet.org

The Digital Disconnect: The Widening Gap between Internet-Savvy Students and Their Schools, http://www.pewinternet.org/reports/pdfs/PIP_Schools_Internet_Report.pdf

"College Students and the Web: A Pew Internet Data Memo," September 15, 2002, http://www.pewinternet.org/reports/pdfs/PIP_College_Memo.pdf

The Internet Goes to College: How Students are Living in the Future with Today's Technology, September 15, 2002, http://www.pewinternet.org/reports/toc.asp?Report=71

Counting on the Internet: Most expect to find key information online. Most find the information they seek. Many now turn to the Internet first, December 29, 2002, http://www.pewinternet.org/reports/pdfs/PIP_Expectations.pdf

The Ever-Shifting Internet Population: A new look at Internet access and the digital divide, April 16, 2003, http://www.pewinternet.org/reports/toc.asp?Report=88

E very so often a new theme surfaces among the many presentations and discussions at the Charleston Conference. Even though in previous years some aspects of scholarly communications were discussed; in 2003, the current state of scholarly communications and the impact that libraries and librarians can have on it came through in numerous sessions. A sample of some of the major issues are Open Access, alternative publishing models like SPARC and DSpace, as well as other library publishing initiatives. The fact that models are changing and funding is changing keeps scholarly communication an interesting topic to watch.

PRICING AND OPEN ACCESS

John Cox, Managing Director, John Cox Associates, Ltd.

A Dysfunctional Market

Most of the commentary in our trade press and on listservs has been disparaging about publishers, particularly those in the for-profit sector. I make no excuse for too many lousy publications, or price gouging, or poor customer service. But our market is dysfunctional, and we are all complicit—publishers, librarians, and academics:

- Journals only exist because there are papers submitted to them to publish. Michael Mabe's analysis of the data suggests that roughly 100 additional articles per year are enough to spawn a new journal. Publishers only respond to that demand. In my time at Carfax, we turned down tens of proposals from academics for new journals for every one that we felt was worth launching.

- There has been a fragmentation in disciplines, and in the journals that reflect this fragmentation, as highly specialized subdisciplines are not adequately reflected by the large, established, broad journals.

- Librarians have been unable or unwilling to punish those publishers who have been guilty of excessive pricing and have failed to convince the university community that they need more funding.

- Librarians have directed their rhetoric at an alleged distinction between nasty commercial publishers that suck money out of the scholarly community and saintly non-profit publishers that only put money in, instead of addressing the funding issue and behaving like proper consumers.

- Much of the discussion about scholarly communication is undertaken as if it is a wholly self-contained capsule with no duties to the wider community or acknowledgment that the market for research literature extends into business, professional, and educational markets and ultimately is of relevance and importance to the man and woman in the street.

- The process of academic research and publication is not an island. Those nasty commercial publishers pay tax, which funds much scholarship and research, and pay dividends to university endowment funds. Non-profit publishers in the United States do not pay tax, so make no contribution to institutional expenses.

This relative lack of price resistance has led to dramatic increases in journal costs in the last three decades. Overall, individual journals are more than 30 times more expensive today than they were in 1970. This represents an average annual increase of 13%. There is a cluster of reasons, and considerable evidence, that much of the pressure on prices emanates from

- the growth of research at roughly 3% per year, leading to increases in pages and issues published;

- the cancellation of subscriptions; and

• the increasing trend of institutions to recharge to the journal the overhead incurred by the editorial activities of its staff.

Nevertheless, in 2003 the overall average rate of increase in individual prices was only 6.4%. This is clearly the result of new pricing and purchasing models for electronic information and the disquiet within the academic community itself that is evidenced by SPARC, Create Change, Public Library of Science, and the interest being shown in open access for scholarly literature. It is also the result of the development of resource sharing into formal purchasing consortia. An economist's view is that purchasing consortia will actually distort the market, but it is clear that, in an imperfect market, librarians now have the opportunity collectively to deploy their purchasing power and secure better value for their money.

Open Access—A New Financial Model for a New Breed of Publisher?

Open access has now become the lightning rod for those who want to overthrow the existing business model, or more precisely, to get rid of commercial publishers. Michael J. Held, executive director at Rockefeller University Press, in a thoughtful editorial in the *Journal of Cell Biology*, pointed out that open access is unproven, however superficially attractive the idea of free access to information might be. He points out that the costs of producing any journal are not trivial and include peer review, copyediting, production, distribution (including worldwide online access), search capabilities, and archiving technologies. He sees no reason at the present time to destroy the subscription model until it is clear that these new models are viable.

In its response, the Public Library of Science (PLoS) agrees that the investment in peer review and quality online and print publication has been the vital contribution publishers have made to the process; all that PLoS asks is that those costs be seen as the final step in the research process and as such be funded as part of the project. PLoS is a serious and significant test of this theory and should be treated with respect, as should BioMed Central, the other major—and commercial—exponent of open access. But it remains to be proven if such a business model can be applied generally across scholarly journal publishing and replace a model that has operated for 300 years.

In my studies, including a current project looking at publication costs as part of an EU-funded study of open access, it is clear that the only costs that are removed by open access are those associated with subscription management and distribution. And that only applies if the journal is online only. If a print version is still available on subscription, as with the PLoS model, then those costs cannot be removed. The cost of that "first copy" still remains. Moreover, new costs are incurred, in managing payments from authors or institutional "memberships"—that is, subscriptions by another name. Simply making the material available is not enough; it needs to be marketed, simply to ensure that the intended readership knows about its existence. This is not trivial.

Furthermore, I have been surprised to discover that paying editors and referees for the work they do is more widespread than I had imagined. Reviewers' fees of between $50 and $150 are not uncommon. The commonly accepted position that academics author and referee works without any financial reward is an oversimplification, just as the view that all mergers lead to higher prices is at best an incomplete assessment. But then whoever wanted facts to disturb their prejudices!

At a meeting in April at the Howard Hughes Medical Institute in Maryland, a group of funders, scientists, lawyers, and publishers came up with a definition of open access for individual research articles:

- The author and copyright holder grants all users the free right to access and to copy, transmit the work publicly, and make a small number of printed copies; and

- The work must be deposited in electronic form in a non-profit online repository that seeks to enable open access, unrestricted distribution, interoperability, and long-term archiving.

It is not clear why the online depository is an essential component of online access. Equally puzzling is the retention of copyright by the author as an essential pre-condition of open access. Surely all that is required for open access is that information be made openly and freely available online.

One thing I do know is that a number of major commercial publishers are involved in contingency planning if open access reaches the "tipping point" at which the whole industry will switch business models. Open access will not lead to the demise of the large commercial publisher. If anything, those publishers might well pick up the idea and run with it while the rest of the community continues its debates. Let us wait and see whether open access is a substantive and sustainable development or little more than another bout of rhetoric that enables us to ignore the very real stresses in scholarly publishing.

FAIR PRICING, INFORMATION ASYMMETRY, AND A PROPOSAL TO EVEN THE PLAYING FIELD

Philip M. Davis, Cornell University

Introduction

I was prepared to present a paper at the conference about the crisis in scholarly publishing representing a tragedy of the commons, whereby the individual interests of publishers, scholars, *and librarians* are all in conflict with the best interest of the public good. The talk was all doom and gloom and quite depressing. Instead of delivering something as dark and dreary as the skies over upstate New York, I decided to deliver a ray of sunshine and hope—something that we can do that may lead to a real difference in pricing, something that is perfectly legal, and something that would not require librarians to conspire.

By the way, if you are interested in the tragedy of the commons, that article will be published this month in the library journal *Portal*.

Fair Pricing

It Doesn't Just Come Down to Price

Last year at the Charleston Conference, Stephen Rhind-Tutt from Alexander Street Press argued that pricing models are a red herring—it really comes down to what is a fair price. He writes:

> Pricing models have one purpose—to generate prices that are acceptable to both publisher and customer. It is essential to focus not on searching for the perfect model, but to come up with flexible models that result in the best prices. After all it's about prices, not models.[1]

I used my session to argue that fairness has *everything* to do with the model—not the actual price—and to present something librarians can do to encourage fair pricing models.

Fairness Is a Universal Quality

Fairness is a universal quality among humans, irrespective of culture, and has been demonstrated recently in monkeys. In a letter appearing in September 2003 in the journal *Nature*,[2] Sarah Brosnan and Frans de Waal from Emory University reported a simple experiment. They rewarded monkeys with a piece of cucumber for doing a menial task (returning a token to the researcher), which the monkeys performed diligently each time.

In the second part of the experiment, the monkey's *neighbor* received a grape (something they like to eat much more than cucumbers) for performing the same task. After seeing this, the first monkey was much less willing to perform the task.

In the third part of the experiment, other monkeys were given grapes for doing nothing at all. The monkeys involved in performing the tasks refused to work for mere cucumbers, often throwing the token at the researcher or refusing to eat the reward, which they would have done under almost any other set of circumstances.

This experiment illustrates that monkeys also measure rewards in relative terms, comparing their own rewards to those of others, and respond very negatively if their colleague gets a better deal.

Behavioral economists have used the "ultimatum game" to illustrate this principle of fairness in humans. In this game, two people are given $100 to split. Only one person (the proposer) decides on how the money should be split (50-50, 70-30, etc.) and makes the other person a take-it-or-leave-it offer. If he or she accepts, both people walk away with their share of the money. If he or she refuses, both walk away with nothing.

In theory, the receiver should accept any amount of money—even a dollar is better than nothing. But in practice this rarely happens. Most people would rather reject a bad deal than watch someone else walking away with too much. Essentially, people are willing to punish those they believe are acting unfairly, even when doing this brings no benefit to them. This type of behavior is what economists call the principle of "strong reciprocity," and it makes markets work more fairly. In the ultimatum game, the proposer usually ends up offering something relatively close to an equal split to ensure that the other accepts.

These behavioral studies suggest that it is all about the pricing model and not about the price.

Fairness Requires Information Transparency

Fairness requires information transparency. Monkeys would go on accepting pieces of cucumber while their mates were receiving juicy grapes just as long as no one knew what the others were receiving.

In the same way, we could argue that preventing libraries from sharing information on how much they paid for a certain product through confidentiality ("gag") clauses protects everyone's sense of fairness—if you don't know that someone else got a better deal, and the publisher gave you the impression that you fought them every step of the way, you may believe that you got a fair deal—just as long as you don't find out that someone else got a better deal.

One of the conditions for a perfect (or efficient) market is the availability of information to all parties. When publishers know more than the librarians—and can *control* the flow of information among librarians—we start getting into a very dysfunctional relationship.

The concept of information asymmetry is very important in the field of economics, so important that three American researchers split the Nobel Prize in Economics in 2001 on their analyses of markets with asymmetric information between buyer and seller, or in markets with incomplete information.[3]

Being Punished for Promoting Information Transparency

In the following discussion I present three examples in which individuals or organizations were punished for promoting information transparency. These examples illustrate that the stakes are very high and there is much to lose as consumers.

Example 1: Isuzu versus Consumers Union

Consumers Union, the non-profit public interest group that publishes *Consumer Reports*, regularly tests new cars and light trucks. During their emergency avoidance maneuver test, the Isuzu Trooper and Acura SLX tipped up on two wheels. *Consumer Reports* rated these sports utility vehicles as "not acceptable" and advised consumers not to purchase them.[4]

Shortly after publication of the test results, Isuzu sued Consumers Union for libel and product disparagement in federal court. Three years later, after a lengthy and expensive jury trial, Consumers Union was found not liable.[5] Their tests were scientific and the reports factual.

Consumers Union is still fighting a suit brought by the Suzuki Motor Corporation for giving the Suzuki Samurai a "not acceptable" rating back in 1988 for the very same reason. Yet Consumers Union was not its only critic—*The New York Times, The Washington Post,* and *Off-Road* magazine also raised concerns about this vehicle's stability. *The Philadelphia Daily News* wrote, "Make a sudden, abrupt maneuver at speed and you're courting Highway Hari-Kari."[6]

There doesn't seem to be any question about the facts. The U.S. Department of Transportation finds that SUVs (as a class of vehicles) are much more likely than any other vehicle on the road to roll over in accidents.[7]

Example 2: Employees in the Dark about Salaries

In her book, *Nickel and Dimed,*[8] author and journalist Barbara Ehrenreich analyzes why it was so difficult for low-wage employees to find higher-paid employment. She describes what is called the "money taboo," a norm in our culture whereby it is uncomfortable to openly discuss our salary with others (even our bosses).

Despite the fact that it is completely legal under federal labor laws to discuss pay, some companies make it a policy to forbid their employees to do so. A *New York Times* article describes several women who have been fired for comparing their pay with their colleagues—in many cases finding that they get paid less money than their male colleagues for doing the same work.[9]

What these individuals were trying to do was figure out if they were being paid fairly—fairly in relation to other employees. Both our culture and some business practices work against transparency in the hope that ignorance will prevent us from feeling that we are being treated unjustly.

Example 3: Gordon & Breach versus AIP, APS, and Henry Barschall

In the mid-1980s, Henry Barschall, a physicist at the University of Wisconsin-Madison, published a series of articles and letters comparing the cost of physics journals. Because journals differ by size, length of articles, and character font, among other details, Barschall compared the journal price per 1,000 characters. In a later article, he expanded his comparison to include ISI's impact factor. His articles were published in *Physics Today*[10] (by the American Institute of Physics [AIP]), and *Bulletin of the American Physical Society*[11] (APS).

The publisher, Gordon & Breach (G&B), did not fare well in the comparison, and instead of engaging Barschall in public discourse, G&B charged the AIP and the APS with false and misleading advertising and unfair competition and attacked Barschall's integrity and motives for conducting his research.

In 2001, after 12 years of lawsuits and appeals in Germany, Switzerland, France, and the United States, the lawsuits were finally dismissed. Barschall unfortunately did not live to see his victory.

And although this was a victory for those involved, another society publisher, the American Mathematical Society (AMS), dropped its defense of a G&B suit in Germany because it did not feel that it could afford the cost of defending its survey of journal pricing.

These three examples illustrate that the stakes are very high, there is much to gain from pricing transparency, and there is much to lose when it is threatened to be taken away.

Transparent Pricing Leads to Lower Market Prices

In any consumer marketplace, access to information is very powerful in the decision-making process. Consider someone who wants to purchase a car. Car dealers are trying to secure the highest possible price, and consumers want to pay the lowest possible price. Information about the wholesale price, the list price, and what others have paid gives the customer a great deal of bargaining power in the negotiation. In the case of car prices, a non-profit group, Consumers Union, is responsible for collecting and disseminating this information.

Without information on what others have paid for the very same car, the consumer is at a distinct disadvantage compared to the knowledgeable consumer. Lack of market information leads to higher prices for all customers.

It is not difficult to move this analogy to the relationship libraries have with some commercial publishers. In many of our largest contracts, we have to work to negotiate against confidentiality clauses for price and licensing terms. Based on market economics, individual institutions that cannot share information with others put themselves (and all libraries) at a distinct disadvantage compared to a model of open sharing of information.

Proposal to Create an E-Resource Value Site

I am proposing the construction of a publicly available, distributed database in which libraries will be able to share their price, usage, and details about themselves with other libraries. Publishers are already knowledgeable about what individual institutions use and pay for a particular title or package. The creation of a shared database would provide a more level playing field for librarians. In essence, it would make any publisher pricing strategy more transparent.

Ideally, participating institutions or consortia would provide:

1. cost data

2. usage data, and

3. descriptive information about the institution or consortium (e.g., FTE and Carnegie Classification).

Once a few libraries have participated in sharing their data and prices, it wouldn't be difficult to have this e-resource value site calculate, rank, and present data based on several criteria such as cost per site or cost per FTE. If you are participating in a consortium, individual consortia could be compared.

In addition, descriptive information about individual titles or products could be used as fixed variables (e.g., number of articles published in a given year). This was the basis of Henry Barschall's original work evaluating the cost of journals.

Please note that I am not talking about keeping track of all electronic resources, just those resources where the publisher insists on keeping their pricing model opaque and hidden from the public. These tend to be the same publishers that require months of laborious negotiations each time their contract comes up.

Participation Does Not Require Collusion

The model of sharing local data with other participating libraries does not require all libraries to participate—those for whatever reason who choose not to participate would still be able to view the data. Benefits to each library, and to libraries as a whole, could be achieved by just a handful of initial participants.

In general, data from multiple institutions would be advantageous. Many of the journals, databases, and bundled products that are considered for cancellation are associated with low use and/or high price. Being able to compare and aggregate usage across multiple libraries would allow more accurate comparisons to be made.

Reasons for Nonparticipation

At present, electronic subscriptions are bound by a legal obligation between the publisher and each institution (or consortium if it is signing on their behalf). It is necessary for libraries to continue to resist confidentiality clauses that prevent them from sharing details about cost or use with other institutions. Without the ability to share and aggregate data from other institutions, we will all find ourselves paying more money for less information than if we openly shared information. Currently, Project COUNTER requires publishers to produce compliant data but has no governance on how they are used—this is a matter between the publisher and the library. Those institutions that are in open-records states or have not already signed confidentiality clauses are in an ideal position to provide the initial leadership for this project.

Summary

In summary, the open sharing of local cost and usage data would provide immediate and beneficial effects on the scholarly publication market. When libraries have as much information as the publishers, we are individually and collectively in a much better position for bargaining. The e-resources value site could provide a prototype to test this idea. I believe that this proposal would work toward the mission of Scholarly Publishing and Academic Resources Coalition (SPARC) and Association of Research Libraries (ARL) libraries. It would be cheap and easy to build and would not require all librarians to collude to see beneficial effects. While the ideal solution would be to work toward transparent pricing models for all publishers, this initiative may provide those who insist on confidentiality in pricing with a little bit of encouragement.

Notes

1. "Pricing Models for Electronic Products—As Tangled As Ever?" in *Charleston Conference Proceedings 2002*, ed. Rosann Bazirjian and Vicky Speck (Westport, Conn.: Libraries Unlimited, 2003). Available at http://www.alexanderst.com/articles/article04.htm (accessed June 18, 2004).

2. Sarah F. Brosnan and Frans B. M. de Waal, "Monkeys Reject Unequal Pay," *Nature* 425 (September 18, 2003): 297.

3. "Nobel Prize in Economics, 2001" [Online], available: http://www.nobel.se/economics/laureates/2001/index.html (accessed June 18, 2004).

4. "Not Acceptable: Isuzu Trooper/Acura SLX," *Consumer Reports* 61, no. 10 (October 1996): 10.

5. Consumers Union Cleared of Liability in Isuzu v. CU, press release, April 12, 2000 [Online], available: http://www.consumersunion.org/products/verdict.htm (accessed June 18, 2004).

6. "Suzuki vs. CU: What You Could Lose," *Consumer Reports* (September 2003): 5. See also UPDATE ON SUZUKI MOTOR CORP. ("Suzuki") v. CONSUMERS UNION OF U.S., INC. ("CU") , press release, June 10, 2003 [Online], available: http://www.consumersunion.org/products/suzuki-503.htm (accessed June 18, 2004).

7. United States Department of Transportation, National Highway Traffic Administration, *Traffic Safety Facts 2001*, Figure 15. Percent Rollover Occurrence by Vehicle Type and Crash Severity, 65 [Online], available: http://www-nrd.nhtsa.dot.gov/pdf/nrd-30/NCSA/TSFAnn/TSF2001.pdf (accessed June 18, 2004).

8. B. Ehrenreich, *Nickel and Dimed: On (Not) Getting by in America* (New York: Henry Holt, 2001).

9. M. W. Walsh, "The Biggest Company Secret: Workers Challenge Employer Policies on Pay Confidentiality," *New York Times,* July 28, 2000, C1.

10. H. H. Barschall, "The Cost of Physics Journals," *Physics Today* 39, no. 12 (December 1986): 34–36. Available at: http://barschall.stanford.edu/articles/pt8612.pdf (accessed June 18, 2004); H. H. Barschall, "The Cost-Effectiveness of Physics Journals," *Physics Today* 41, no. 7 (July 1988): 56–59. Available at: http://barschall.stanford.edu/articles/pt8807.pdf (accessed June 18, 2004).

11. H. H. Barschall and J. R. Arrington, "Cost of Physics Journals: A Survey," *Bulletin of the American Physical Society* 33, no. 7 (July 1988): 1437–47. Available at: http://barschall.stanford.edu/articles/baps8807.pdf (accessed June 18, 2004).

OPEN ACCESS: FROM "VISION SPLENDID" INTO "THE LIGHT OF COMMON DAY"

Frederick J. Friend, Joint Information Systems Committee

In the ode "Intimations of Immortality," William Wordsworth describes the change in the "vision splendid" of his youth as he moves into the reality of life in "the light of common day," but he finds that his early thoughts "are yet a master light of all our seeing." In the open access movement we have not lost the "vision splendid" of access for the whole of humankind to all information. The "light of common day" is making the vision real rather than causing it to fade, and our early thoughts are still "the master light." In this chapter I describe the work being undertaken to implement the two open access strategies in the Budapest Open Access Initiative, concentrating upon the work of the Joint Information Systems Committee (JISC) in the United Kingdom.

The vision described in the Budapest Open Access Initiative (BOAI) has its origins in the opportunities provided by technological change, particularly the opportunities provided by universal access to the electronic networks. Universal access to the networks is still constrained in many countries by unreliable electricity supplies, shortage of computer equipment, and the high cost of using monopolistic telecommunications networks. Those problems are very real, but they are being addressed, and governments across the world are coming to realize the importance of good connectivity to the Internet as a driver for economic and social development. Individuals also are avidly absorbing content and using search engines like crazy in the pursuit of personal and educational development. Whereas eating more than our share of the world's supply of food can mean less for others, eating more of the world's share of information leaves just as much information left for everybody else. At least it does if the information is free to the user. "There's the rub," to quote another English author. So much of the world's information is locked away behind price barriers, copyright barriers, or technical protection barriers. I applaud the work of the World Health Organization in collaboration with publishers to make certain medical journals available to doctors in developing countries, but such charitable endeavors only lift the lid of the cooking pot of information, giving the information-poor a smell and a little taste of the good things inside the pot. So much more intellectual food is locked away in the Internet parlor. Information is vital to us all; there has to be a way of making all information available to every member of the human race.

The reason the "vision splendid" of open access does not melt away in "the light of common day" is that open access advocates are totally realistic about the cost of making information available. Issues concerning the cost of information are being addressed up front. The cost of the research that produces academic information is largely met by the world's taxpayers, through the funding of universities and research agencies. What has often not been met is the cost of making that information available, that is, publishing it, and this cost has usually been recovered from the user of the information, whether directly or indirectly through library expenditure. So for open access for users to succeed there has to be an alternative way of meeting the cost incurred in making academic information available. The two strategies outlined in the Budapest Open Access Initiative provide two different ways of meeting that cost. The "self-archiving" strategy provides a way of meeting the cost through expenditure by academic institutions on institutional repositories. These repositories cost varying amounts of money to set up and maintain depending on the level of existing infrastructure, but institutions recognize that there is a cost to be met. Many universities are looking at the cost of repositories in the context of their overall expenditure on information provision. The second BOAI strategy, the establishment of new open access journals or the conversion of existing journals to open access, proposes that the cost of publication should be transferred from the user of information to the author or funding agency. Whereas in the past the cost of research was seen as separate from the cost of publication, the link between the two is increasingly being recognized. There is decreased value in funding research if the results of research are not being used as fully as they might be. The high use of open access content already available demonstrates that there is a huge demand for academic content not being met by the present payment model. Open access to publications derived from research enables greater value to be derived from the research process.

How is the "vision splendid" faring in "the light of common day?" How are the two BOAI strategies working out in practice? Let me outline the global situation first, because the open access movement is a global movement, and then describe the work of the Joint Information Systems Committee in the United Kingdom. Those of us who wrote the text of the Budapest Open Access Initiative have been greatly encouraged by the interest in open access from the academic community across the world. A few open access journals have existed for many years, but in the past two years there has been an explosion of interest in open access. The interest in open access may be because it is perceived to be either an opportunity or a threat, but either way it is being taken seriously. That is good, because we need the involvement of many people to work through the problems and make open access a reality.

To produce benefits, open access has to be a collaborative activity involving all stakeholders in information from the author to the user, including intermediaries like publishers and librarians. The interest in open access is also coming from a wide range of countries on every continent. Wealthy countries as well as poor countries can benefit from open access to information. Institutional repositories are being established in many universities across the globe, and many organizations publishing academic research are looking seriously at the open access economic model. Typical initiatives have been the recent Berlin Statement in support of open access from the German funding agencies and the announcement of Australian government funding for institutional repositories in their universities. And the launch of the new journal *Public Library of Science* has received more interest than the launch of any journal ever published. We could look at any single such initiative and say that it is a "flash in the pan," but there are too many initiatives in too many countries for the open access movement to be dismissed as irrelevant.

Let us examine the situation in the United Kingdom in more detail. The most public announcement about open access in the United Kingdom came from the Wellcome Trust in October 2003. Two aspects of this were not obvious from the public announcement. First, the announcement was the culmination of a great deal of research by the Wellcome Trust staff over the previous two years. This was not an announcement made lightly without serious investigation. Second, the Wellcome Trust announcement was very similar to the Bethesda Declaration made by the leaders of U.S. medical funding agencies in April. Wellcome was acting independently, but it had come to the same conclusions as other funding agencies that support for open access is good for the funding agencies and for the research they sponsor. No other funding agency in the United Kingdom has taken a decision as yet, but several are considering their attitude toward open access. The organization I represented at the conference is taking a key role in discussions with academic leaders. The Joint Information Systems Committee (JISC) is the agency of the UK Higher Education Funding Councils charged with promoting access to information for UK students and staff. The JISC has a wide brief for the academic networks and the content carried on the networks, and you may know of the JISC's national journal purchasing program, called NESLI. In the context of promoting access to information it was natural that JISC would take an interest in the opportunities presented by open access while continuing its program for the purchase of content.

The JISC is funding several initiatives to take forward each of the strategies in the Budapest Open Access Initiative. The largest amount of money is going into a program called Focus on Access to Institutional Resources (FAIR), which is designed to help UK universities in their decisions about the infrastructure for institutional repositories. The 14 projects are not only concerned with content published in conventional books and journals but also cover access to UK doctoral theses and internal university documents, such as committee papers. One project, ROMEO, has been charged with investigating the copyright position on pre-prints and post-prints deposited in university repositories, and the findings from this project are already proving of value to universities in other countries. The JISC wishes to encourage the use of university repositories for pre-prints or post-prints of journal articles, but the decision whether or not to self-archive must be left to individual authors in consultation with their university authorities. The JISC can encourage, but it cannot and should not command. We are confident, however, that once the infrastructure is in place in all our universities, authors will deposit the text of their published articles in those repositories.

In relation to the second strategy in the Budapest Open Access Initiative, the action by JISC that has received the most publicity has been the funding of publication payments for UK authors publishing in BioMed Central journals. This is a 15-month initiative designed to test the effect of the new economic model. Although authors have to pass the peer-review process, this initiative has already led to an increase in the number of UK authors taking the open access route. The early success of this funding and the wish to be evenhanded in our dealings with publishers has led the JISC to draft a new proposal to invite other publishers to bid for transition funding for open access journals. The criteria for the award of further grants from JISC will include a commitment by the publisher to move toward an open access economic model. Funding by JISC cannot subsidize the open access economic model in the long term, but it can reduce the risk for publishers in making the transition from subscriptions to publication payments. It cannot be stressed too strongly that the open access movement is not anti-publisher, and we wish to work with publishers in ensuring the survival of high-quality journals in an open access world.

The discussions JISC staff have been holding with publishers in the United Kingdom to explore the open access economic model have received less publicity. We hold these discussions in confidence, and the comments at the meeting are non-attributable, so that we have a forum in which issues can be explored without commitment. Particularly valuable in these discussions has been the involvement of the Association of Learned and Professional Society Publishers (ALPSP), several of whose members are actively considering open access publication on the "hybrid" model. Institute of Physics Publishing has a long-standing open access journal, and recent public announcements have been made by Oxford University Press for one journal and the Company of Biologists for their journals. Several other publishers have been assessing the implications of open access for their businesses. In these discussions with publishers, JISC staff has been working closely with staff of the Open Society Institute (OSI), SPARC, and SPARC Europe. There is nothing in our experience so far to suggest that the open access economic model is not viable, but we need more trials to be sure that our "vision splendid" will stand up to "the light of common day."

I have tried to make this a realistic presentation on the progress of open access, and to be realistic I must identify where I think the problem areas are. The JISC and OSI are jointly commissioning a survey of author attitudes toward open access, a survey that should tell us more about the problem areas, but let me identify two significant problems with each of the BOAI strategies. With self-archiving in institutional repositories, the first problem is the reluctance of authors to deposit copies of pre-prints or post-prints in their local repository. I believe that this reluctance is due to author uncertainty about the attitude of publishers to self-archiving, despite the fact that many publishers permit self-archiving. The perception is still there that publishers do not like university repositories and that an author's publication prospects will be harmed through self-archiving. The second problem is one for the owners of the repositories, and that is the cost of ensuring the long-term preservation of the content. It is an issue the universities will have to address. The cost of ensuring long-term preservation is also a problem for the second BOAI strategy. If the cost of publication is met through author payments, how will the open access economic model cope with the cost of long-term preservation? Likewise, how will the open access economic model cope with the cost of subsidizing author payments for authors from poor countries, where a professor's annual salary may be less than the cost of one open access publication payment? At the moment this cost is being met by publishers of open access journals or by grants from OSI, but is this a sustainable model?

I would not wish to end this chapter with the thought of problems in our minds. The interest in open access is leading to initiative that make open access more rather than less real. There are solutions to the problems I have identified if the will is there to make open access work. I believe that open access to information is a way to improve the economic, social, and educational welfare of humankind, and if it is that important, it is worth working to achieve. It is clear that no single organization can make open access work. It requires the commitment of authors, funding agencies, publishers, and librarians. There is a "vision splendid," and it is still there in "the light of common day," if only we can work together to realize it. I began with some words written 200 years ago. Let me close with some words from a modern television advertisement. The Linux operating system ad contains the words: "The future is open." Those words are true!

SCHOLARLY COMMUNICATION AND THE CHANGING LANDSCAPE OF SCHOLARSHIP

Joyce L. Ogburn, University of Washington Libraries

This chapter covers the changes that are occurring within scholarship, the relationship they have with scholarly communication, and the role of libraries in this evolving landscape. It discusses initiatives that the University of Washington (UW) Libraries is pursuing with regard to scholarly communication and support models for new scholarship, as well as how the UW is creating programs to combine the new kinds of scholarship with the new concepts, strategies, models, and technologies that have developed.

The emergence of new forms of scholarship and strategies such as institutional repositories can be seen as falling under the larger umbrella of scholarly communication, an overarching theme of this chapter.

Scholarly Environment

As we all know, scholarship has begun to expand quite rapidly—there's more being produced all the time. Research and publishing are growing exponentially, and libraries can barely scratch the surface in their collecting efforts.

Scholarship is evolving into new forms, and scholars are producing works we wouldn't have recognized 10 years ago. In some cases scholarship is heavily interwoven with and inseparable from multimedia, images, data files, simulations, and the like. Some scholars are even researching and teaching about the evolving cyberculture and aspects of born digital materials. Of course many are also creating works that are digital versions of scholarship with which we are more familiar, such as journals or individual articles.

More often than not scholars who are creating new scholarship are placing their investment of time and resources in the creative act without necessarily thinking about the implications their work has for libraries, the scholarly record, or preserving their work for future generations.

Digital Scholarship

Although there are different rates of growth of digital resources among subject disciplines, increasingly scholars in all areas are working intensively in digital formats creating new works, new research, and innovative teaching materials. This is what one may call digital scholarship. Digital scholarship can be defined as

- knowledge or art that is created, produced, analyzed, distributed, and/or displayed in a digital medium for the purpose of research or teaching;

- creation of digital technology, tools, and services to solve problems in scholarship; or

- the study and analysis of digital resources and culture.

Much of this scholarship is never intended to be formally published, nor is it meant to address directly the problems that we are experiencing with the current system of scholarly communication. Though these new kinds of scholarly data, presentation, and distribution represent a shift away from publishing and the kind of scholarship that we have traditionally collected and preserved in libraries, they are a natural evolution and adaptation of digital technology to scholarly work.[1]

Digital scholarship is being produced regularly through programs such as the Institute for Advanced Technology in the Humanities at the University of Virginia[2] and the California Digital Library's eScholarship program.[3] Examples also include Internet sites developed and managed by scholars, such as PoliticalWeb.lnfo.[4]

Endangered Scholarship

Because digital scholarship appears to be different from traditional forms of scholarship, it faces many hurdles and questions in the academy:

- Will digital scholarship be valued and accepted for promotion and tenure?

- How will acceptance vary among disciplines?

- What role will peer review have in evaluating and validating this new scholarship?

- What are the new measures of authority and quality?

- Will there be other rewards for engaging in innovative projects and changing the landscape of traditional scholarly communication?

- Without a long-term support plan, are valuable intellectual assets in danger of disappearing from the scholarly record?

If we agree that something needs to be done to maintain and make available these endangered works, how can libraries play this role with new scholarship?

Digital Scholarship, Libraries, and Communication

Digital scholarship falls within the mission of libraries to support and preserve the products of scholarship. Librarians need to acknowledge developments and changes in scholarship, the growing importance of digital scholarship in some fields, and the increasing recognition of its value to overall scholarship. Librarians also need to realize that for some scholarship it makes no sense to do it any way other than digitally. It is inevitable that the shift to digital scholarship will happen more quickly where it will be fully accepted and rewarded. And clearly this is the future of much of the substance of scholarly communication. At the University of Washington Libraries our Digital Initiatives Program has been working in this area with faculty on request, primarily dealing with text and images, but in some cases with more complex data.

The University of Washington has also had an active program in support of change in scholarly communication, and the Libraries personnel have engaged in the typical activities such as holding forums, developing a Web site, conducting one-on-one discussions with faculty and other campus personnel, presenting briefings at department meetings and new faculty orientation sessions, and writing articles for the library newsletter. The challenges of supporting change include engaging faculty and keeping their attention; making scholarly communication a campus issue, not a library issue; reconciling visions of different groups and moving in concert; and keeping conversations relevant and fresh. Often our interactions and communications are viable means to tell others what we want them to hear about scholarly communication but not to find out what they want to tell us. I return to this point later.

Digital Libraries

The next area to discuss is that of digital libraries and how they relate to scholarly communication and digital scholarship. The phrase "digital libraries" means different things to different people. One could say that it has taken at least four paths: electronic publishing, computer science research, electronic text centers and digitizing projects, and library-based services and projects devoted to reformatting of collections. Ultimately, libraries should be knitting together these digital library threads and including digital scholarship. We need to place our digital library efforts firmly within the context of evolving scholarship, the mission of libraries, and our support for scholarly communication. If we do that, we can cast digital library efforts into two goals.

The first goal would be promoting and supporting scholarship in a digital environment. This goal requires that libraries enable new models and forms of scholarship, expand access to both the old and the new forms, support methods that can create change in scholarly communication, and help prepare and support a new generation of scholars. A second goal would be to take library services to a new level. To do that we need to exponentially increase knowledge discovery and use, extend our services outside the walls of the library, find and serve new audiences, and preserve and study the "born digital."

The UW Libraries has been implementing several approaches to develop and support this integrated vision of digital libraries. One of the things we did several years ago was to change the charge of our Digital Initiatives Program by establishing new goals to support change models in scholarly communication and new forms of scholarship; to explore new ways to support, capture, disseminate, and preserve digital scholarship; and to foster experimentation and specialized scholarly projects. That step enabled us to move forward with concepts that are now embraced by the term *institutional repository*.

Institutional Repositories

What is an institutional repository? At its most basic level it is a place where the digital content of our institutions can be stored, found, and preserved. The recent national movement on this front began with the recognition that we need a place to archive, manage, and service the important digital assets and scholarship being created on our campuses.

An institutional repository exists for locally created content of an institution and relies on and assumes commitment of the institution for the long term. Although its purpose is to serve locally created content rather than a subject base, it is not incompatible with having discipline-based collections within the repository or derived from the repository.

One could ask, why a repository? As the quantity of born-digital scholarship is increasing, universities are faced with the enormous challenge of how to manage it over time. Some digital material should be saved as part of the permanent scholarly record, and some must be saved due to statutory requirements as part of our institution's archives. Institutional repositories can also lead to new ways to support evolving scholarship by providing a place for new kinds of scholarly communication, publishing, research, and teaching, and by promoting innovation and experimentation.

The direction established by having an institutional repository is a change for libraries, which have collected the research output of faculty, staff, and students in very prescribed and well-known forms, such as published books and articles, microfilm, theses and dissertations, and faculty papers. Increasingly teaching and research materials are created, integrated, and used digitally. If we want to preserve these new kinds of scholarship, we need a means and place to do so. If this is done right, institutional repositories can help communities of scholars share their materials with each other across institutional boundaries, in ways that expand on traditional scholarly publishing models.

Moreover, institutional repositories could also keep our scholarly materials in our hands and will give us the mandate to preserve the stuff of our institutions for our institutions and our future scholars. One can hope that this will also shift power from publishers back to scholars and the academy.

Advantages, Disadvantages, and Barriers

In many ways the advantages of institutional repositories mirror those that libraries offer their institutions already. An institutional repository ensures long-term viability and access to an entire corpus of the institution, promotes sharing of resources, and makes preservation a high priority. It provides organization and description, creates exposure, and promotes discovery of important materials. Furthermore, it has the potential to create efficiency for the organization and the individual scholar.

There are also, of course, potential disadvantages. Some scholars may prefer to support a subject repository since it identifies more with their discipline or scholarly society than their institution. Some researchers aren't ready to share their output and may resist contributing their time and material to a repository. Many libraries are going to feel overwhelmed by the commitment to archiving everything and dealing with the support issues that that commitment raises. Institutional repositories are hard to get off the ground, and failure may endanger the contents of a repository. The scholarly community risks losing unique resources if there is not careful planning and adequate resources; however, the attempt to have an institutional repository still may be better than what we have now, which is no plan or system at all.

Many potential barriers may prevent libraries from supporting digital scholarship and institutional repositories, including competition for resources, competition for time and attention, and ambiguity of roles on campus and in the library for managing digital assets. Developing support on campus is critical—the need and urgency or the role of the library in this endeavor may not be readily acknowledged. People and units that should be consulted are many and could include the graduate school, academic computing, various centers and institutes, programs, departments, and colleges. In the library, one needs to sort out the role of the archives, collection development, systems, digital library program, and other departments.

The concept of the institutional repository has received criticism for its limitations, and it is sometimes posited that discipline-based initiatives are the better way to go. It's not an either/or proposition. Institutional repositories will likely coexist with or provide content or preservation services for subject portals, repositories, and other similar approaches intended to support discipline-based scholarship. They may not be the best way to capture and preserve all material but serve at the very least as a jumping-off point for illuminating the challenges inherent in the new ways that scholars are working and for jump-starting discussions at our institutions about the life cycle support of scholarship, including the problems with scholarly communication as it now stands. The attempt to start an institutional repository can focus attention on the problem of preserving new scholarship and can get the institution and its scholars thinking about the value and the future of their digital assets.

Implementing an Institutional Repository

To develop an institutional repository, at the very least one needs

- find good models and tools,

- review current service concepts and applications to see what can work in conjunction with a repository,

- look for partners and content on campus for experimentation and pilot projects,

- examine rights issues and not make these a barrier to participation,

- start addressing archiving and preservation obligations for these complex resources, and

- identify resources and funding.

The UW Libraries chose to work with DSpace as a model and tool set for building an institutional repository because it promises to provide the stable long-term preservation mechanisms required to archive the digital assets of our institution. Its aims jive with the goals of developing sound digital libraries and institutional repositories by capturing, distributing, and preserving digital scholarship. Its model provides a solid, secure basis for developing additional digital library services.

DSpace seeks to provide core services that will meet the basic needs of many with basic functionality. It is also open source and employs a federated model to distribute the load of development, policy making, and creation of best practices. Its heart will be preservation and durability (the "D" in DSpace stands for durable, not digital), and it will be a reliable and trusted repository and service to support the life cycle of scholarship.

Finally, DSpace is based in communities and presupposes that they will be supported by organizational or administrative structures, not ad hoc groups that come together on a temporary basis. Communities can be departments, colleges, centers, institutes, and so on, but they aren't individuals. The idea behind communities is to secure institutional commitment beyond individual faculty member interests or careers. Policy development is made in conjunction with the communities, and they share in the responsibility to set their policies for peer review, selection, retention, and the like.

Although on the technical level DSpace is dealing most effectively with textual material at the moment, it will support anything digital such as datasets, Web sites, software, course materials, and audiovisual material. The UW Libraries is facilitating conversations between DSpace and a UW Computing and Communications Department project called the Digital Well, which can house large chunks of data and support streaming video and may be able to expand the current capabilities of the DSpace architecture.

We are working on three DSpace communities at the moment. We have placed in DSpace the image files of the Early Buddhist Manuscript Project, based in the Jackson School of International Studies; we are developing a strategy to manage Web sites from faculty in the Department of Communication; and we are talking with the Information School about building a joint community.

The Scholars' View

While we need to continue to share our visions of a sustainable and successful system of scholarly communication, we also need to tune in to the language of our scholars and listen to what they have to say about their needs and their vision. The UW Libraries took yet another step to help determine what directions we need to take and to find out what our scholars want.

In September 2001, Don Waters, program officer for scholarly communication at the Andrew W. Mellon Foundation, posed this question to a group of new library directors: "How can libraries be more effectively positioned in scholarly life at a time when there is so much flux?" The UW Libraries answered this provocative question with a proposal to the Mellon Foundation to host a retreat and begin a planning process for the university. We were honored to receive funding from the Mellon Foundation and were able to hold the retreat in March 2003. The purpose of the retreat could be summed up by this question: "What are scholars' needs and wants with regard to digital scholarship, collections, and technology, and what strategies should the university and the libraries take to advance such scholarship and learning?"

The retreat was designed to provide scholars and planners with an opportunity to engage deeply in the exploration of and visioning about digital scholarship and new models of support, not for the libraries to tell the faculty what we wanted them to hear. A faculty planning group helped shape the retreat content and structure. The Libraries built a Web site devoted to the retreat that included resources and links to other initiatives of which we were aware. We provided other background material such as short articles for participants to scan ahead of time. We planned to bring together in one place scholars in the humanities and social sciences along with key campus organizations, such as Computing and Communications, the UW Press, and UW museums to hear what was said and participate in creating a shared vision. The provost and the president hosted a pre-retreat reception to give the participants a chance to meet each other and to deliver short but inspiring speeches.

Prior to the retreat, participants were asked to complete a survey on what they had been doing in the digital scholarship arena, their insights on barriers and needs, and a list of the projects they considered to be digital scholarship. One of the faculty planners designed the survey from the viewpoint of a faculty member. The results were made available via the Web site and comprise an informal registry of our institutional work.

At the retreat, the tone was established with plenary sessions that included information about the current challenges of digital scholarship, along with recent opportunities and initiatives under way. Some initial questions were posed for participants to ponder, such as:

- What are you creating and how? Where are you keeping it? How can others find it?

- Who needs to use it? How will they use it? How will they find it?

- Can your work be a model for others?

- Will the promotion and tenure system embrace your scholarship?

- How will you preserve it as a scholarly work and in the scholarly record, and for how long?

Over the two days, participants worked in small groups of six to eight individuals to discuss these questions and more, including:

- What is driving digital scholarship?

- What are the current constraints and inhibitors?

- What is your vision for digital scholarship and models of academic support?

- What needs to be done to attain the emerging vision?

- What will move us along as an institution and as individual scholars toward next-generation scholarship?

- What should the UW Libraries be doing?

- Where should the UW invest resources and new funds?

Participants were brought together to discuss the results of their small group conversations—to synthesize, evaluate, respond to each other, and share more ideas. The larger sessions were used to flesh out conceptual models of support.

Outcomes from the Retreat

There were many anticipated and unanticipated outcomes from the retreat and the pre-retreat activities. Here are a few highlights:

- Many faculty didn't know each other and were unaware of the extent and scope of activities at the UW. They discovered each other and the diverse nature of activities at our institution. They found they shared models and similarity of efforts across disciplines.

- Faculty confirmed that they greatly value the Libraries as a broker and knowledgeable player, able to bring people together because librarians know what people are doing all over campus. The Libraries was perceived as a valued partner in research and teaching, and faculty appreciated its role in helping to create and preserve their work.

- Several models were developed for support of digital scholarship, including services ranging from tool building to preservation. Some participants went so far as to view digital scholarship as an emerging discipline worthy of study, not just a new way of working or just a practical or technical concern of scholarship.

- The scholars desired a registry of each other's work to invite collaboration and cross-fertilization. They also thought it was important to move digital scholarship forward and increase activity—they wanted more support and recognition from administrators, along with a change in the rewards structure, to foster and support this work.

- The retreat encouraged more collaboration among potential partners such as the Libraries, the Information School, the Digital Well, and the University of Washington Press.

- All attendees were willing to participate in future meetings, grant writing, or other activities that would move campus initiatives forward.

To quote one comment from among many:

The digital scholarship initiative will bring (or at least help to bring) focus to an emerging need and opportunity to many scholars on campus who have been struggling individually with attempting to articulate and elucidate this area of study. Both the opportunity and challenges are enormous for making significant contributions in scholarship previously impossible without digital technology.

The retreat was deemed a great success by the participants. There were a number of reasons given, including the following:

- **Support**—There was strong support from the provost and president from the inception, and their involvement in the pre-retreat reception lent enthusiasm to the undertaking. Funding from an outside foundation lent prestige to the event.

- **People**—Faculty did much of the program planning and identification of fellow participants. There was broad participation by a range of stakeholders, including graduate students. Librarians facilitated the lively discussions among the scholars but allowed them to drive much of the conversation. The planners also made sure that the retreat was about the faculty and their scholarship, not about the Libraries.

- **Structure**—A robust Web site was created to facilitate planning and sharing of information. The structure of the retreat made it easy to participate and allowed plenty of time for discussion, interaction, and relaxation. Small groups were composed of people who did not know each other beforehand, which led to interesting synergy and a mix of perspectives. Balance among plenary sessions, group reports, and small group work kept conversations fresh and invigorating.

- **Closure**—Very importantly, we brought closure to the retreat by having a product and clear ideas at the conclusion.

Models

Several models for academic support for digital scholarship emerged from the retreat. One was a center for digital scholarship. It was envisioned as a support service that would facilitate digital scholarship; assist with project planning, grant writing, and metadata; provide a place to do digital scholarship; create a registry and tools; promote best practices; and organize digital fairs and other information-sharing venues. The center would be both physical and virtual and would most probably be housed and hosted in the Libraries. The vision for the center was a natural extension and evolution of the work that the Libraries has already been doing and fits within our mission.

A second model proposed was an Institute for Digital Scholarship, which would address research and teaching about digital scholarship. This model was the most controversial idea that emerged—not all scholars agreed that digital scholarship was more than a new way of doing their work. The details of this model and the debate over its importance are a story for another day.

Further conversation, input, and planning are continuing on these models. In the meantime, the Libraries is moving ahead on some tangible outcomes and ideas emanating from the retreat, such as hosting seminars to share vision, challenges, tools, and results with our staff and the rest of the UW community, and seeking funding for testing the center model.[5]

Conclusion

Digital scholarship may one day supplant or at the very least grow as important as traditional scholarship. By supporting the new wave of research and scholarship librarians carve out a hefty agenda for themselves, but by doing so we may also be supporting change in scholarly communication. No one has all the answers on how to do this or knows how these strategies will play out over time, but the decision to support emerging forms of scholarship is one that we must make, or we risk losing this scholarship altogether, either by having it uncollected and unsupported or by losing it to the commercial publishers, who will exercise their control over this new scholarship and sell it back to libraries at ever-increasing prices.

This chapter has described the convergence of multiple activities that center around scholarship and scholarly communication. The future of libraries and of scholarship is bound together in these new endeavors, and libraries have no choice but to take the lead in new models of support, whatever form they should take. If we don't, libraries will betray our missions, our scholars, and our institutions, and ultimately will lose the battle in the fight to keep scholarship with the scholars.

Acquisitions and collections librarians, with their long and successful history of collaboration and working with scholars and publishers, are well positioned to begin experimenting with supporting new kinds of scholarship. They are encouraged to step up to the challenge and lend their expertise to the exploration of this new territory.

Notes

1. The topic of digital scholarship and its place in the academy has been covered in depth in three recent publications: Abby Smith, *New-Model Scholarship: How Will It Survive* (Washington, D.C.: Council of Library and Information Resources, 2003), available: http://www.clir.org/pubs/reports/pub114/pub114.pdf (accessed June 18, 2004); John M. Unsworth, "The Crisis in Scholarly Publishing in the Humanities," *ARL Bimonthly Report* no. 228 (June 2003): 1–4, available: http://www.arl.org/newsltr/228/crisis.html (accessed June 18, 2004) and Deborah Lines Andersen, ed., *Digital Scholarship in the Tenure, Promotion, and Review Process* (Armonk, N.Y.: M. E. Sharpe, 2004).

2. http://www.iath.virqinia.edu/.

3. http://www.escholarship.cdlib.orq/.

4. http://politicalweb.info/home.html.

5. Information about the retreat can be found at the UW Libraries site devoted to Digital Scholarship: http://www.lib.washinqton.edu/diqitalscholar/. The Libraries scholarly communication Web site is located at http://www.lib.washinaton.edu/ ScholComm/.

PROMOTION OF SPARC AND ALTERNATIVE PUBLISHING MODELS IN COLLEGE LIBRARIES

Rebecca Stuhr, Grinnell College Libraries
Alison Ricker, Oberlin College

Introduction

The much-talked-about serials crisis has evolved over the past 20 years as a result of a rapid rate of inflation and stagnant and declining library budgets. Expectations that the electronic medium would reduce costs have not been realized, and in fact, this new medium has resulted in increased costs. This chapter focuses on the response from college libraries to these and other pressures, specifically related to the emergence of scholarly publications intended as alternatives to high-priced commercial journals.

The rise of electronic publishing brought with it the complications and restrictions of licensing. Although librarians, publishers, and vendors are working together to develop workable licensing models, the environment is far from perfect. License stipulations often restrict use of the published material beyond fair use guidelines, and licensing means that libraries do not own the material for which they are paying higher and higher prices.

Add to this the growing restrictive nature of copyright, and we have conditions that are not favorable to broad access to the published record. As a result, librarians and scholars have worked together to create alternatives to fee-based journals. SPARC was one of the first high-profile initiatives to address the serials crisis. Developed by the ARL, SPARC's aim is to support the creation of lower cost, non-profit journals that would compete directly with expensive commercial counterparts.

SPARC embraces the open access movement (see the Budapest Open Access Initiative [BOAI] site, http://www.soros.org/openaccess/forum.shtml), which seeks, among other strategies, to develop peer-reviewed journals that have no subscription fees. SPARC has sponsored a number of these journals, but the open access movement's most prominent publishing enterprises are BioMed Central (http://www.biomedcentral.com) and the Public Library of Science (PloS, http://www.publiclibraryofscience.org/). The Directory of Open Access Journals, sponsored by Lund University Libraries (http://www.doaj.org/), lists, as of December 2003, 601 (up from 540 in October) peer-reviewed open access journals in all disciplines. This number has been growing steadily.

A third alternative, and one that goes hand in hand with the journal movement, is institutional or self-archiving of pre- and post-publication scholarly papers. Self/institutional archiving of the published record is supported by the BOAI. Clearly, SPARC is seeking to increase competition in the marketplace to bring down subscription costs. What does the open access movement offer beyond this? It encourages the broadest dissemination of the scholarly record. It offers a speedy publication timetable with the possibility of rapid publication following a successful peer-review process. Open access addresses restrictive licensing as well as the imbalance of library acquisition budgets toward periodicals and more particularly toward periodicals in the sciences.

Unresolved Questions

Do we know if open access is an unqualified good for scholarly communication? We are still so early in the development of this model that it is impossible to say. Can we say that it is risky? It seems likely that there will be more harm done to scholarly communication if we don't follow this movement through to see what it has to offer. This may be true especially for scholars in those parts of the world where the published record has never been readily available due to institutional inability to pay.

There are issues of concern in this still-nascent model of publishing. Untenured faculty want to publish in acceptable journals, and most faculty may hesitate to risk the possibility of not being able to publish by negotiating with publishers to retain copyright or to publicly archive their articles in an institutional repository. There remains a high degree of uncertainty associated with the preservation of electronic-only publishing. Librarians must take into consideration the long-term accessibility of these journals. And finally, although the hope is that alternative publishing models will create positive changes in the environment of scholarly publishing, there is no desire to disenfranchise existing publishers.

Developments at Grinnell

Following is a brief chronology of the steps taken at Grinnell College, a four-year liberal arts college located in Grinnell, Iowa, to support open access and alternative publishing models.

- March 2003: The science librarian (Kevin Engel) and collection development librarian (Rebecca Stuhr) investigate memberships in SPARC and BioMed Central. Discussions are held within the library, and a department cancels a high-cost journal that provides funding for memberships.

- May 2003: Stuhr and Engel give a presentation on open access and SPARC at a meeting of the science division.

- July 2003: Grinnell College Libraries subscribe to Serials Solutions, which is currently working with BioMed Central to link from other sources to BioMed Central journals.

- August/September 2003: Catalog SPARC open access partnership journals; subscribe to a SPARC alternative journal (for a total of two); catalog over 40 of the BioMed Central journals; search DOAJ to identify additional open access journals.

- October 2003: Stuhr and Engel meet with the science, humanities, and social studies divisions to discuss open access and SPARC membership. (See http://www.lib.grinnell.edu/research/alternative_publishing.html.) The libraries catalog the electronic version and subscribe to the paper version of *PloS Biology*.

- Still to Do: Continue discussions at individual, departmental, and divisional levels; keep up with changes within the movement; pursue the creation of an institutional archive.

Survey Results of Oberlin Group Libraries

We surveyed the Oberlin Group Libraries, a group of 75 private liberal arts colleges with student FTE enrollments between 990 and 3,700, in October 2003 to gauge their participation in various alternative publishing initiatives. Twenty-seven members responded to the questionnaire, a 36% response rate. Membership status in SPARC, BioMed Central, and BioOne was seen as a key indicator of the level of support libraries provide to either open access or alternative publishing models.

Of the 27 respondents, 16, or nearly 41% of respondents, are SPARC members. The SPARC Web site indicates that 26 of the Oberlin Group libraries overall are SPARC members, 20 of them through their Oberlin Group membership. Ten of the Oberlin Group SPARC members did not participate in this survey.

BioMed Central membership was limited to seven libraries, and primarily through a consortium; only one respondent (Grinnell) joined BioMed Central directly. Access to BioOne publications is more prevalent; only five respondents indicated no access at all, and 18 stated that access was through a consortium.

Clearly, and not at all surprisingly, consortia are crucial to the success of college libraries that wish to promote alternative publishing models. Budgetary constraints were cited as the primary reason for not joining one of the three organizations. Only one respondent indicated that the content of the resources offered by SPARC, BioOne, or BioMed Central was "too specialized or technical for our needs."

Much of the survey focused on specific SPARC alternative journals, open access titles, and the extent to which libraries have promoted their use through subscriptions, cataloging, and other modes of access. Despite SPARC membership by 16 libraries, only 4 of the 19 SPARC "alternative and leading edge" journals have been cataloged by 14 or more of the respondents. Lack of funds, again, was a major stumbling black. Most libraries did not have subscriptions to the targeted commercial publications that could be canceled, theoretically freeing money to use on the alternative titles. BioOne, a SPARC partner in the scientific community, was the primary exception; 21 of the respondents subscribe to BioOne and have actively promoted its use on their campuses.

Publicity efforts for BioMed Central, the PLoS, and other SPARC partners most often took the form of e-mail announcements to interested parties and discussions with individuals. Meetings with specific departments were undertaken by one-third of the respondents. These meetings were cited as critical for conveying the complexities of serials pricing issues, often in the context of serials cancellation projects, and enhancing dialogue with faculty on alternative modes of scholarly communication. Plans for institutional repositories of faculty publications are in the infancy stage at one-third of the responding campuses and nonexistent at the other colleges. "Infancy" is perhaps too strong a description; attempting to conceive might be more accurate! Creating repositories as a means of primary publication was not cited by any librarians as a model that their campus is ready to adopt. Indeed, all of the narrative comments indicated a mix of caution with a willingness to explore all options. When asked, "do you envision a specific or unique role for liberal arts colleges?" (related to open access and alternative publishing models), one librarian exemplified many comments by stating: "We have a responsibility to make the faculty aware of alternative publishing models and scholarly communication issues. Liberal arts colleges have unique needs rather than a unique role [given that] our faculty are active scholars though not a research university."

Liberal arts colleges seek to become "active participants in the process of expanding open access," stated another respondent. Collaboration with faculty and within consortia will undoubtedly make that participation more effective and help accelerate the shift from reliance on traditional models of publication to new means of disseminating and archiving the primary publications of college faculty.

ALTERNATIVE MODELS OF SCHOLARLY COMMUNICATION AND PUBLISHING

Greg Tananbaum, President, The Berkeley Electronic Press

The current scholarly journal landscape has considerable strengths and a number of fundamental problems. On the plus side, peer review provides clear quality signals, there is an established hierarchy of publishing outlets, and the continuing transition to combined print and electronic delivery mechanisms widens availability of important research. Conversely, long time delays, substantial subscription costs, and the lack of viable publishing outlets for nonstandard materials create serious barriers to effective dissemination.

As with most things in life, money matters. From 1986 through 2000, ARL libraries saw their serials spending increase 226%. In that same time frame, the number of serials these libraries purchased actually fell by 7%. Since 1998, business and economics journal prices have risen by 61%, general science journals by 56%, engineering journals by 52%, and so on. Particularly troubling for many universities is that they are the primary source of human capital for journals. A majority of authors, editors, and reviewers are drawn from academia. The source of funding for that human capital is the academy. The source of revenue for the journals created using that human capital is also the academy. This "double dip" means that the universities are, on some level, subsidizing the journals' operations.

Some institutions are seeking to address this problem by taking a more active role in publishing ventures. In addition to halving the double dip, the goals of these ventures include providing outlets for monographs and other specialty publications, ensuring persistent access to information, presenting a better representation of scholarship created within the institution, and, perhaps, staking or furthering a leadership claim in a specific subject area. "University-as-publisher" projects fit broadly into three categories: new peer-reviewed journals (e.g., University of Arizona's *Journal of Insect Science*, University of Warwick's *Geometry & Topology*), subject-based portals (e.g., Cornell's Project Euclid, Washington University's EconWPA), and institution-based archives (e.g., University of California's eScholarship Repository).

A number of questions surround university-sponsored journals. Should the institution solicit editors or wait for bottom-up interest to dawn? The more successful implementations to date have come via the latter path. What motivates these editors? Typically, it is a combination of altruism (wanting to improve the flow of information within the discipline), frustration with the inherent problems of the mainstream publishing model, and ego (a desire to lead the revolution). What role does the university press play? In many instances, the press's imprimatur and experience dealing with editors are valuable additions to the project. Should journals be digital only, or have a print component? In this matter, the jury is still out. The University of New Brunswick's Electronic Text Centre seems to have a good approach. In its seven years of existence, it has been open to experimentation with new and existing journals, electronic publications and ones with print counterparts, open access and fee-based, faculty-centered and learned society-sponsored, even French and English. It is this spirit of experimentation that will ultimately help address the questions I have broached here.

A first cousin to university-sponsored journals is the armada of open access journals coming from non-profit and commercial organizations. Among the most prominent are PLoS, BioMed Central, and ELSSS. These projects challenge the traditional publishing orthodoxy and will ultimately provide valuable insights into the establishment and maintenance of university-sponsored initiatives.

Beyond journals, "university-as-publisher" projects also include subject-based portals and institution-based archives. Subject-based portals often encompass both peer-reviewed and pre-print materials. They typically include input from learned societies and/or small publishers working in concert with the institution. Subject-based portals may pull information from different Web sites rather than actually "publish" unique materials.

As president of The Berkeley Electronic Press, I have a front row seat to the eScholarship Repository, the largest and fastest-growing institutional repository in existence today. Our partnership with the University of California's California Digital Library (CDL) arose from a perfect confluence of technology and opportunity. The Berkeley Electronic Press system, EdiKit, provides editorial management and publishing support for a variety of publication types (e.g., peer-reviewed journals, working papers, monographs). It is flexible and easily customized. CDL had a vision in late 2001 to construct a repository showcasing the depth and breadth of research conducted by UC faculty but lacked the technical infrastructure to get the project running. In late 2001, we decided to team up to construct an institutional repository. We recognized that any system we rolled out needed to accomplish certain things: It had to provide participating research units with unique spaces that fed into a single collection, uploading of both new and legacy papers needed to be as easy as possible, nonstatic resources should be included, an alerting component for readers should be constructed, and data had to be OAI-compliant to promote interoperability.

By April 2002, the eScholarship Repository was set to launch. Among its key features are

- automatic conversion of documents to PDF;

- the ability to publish nonstatic resources such as sound and video files, datasets, and executables;

- acceptance of a wide variety of publication types (e.g., articles, pre-prints, monographs, reports);

- the ability to publish HTML;

- a peer-review module;

- full-text searching;

- saved searches;

- personalized e-mail notification of newly published content;

- browsing by date or author;

- access/subscription control;

- customized controlled-vocabulary picklists for data entry;

- branded publication sites for participating research units;

- customized document cover pages;

- automated e-mail interface between author and publication administrator;

- usage statistics at the publication and paper level;

- a flexible document hierarchy;

- "push" e-mail capabilities;

- OAI compliance;

- data exporting as XML; and

- data transfer to third-party indexing services.

The eScholarship Repository was pitched to research unit heads with a very concise set of benefits. It would provide increased visibility of the research and the research unit, particularly by highly placing materials in search engines such as Google. Usage statistics would give authors and unit heads an understanding of what was actually being read. The technology would lessen reliance on local IT staff. Finally, it would offer a permanent home for these materials.

Another key factor motivating groups to participate is the software's ease of use. A paper may be uploaded by an administrator, converted to PDF, and posted within three minutes. It is similarly quick and simple to archive associated files such as sound, video, datasets, and executables. By clicking "publish," objects are indexed, tables of contents are rebuilt, HTML "cover pages" are created, and so forth—again, with no technical skill required.

The benefits of participation have combined with this ease of use to yield early success for the eScholarship Repository. While only a dozen research units were active at launch, more than 125 were participating by November 2003. Another 30 are in queue to join. More than 300,000 full-text downloads have been tallied, a figure currently increasing by more than 10,000 per week.

The eScholarship Repository and other successful publishing alternatives share a number of commonalities. Each has a clear charter detailing what it is trying to accomplish. Each shares a base of motivated participants among library, administration, IT, and faculty. Each has maintained low technological barriers to participation. And finally, each seeks to create a viable alternative to specifically address frustration with the current state of scholarly publishing.

As new models emerge and evolve, a number of questions remain:

- Will repositories and portals complement or compete with commercial journals?

- Can current implementations move from pre-prints and reprints to first-run peer-reviewed content?

- Will alternative journals emerge in the mainstream disciplines?

- Will the electronic medium entice or dissuade scholars?

- What is the long-term funding strategy?

I look forward to addressing these questions at future Charleston conferences.

W ithout electronic publishing, there would not be as
much of an issue of archiving. Traditionally, archiving
means saving print copies and finding some place to store them.
Now librarians are making decisions about the nature of electronic archiving as well as determining what to archive. The budget crisis has had a major influence on purchasing decisions, and
archiving concerns arise out of decisions about whether to purchase both print and electronic copies. Trust has also been an important issue in resolving archiving questions. Here several
librarians and publishers address such archiving issues as the use
of national libraries, digital archives, and archiving with a trusted
third party.

Archiving

GET IT AND KEEP IT

Matthew J. Bruccoli, University of South Carolina

My topic is the proper use of books and the opportunities for libraries to acquire and preserve printed material that will become increasingly rare and expensive and even unprocurable. Library acquisitions funds have been diverted to electronic texts, which do not require shelving. I speak with asperity because as editor of the *Dictionary of Literary Biography* I am the recipient of frequent complaints from librarians that the 350 volumes take up too much room. The *DLB Yearbook* has been terminated to pacify these parishioners, and I am mad as hell about it.

Nicholson Baker's *Double Fold* revealed that there was a librarian conspiracy to destroy printed materials, especially newspapers that take up too much room. Mr. Baker has used his own money to support the American Newspaper Repository, where he has the only runs of such obscure newspapers as the *New York World* and the *Chicago Tribune.* Speaking of lost newspapers, I have been searching for the 1924–1926 issues of the *Pottsville Journal* since 1970. Anyone who thinks that a microfilm when it exists is as good as the real thing for purposes of research has never engaged in serious research. Moreover, we don't know how long microfilm will last. But I do know that the microfilms of telephone books at the New York Public Library are deteriorating or disintegrating and that the originals are gone.

The task of a research library is collection building, which means purposeful preservation of the real things. That requires an acquisitions plan for the books and newspapers and journals and typescripts and manuscripts and, God help us, the computer printouts and even hard drives. I was trained at the University of Virginia by John Cook Wyllie, the best librarian I've ever known, whose acquisitions plan was to get it all and keep it, because there is no way of knowing which of today's obscure publications will be tomorrow's treasures. Mr. Wyllie also believed that two copies are better than one. Failing the Wyllie rationale, it is imperative that research libraries have a policy governing what to keep in special collections and on what to spend always insufficient funds. This is a form of wagering on futures. USC has a list of 50-odd contemporary writers for whom we buy a copy of the first American and first English printings of every book as well as advance or proof copies, if available. I regard this as too conservative. If 10% of the authors on the hit list turn out to be winners in terms of literary standing and rare book value, the gamble will be successful. Thus, if in 1925 a library had prepared an acquisitions list that included F. Scott Fitzgerald, a highly risky gamble, the $2 purchase of *The Great Gatsby* would be worth up to $150,000 now. The USC copy of *Gatsby* cost $30 in 1958. The *Gatsby* first printing without jacket is worth $5,000 to $10,000; the jacket adds at least $100,000 to the price. Libraries routinely discard jackets. They should not. Jackets are a form of literary history. The artwork can suggest the cultural or social influences of the book in its time; the blurbs document the critical reception and the mechanism of literary politics.

I know of no library that has systematically retained publishers' catalogs. This carelessness has produced a terrible hole in literary history. Literary history is book history and publishing history.

Despite the omnipresence of the personal computer, reading is still best done with printed books. E-books that were supposed to replace real books flopped because the book is the most usable package ever invented. The orders for the Scribner electronic texts for Fitzgerald and Hemingway have been less than 1% of the book orders. If Gutenberg were to produce his first book in 2003, it would be celebrated as a miracle. Nonetheless, I sometimes feel like the owner of a livery stable watching Henry Ford drive by in his Model T.

Readers go on reading and buying books. Amazon and the other dot-coms are making new and used books available to people who formerly were bookless or library-less. At the same time the dot-coms are killing the used book shops. Yet Barnes and Noble and the other chains show increasing sales and profits. Book publishing is big business; foreign conglomerates are gobbling up American publishing houses. The complaints that books are overpriced are untrue for hardbound books but true for paperbacks. When I was a boy, clothbound novels were $2.50 or $3.00 and paperbacks were $0.25. Now the clothbounds are $25 to $30, a tenfold increase. But paperbacks are now $5 or more, a twentyfold increase. Paperback inflation means larger royalties for authors as well as greater profits for publishers. But it is bad for readers because most book purchases, especially of paperbacks, are impulse buys; buyers are less impulsive about $5 paperbacks.

The so-called paperback revolution that commenced in America in 1939 changed literature and literacy as well as the profession of authorship. Yet no library has attempted to build a complete collection of the American paperback imprints from 1939 to 1959. The greatest cultural giveaway of all time was the Armed Services Editions, which distributed 1,322 titles during World War II. There are only two supposedly complete ASE sets in libraries; USC has acquired 1,308 of these 1,322 titles one by one. When I started collecting ASEs they were two for a quarter. Now single copies bring up to $300, and some are not findable. There is a lesson there.

WHO CAN WE TRUST: NATIONAL LIBRARIES?

Natalie Ceeney, The British Library

I was delighted to receive an invitation to speak at the Charleston Conference. We have heard some fascinating presentations about the future of the information sector and about digital preservation in particular. Almost every speaker has posed the question, "How are we going to ensure that today's digital material is available for tomorrow's researcher?" Over the last decade, everyone who uses information has been flooded with it. It is freely available at their desktops—at home and at work. Any mystique surrounding the accessibility of information has been removed completely. People trust that information will be around whenever they need it, but few give any thought as to who is going to safeguard it for them. What I want to explore today is just how challenging this future-proofing of information is. I see this as a genuine question of trust; we all have an interest in ensuring that our digital heritage is preserved in perpetuity, but the question we all need to ask ourselves is who it is that we trust to lead it. I hope I shall be able to give you an insight into a national library's perspective, and specifically that of the British Library—the only national library of which I can claim any direct knowledge. Our role in digital preservation is key to how we view our position in the information sector of the future.

Given that the United States doesn't have a national library that compares directly with that of the United Kingdom, I should say a word or two about what a national library is. It is hard to explain something that you see as a given, especially as my first observation is that there is no common definition of a national library! The British Library is, perhaps, unique in its wide range of activities and services. It collects widely across disciplines, formats, and geographical boundaries. Some national libraries specialize by sector or by country. National libraries differ widely in their origins, though they are rarely born of governments in spite of being funded centrally. Most have long histories, with many of the European libraries' roots in the collections of wealthy individuals or monarchs. But if they vary in almost every other respect, what national libraries do have in common is their mission. The vast majority of national libraries see their role as preserving their country's research output and underpinning its future research infrastructure.

Having attempted to define a national library, I would now like you to visualize the world 10 years from now. Visualize a researcher in that world, undertaking important research that depends on information about today's world—2003. Pick your own subject. It could be a medical breakthrough that utilizes clinical trial data created in 2003. It could be climate change. It could be global security, or immigration issues, or the work of a famous author, as yet undiscovered.

Now think of the sources your researcher is going to need. A scientist will need peer-reviewed journals, but they will comprise a fraction of his research material. He might also want scientific databases, pre-print archives and conference reports. If a researcher is working on climate change, he will want to know what is being published on that subject in 2003. So he might log on to Web sites and expect to find the same functionality that the site offered originally. He might want to know how CNN reported climate change, and what the print journalists were saying about it. A social scientist might need the Web—official and unofficial, news broadcasts, newspapers, government publications, journals, and e-mails. A researcher in the arts or humanities would be looking for books, journals, and perhaps e-mails. (How many contemporary writers chart their progress through letters?) How confident are you that these sources will all be available to our researcher?

I would like to remind you of some of the significant challenges we are facing. On a positive note, we are accomplished at preserving paper-based material. We have a wealth of experience, and we know exactly how much it costs. The British Library has calculated that for a single printed item, from cataloging through to long-term preservation, we can expect to pay $229 for 100 years' storage. We can also rely on the fact that "benign neglect" works! We can leave a book on a shelf, as long as the conditions are neither too hot nor too humid, and it will remain readable. The British Library's oldest material dates from the third century B.C., and it is perfectly intelligible. What is more, we have never been confronted with the challenge of selecting which material to store because we have been able to store almost everything. As a result, the greatest challenge we face is running out of storage space!

We are, however, less equipped when it comes to electronic material. We are facing an incessant and powerful tide of new information, and we lack the experience to deal with it. The average lifespan of a Web page is four weeks; this means that we have to be proactive. Benign neglect does not have a chance. Technological obsolescence also presents a huge challenge. Magnetic tapes and punch cards deteriorate with time. Old reading devices do not exist any more. We have problems now opening a document written two years ago on an old version of Microsoft Word. To give you some idea of scale, research carried out at the University of California, Berkeley, suggests that each year, the world produces 250 megabytes of new material for every person on earth. Just a fraction of this is printed on paper. We therefore have to be selective about what we preserve, which means that to some extent, we have to pre-judge the research needs of future generations. Deciding what is trivial and what merits preservation poses a major challenge. Even 20 years ago, we, like other libraries, were relegating research on climate change to deep basements, as we didn't think that it would ever need to be accessed. Who would have thought that climate change would acquire its current significance? In a paper world, we can preserve almost everything. In an electronic world, we can't.

Think about the kind of information we might lose that could be critical to tomorrow's researcher. Electronic material tells its own story. It can be updated in minutes, enabling a researcher to follow the development of events, research, products, or services in unparalleled depth. Online news is perhaps the most obvious example of this, but there is an enormous range of electronic information that is at risk. There are vast amounts of business data, the loss of which could lead to problems of liability. The UK government has committed to providing access to all its services electronically by 2006, which will mean that many government records documenting interactions among the state, citizens, and business will be electronic. There have been heroic efforts to capture major global events, like Norbert Specker's archive of online news publications from 9/11 and the subsequent 48 hours. It is incredible to think that this is perhaps the only archive of its kind. The most notable events will, of course, be preserved. But if we are in the business of preserving the integrity of our intellectual heritage, we have to ensure that we make the broadest possible provision for tomorrow's researchers.

We all appreciate the importance of e-mail as a means of conveying vital information. The Hutton Inquiry, a significant and high-profile government inquiry into the death of the government weapons expert, Dr. David Kelly, has had a significant number of e-mails submitted as documentary evidence. E-mail has replaced the printed memo and the letter. The replacement of handwritten work by electronic methods also threatens literary research. Today's writers are unlikely to produce manuscripts. The British Library holds a number of existing manuscripts, including an early version of James Joyce's *Ulysses*. It is especially significant because the writer's crossings-out and changes are still evident. New technology means that we are far more likely to see the finished product on disc. We would be unable to chart an author's literary progress without delving into his or her hard drive.

One of the greatest treasures of British history is the Domesday Book, and it provides an interesting example of the challenges presented by technological obsolescence. Produced from a survey carried out in 1086 on the orders of William I, the Domesday Book describes in incredible detail the landholdings and resources of late-eleventh-century England. One contemporary observed that "not even one ox, nor one cow, escaped notice." It documented Britain's resources on a scale not seen again until the nineteenth century. The original Domesday Book, now bound in five volumes, is held at the Public Record Office in London, and is perfectly readable. Nine hundred years after it was created, the BBC launched an ambitious project to celebrate Domesday. It produced a computer-based, multimedia archive of life in the mid-1990s at a cost of $4 million. The BBC stored the project on two special discs. Unfortunately, the computers that could read these discs became obsolete less than 15 years later, and the information was unreadable. However, specialists from Leeds University and the University of Michigan developed software to emulate the original equipment and "unlocked" the Domesday Project. The message here is not that we lost the Domesday Project. We didn't. But it took a large-scale, expensive project to retrieve it. While this is feasible for high-profile projects, we cannot afford to expend this amount of resources on every piece of research that we lose.

I would now like to look at what the challenge really means in practical terms. We all know that the major issue is money. We have to look to a shifting economic model, as digital preservation necessitates new areas of investment. Little work has been done to date on assessing the likely costs, and nobody really knows who should pay them. We do not yet understand the life cycle of a digital item. We should consider that these costs are additional; it has become very clear during this conference that paper is not disappearing, and it is important that we maintain active programs for print material.

We also need to consider the new skills required to face the digital challenge. These will be quite different from the traditional range of skills associated with the information sector. We will need cutting-edge technology to go about collecting, storing, and providing access to digital material. For example, how do we go about ensuring that a PDF document created today will be readable in 100 years' time? How do we preserve the functionality of the Web? How do we preserve records of e-science so that we can see not only the latest research but also the audit trail of its creation? There is also a need to build on existing skills in collection management, brought up to date in a digital world.

We have to develop selection criteria by predicting the way future researchers will behave. We need to develop the same skills of acquisition and cataloging, though in a different environment. Fundamentally, we need to ask what curatorship really means in this new environment.

I think the crucial issues in all this are leadership and trust. No single institution has yet nailed its colors to the mast and stated which technology model it intends to use for digital preservation: emulation, migration, a combination, or something totally new. Somebody has to be responsible for establishing technological best practice. There are other leadership issues, too: Who is going to make crucial decisions of content? Who is going to decide what digital curation means? Somebody has to be accountable for these decisions, and it is a daunting prospect. We have to be able to trust whoever is making these vital decisions. If we consider our customers and stakeholders for a moment, we can revisit why this issue of trust is so important.

Librarians need to trust that the mode of preservation will work. We need to build confidence in the information community that the digital copy can also be the preservation copy. The statistics suggest that librarians will not cancel print subscriptions until they can trust e-archiving. Today's businesses increasingly rely on the fact that their customers have to trust them, and at the heart of this they rely on a wide range of electronically held data. Businesses also have the same digital archive concerns as the rest of us. The general public seems to have little difficulty in trusting that "somebody" is working on digital preservation. As I have suggested, the scale and efficiency of the information age may have lulled the public into a false sense of security. Future researchers will have similar expectations. They will expect access to twenty-first-century information, but they might also expect it to have the same "look and feel" as in its original form. They might find themselves in the ironic position of being able to study a copy of Magna Carta in its original form but unable to access twenty-first-century information with contemporary functionality. We should question whether the material will be there at all, as our assumptions about what tomorrow's researchers will want to access may be wrong. Our challenge is to give future researchers the scope to set their own limits.

If we consider that the public and researchers already trust "somebody" to do this, we need to consider who *we* trust. I have prepared some criteria an organization needs to meet to be trusted to lead in this field. It is vital that digital preservation form part of an organization's core mission. We need to trust that effort and investment will be sustained and consistent. We need to be confident that the organization will be around in the long term in one form or another, and capable of making decisions with a view to the long term. Such an organization has to be neutral and not driven by commercial return or competitive threat. Finally, the organization needs to be willing to invest with the prospect of uncertain returns.

It would be unrealistic to expect authors to take on this challenge. I would argue that research libraries have a key part to play in digital preservation. However, a research library is part of a bigger institution, whose core mission is not necessarily concerned with preservation. There is also the question of funding. The funding crisis facing research libraries around the world is well-documented. Finally, research libraries' parent bodies generate intellectual property and, crucially, they select and purchase the material they require. As far as publishers are concerned, we all appreciate that the publishing industry is fragmented and volatile. In the United Kingdom alone, during the last six years there have been 216 mergers, and between $30 and $40 billion has changed hands. It is notoriously difficult to keep track of publishers. The British Library runs the world's largest document supply center, and passes copyright fees to publishers. We sometimes struggle to track down publishers when we want to pay them! If our trusted organization needs to be stable and long-standing, I think we would agree that publishers are not an option.

That leaves national libraries. As I have already suggested, we see digital preservation as central to our core mission. To a significant degree, we are already trusted. National libraries are funded nationally and have genuine awareness of the source of their legitimacy. They are also becoming increasingly user-focused. We do face challenges. We are willing to invest, but we do not pretend to have the necessary resources. We are aware of the skills that we will require, but we do not currently have them. Digital preservation will require speed, particularly if we are considering Web archiving. National libraries are not usually known for their speed. So although national libraries might be a candidate for leadership, and I would argue that they are probably the prime candidate, we cannot do it alone.

I would like to move on to what the British Library *is* doing to rise to the challenge. We have assumed that there is a leadership problem. We certainly assume that we have a leadership problem in the United Kingdom. We also recognize that we can only do this in collaboration with others. There are strong drivers here, one of the most significant being the needs of our users. We need to work closely with publishers. Publishing models are changing so rapidly that we have to be amenable to all formats. We have a government that funds us and that has an agenda. But the great thing about a national library is that it is not generally perceived as a threat. We work incredibly closely with other national libraries, with UK Research Councils and a lot of other bodies in the sector. This has to be an international effort.

We have to have a favorable regulatory climate. Just a few weeks ago, the UK Parliament passed legislation requiring all material, and not just print, to be "deposited" with the British Library and the other copyright libraries in the United Kingdom. This was the result of a lobbying campaign led jointly by the British Library and publishers. It presents a huge step forward, but also a huge challenge. There is a lot of work to be done to turn this legislation into a workable approach to the deposit of electronic material, in terms of both rights management and technology.

The British Library is also working on a digital object management store, which will take all forms of electronic material and will be highly scalable. Many digital preservation issues remain substantially at a research level, and the BL's Digital Object Management Programme is currently in its definition phase. We are looking at architecture of archival repositories and the attributes of archived collections. DOMs will be implemented gradually, and through collaboration with others. The Library is an active participant in the consortium looking at best practice in long-term preservation.

As far as Web archiving is concerned, I know this is going to be a huge challenge. Although we see it as part of our core mission, we are far from knowing how to do it. We are developing selection criteria for archiving Web sites, which we know will be significant primary sources for researchers in the future. We are particularly conscious of the long-term view; advertisements in leisure magazines like *Vanity Fair* may not have been deemed scholarly material during the 1960s, but they are surprisingly well-used now! We are grappling with the issue of functionality as well as content capture. We recognize the importance of creating an archive that allows the user to experience the function as well as the content on the site. This is a particularly global effort, and there is now a global consortium of institutions working to solve the problem of Web archiving.

Underpinning all of this is rights management, something the British Library takes very seriously. This causes obvious concern to publishers, yet there is little point in having an archive if it is inaccessible. We therefore need to become far more sophisticated in our management of rights in a digital world. If we consider the scale of the archive we need to build, this is going to be extremely difficult. We have already developed a system through working closely with Adobe and Elsevier to exert tight control over rights when e-mailing information, preventing onward distribution, and limiting user rights to those permitted under license. However, we cannot just assume that paper and "e" have the same rules. We are going to need to work hard on understanding what permissions and rights management really means, and how we enforce it in a digital world.

I'd now like to take you back to the researcher I started with. I think most people here were already convinced that digital preservation is crucial to enable tomorrow's research. I think we agree that tomorrow's researcher needs access to today's material—and it needs to be at least as good as it is now. But this is uncharted territory. It needs new skills and new money. I firmly believe that the overriding issues at the moment are trust and leadership. I also believe that national libraries can be trusted to lead. But it is the responsibility of the whole information community to contribute to finding an enduring solution.

CREATING DIGITAL ARCHIVES: THE PERSPECTIVE OF ONE SOCIETY PUBLISHER

Timothy C. Ingoldsby, American Institute of Physics

Learned society publishers perhaps feel somewhat stronger connections to the preservation of the record of scholarship within their disciplines than do commercial publishers. After all, learned societies were created in large part for the purpose of validating the scholarly record of research progress. In the print era, societies were happy to cede archival responsibility to the libraries, under the premise that (to borrow from one compelling example of a digital preservation strategy) "lots of copies keeps stuff safe." In the digital era, societies feel a stronger sense of responsibility to safeguard the archival record of scholarship in their discipline. As such, they have been quick to assert their responsibilities via the development of policies that spell out their roles and responsibilities. When faced with the daunting task of transforming policies into practice, however, many societies have discovered the true financial and procedural implications of their decisions. Examples drawn from the experiences of one publisher illustrate the breadth and depth of the difficulties involved in translating policy into practice.

The American Institute of Physics (AIP) is a publisher of nine titles, a copublisher of two additional titles, and cocreator of the virtual journals in the Science and Technology series. (See Table 1 for a listing of these titles.) We also publish the trade magazines *Physics Today* and *The Industrial Physicist*. In addition to being a publisher, AIP is a provider of publishing services for an additional 18 physical sciences and engineering societies, comprising about 100 additional titles. In our dual role as a significant primary publisher and a publishing services provider to other important societies, we develop positions regarding important publishing issues, like digital archiving, and communicate these positions to our publishing partners and subscribers.

Table 1. Journals Published by the American Institute of Physics

Applied Physics Letters
Chaos
Geochemical Transactions
Journal of Applied Physics
Journal of Chemical Physics
Journal of Mathematical Physics
Journal of Physical and Chemical Reference Data
Low Temperature Physics
Physics of Fluids
Physics of Plasmas
Review of Scientific Instruments
Virtual Journals in Science and Technology

I will begin by describing how archiving used to work and why things are different in the digital era. Then I will explain why learned societies feel a special responsibility for creating digital archives of our publications. I will then describe the efforts of my society to develop, first, a policy governing digital archives for our publications, and then the implementation of the policy. I will close by posing a few questions regarding access to the archival information and offering some tentative answers reflecting the current thinking of my society.

Archiving in the Print Era

As I stated previously, for the past 400 years of the print era, publishers have been happy to benefit from having libraries to perform the archival function. One mission of the research library is preservation, and libraries throughout the world have secured dozens or hundreds of copies of each journal over periods of time, measured in decades and even centuries. But will this same methodology work in the digital age? The reality of digital information is that the maintenance of such information over decades and centuries is likely to be an expensive process. Large duplication of expensive efforts would be required to create, maintain, refresh, and transform hundreds of thousands of digital files published over decades and centuries. The growth of licensing as a mechanism for providing access also complicates the ability of research libraries to perform the archive function in the digital age. Clearly, digital archiving will require cooperative efforts among publishers, libraries, and perhaps third parties as well.

There are many reasons why digital archiving is more difficult. To begin with, digital research/documents are more complex, containing in addition to text and illustrations, ever-evolving multimedia content types such as animations or movies, sound clips, molecular models, and equations developed using symbolic algebra software such as Mathematica. There is no reason to expect that the process of creation of new content types will slow any time soon. As anyone who uses a computer knows, software evolves rapidly, and formats change, requiring frequent conversion of digital files to new formats.

Multiple standards, such as MPEG, QuickTime, and AVI, compete to become "the" standard for movies. Even the basic archival format, SGML, is currently evolving, being replaced by XML. Another important difference is that, unlike print, digital research articles continue to evolve after publication, as additional links to and from citing articles are published.

Publishers are dealing with these issues in a variety of ways. Certainly it is understandable why learned society publishers feel that they must assume responsibility for—or at least play a key role in—the preservation of the digital archive. A glance at any of the mission statements in Table 2 shows the connection that professional societies feel to the record of scholarly research in their discipline. Perhaps this might be one distinction between society publishers and commercial publishers, although I believe—and Elsevier's actions demonstrate—that all publishers feel this same need to preserve the record of scholarship. However, it is not only publishers that have asserted their role in the safekeeping of digital information.

Table 2. Mission Statements of Society Publishers

It is the mission of the Institute to serve physics, astronomy, and related fields of science and technology by serving its Member Societies and their associates, individual scientists, educators, students, R&D leaders, and the general public with programs, services and publications. (American Institute of Physics)
AAAS seeks to advance science and innovation throughout the world for the benefit of all people. (American Association for the Advancement of Science)
The Society's purpose is to advance the science of biochemistry and molecular biology through publication of scientific and educational journals, organization of scientific meetings, advocacy for funding of basic research and education, support of science education at all levels, and promoting the diversity of individuals entering the scientific workforce. (American Society for Biochemistry and Molecular Biology)

Libraries were quick to document the challenges of digital preservation. Their groundbreaking report, prepared by a coalition of interested library societies,[1] issued at the dawn of the digital era, spelled out the challenges and confirmed that digital is, indeed, different. The report envisioned a system of national archives and agreed with the position of many publishers that initial responsibility for the archive rests with the creator or owner. The report also issued a series of recommendations for further study. Many of the recommendations made in this report have yielded valuable results as research projects have been carried out and their results transformed into functioning archival processes and procedures.

The principal task for me in this chapter is to inform you about how professional society publishers have responded to the challenge of digital archive development. Among the accomplishments to date, societies have articulated requirements for archival representation of digital publications, asserted their role of primary (or joint) responsibility for maintenance of the digital archive, begun to establish procedures required to maintain archives over decades, and begun to establish partnerships with other stakeholders (i.e., libraries, etc.). I will give concrete examples of each point by using the archival activities of my institute as a case study.

One Society Publisher's Activities

AIP's involvement with archiving began for a very practical reason. After starting in 1995 with online journal access bundled in with print, AIP wanted to evolve to the point where we could offer the choice of online-only subscriptions to our journals. Conversations with librarians made it clear that a robust, assured digital archive was a necessary pre-condition to convincing libraries to abandon print subscriptions. So we began development of a strong policy asserting our commitment to digital preservation. This policy, "Archiving and Use of AIP Electronic Information,"[2] was established in 1998 and revised in 2003 to reflect our increased understanding of the requirements and realities of developing a digital archive. With a policy in place, we then began development of our digital archive, forming partnerships with interested parties to ensure acceptance by the research community.

AIP's policy was developed in close collaboration with volunteer scientists who serve on our advisory committees and librarians representing academe and federal research laboratories. The resulting policy—one of the earliest policies from any publisher—was hailed as a model by many publishers and embraced by research librarians as a reasonable commitment that would allow them to seriously consider converting their subscriptions to online only.

A review of key sections of the policy will define terms important to the archival process and explain how we have gone about implementing the provisions of the policy. The policy begins with a preamble that states our commitment to maintenance of the digital archive while pointing out the complexity involved in doing so at this early point in the digital era, when there remain many open questions.

The American Institute of Physics has extensively studied approaches to retaining and maintaining its electronic information according to the following policy, exercising its best efforts to adapt to rapidly changing publishing technology and financial models. The Institute and subscribers understand that because of the still emerging nature of electronic publishing, there are many technical and financial uncertainties about how archiving will be accomplished by any publisher, library, or third party. However, AIP's intent to maintain an archive of all its electronic journals is clear. The Institute will plan its technical and financial investments accordingly.

The first paragraph of the actual policy describes the scope of the archive. Note that AIP's secondary information products—mainly our Searchable Physics Information Notices (SPIN) database—are not included at this time.

AIP will retain in an archive all electronic information published by the American Institute of Physics. The archive will include all AIP-owned primary publications hosted on its Scitation service, including multimedia elements of journal articles that have been judged by peer review as being essential to the understanding of the article.

The identification of "essential" multimedia is still in progress. A working group of editors, scientists, and technologists is meeting to develop guidelines for determining what elements need to be preserved and what formats or file types should initially be accepted.

A core belief of the scholarly community is that the record of research progress should remain fixed for all time. The next paragraph confirms that principle, but also recognizes that the digital era improves the ability to report corrections, comments, and other related actions in a fashion that improves access by the reader to these important addenda.

Original source material will not be altered, except in extraordinary cases of production errors or similar situations, in which case there will be a clear record of the change. Source material may be annotated or supplemented by clearly noted errata, references, and other developments that may occur subsequent to original publication.

Three paragraphs into the policy, we find the core commitment of the publisher to the preservation of the archive. It also includes provision for multiple copies of the archive to be held at separate sites.

AIP will hold a primary source material archive and be responsible for the periodic refreshing of this archive (to ensure its continuing availability) and its replication to additional archives. The primary source material archive will not be used for active delivery. At least one complete archive will be maintained outside AIP at a site separate and distant from the primary archive.

This paragraph introduces one of the important archival functions: the periodic validation of the integrity of digital files that comprise the archive. This process is called *refreshing* the archive. Note that, although the archive is separate from the system used for active deliver of the content, this does not mean that the archival material is not continuously exercised. Multiple archive locations safeguard the collection from disaster and changes in political climes—assuming that secondary archives are held in multiple countries. We are nearing agreement with the first two remote sites—a prominent academic research library and an equally recognized federally funded research laboratory. Both agreements allow the libraries to experiment with copies of the files to contribute to the record of knowledge regarding digital preservation.

An archive is of little value if it cannot be accessed, so our policy also includes commitments to continued access, even after a journal is discontinued. Migration is an important concept and a potentially expensive proposition that is further spelled out in the next paragraph of the policy.

AIP will ensure access to relevant retrospective archives via subscriptions or other means. If publication of a journal is terminated, AIP will continue to maintain and migrate that journal's database archive and will charge appropriate access fees.

Migration involves the transformation of archival formats when current standard formats are about to be superseded by technology developments. The next paragraph provides further details about the refreshing/migration tasks.

The archive will be reviewed for refreshing or migration to new information formats at appropriate intervals. The initial archive material will be in the predominant current standard (e.g., SGML-based) with suitable current standard-based storage formats for figures, page images, and other information forms as they develop. Information will be migrated to new formats when current formats are in danger of becoming obsolete or unsupportable, or when new formats provide substantial improvements in features with no loss of content.

From its initial stage, the digital archive has contained multiple formats of information. At present, these forms include Standard Generalized Markup Language (SGML), Tagged Image File Format (TIFF), Joint Photographic Experts Group (JPEG), and Portable Document Format (PDF). Over time, these formats will evolve and software developments will require migration or transformation of original file formats to newly emerging standard formats. In physics, the "experts group" that will monitor standard formats will be managed by the International Union of Pure and Applied Physics, a decision taken at an international workshop held in Lyon, France, in 2002.

There are additional principles in the AIP archive policy, which can be viewed in the Archival Journals section of the AIP Web site (http://www.aip.org/journals/archive/).

Summarizing where we are in the implementation of our archive policy, we are just completing the procedures required to do a refresh of the archive—comparing the official archive tapes to the active files being delivered. We expect this refresh—which involves millions of files on hundreds of tapes—to require three to six months and cost $50,000–$100,000 in staff and consulting time. This illustrates another reason why digital is different: The expense involved in maintaining a digital archive is a new cost that must be borne by publishers and other portions of the scholarly research community. We are also working to set up the "expert groups" that will monitor existing and emerging archival standards.

One important realization that has come to us as we begin to implement the project is that preservation metadata is an essential component of the archive. Examples of preservation metadata include byte counts and checksums for each digital file, version numbers of software used to created the files, etc. We will be creating the metadata during the first refreshing process and will make it a step in the publication process for all articles going forward.

Our formal archive is being developed in keeping with the Open Archival Information System (OAIS) reference model. This model provides a comprehensive framework for creation and maintenance of an archive. The OAIS model describes archival concepts, including archive information packages, content information, data objects, representation information, and preservation description information. It defines a variety of archival functions, including ingest, archival storage, data management, preservation planning, administration, and access. It represents the "gold standard" for archive development. If a publisher who claims to be developing a digital archive is not using the OAIS model, you should ask some hard questions before accepting their claim.

Important Policy Questions

I close this chapter by posing some important policy questions that we are still struggling with. Now that "subscription" has come (in the online era) to mean access to a body of material for a defined period of time:

- How much material is included with the "current year" subscription?

- How is archival access (to material published prior to the "current year" content) provided?

- How is the maintenance of the archive to be funded?

We have preliminary answers to at least some of these questions but don't feel that we have fully come to an understanding yet of just exactly what the "right" answers should be. As more publishers join with library groups to explore these important issues, consensus should begin to emerge.

Notes

1. Council on Library and Information Resources and Research Libraries Group, "Preserving Digital Information: Final Report and Recommendations," May 1996 [Online], available: http://www.rlg.org/ArchTF/index.html (accessed June 18, 2004).

2. http://www.aip.org/journals/archive/.

ARCHIVING WITH A TRUSTED THIRD PARTY: AN ACADEMIC LIBRARY'S PERSPECTIVE

Yvonne Lev, Associate University Librarian, Towson University

Why do libraries need to consider archiving with a trusted third party? Won't publishers take care of electronic journal archiving? What about the option of libraries archiving electronic journals themselves? Why would libraries choose to rely on trusted third parties to archive their journals, and what are the economic implications for library budgets?

Archiving electronic journals became a hot issue in 2003 at Towson University, a medium-sized, state-assisted, metropolitan university of about 17,000 students on the outskirts of Baltimore. Because of the convergence of budget cuts from the State of Maryland and unbundling of electronic and print formats by major publishers—Blackwell, Cambridge, Oxford, Kluwer, Karger, and others—the library had an opportunity to choose one format or the other and still provide journal access to Towson users while saving money. At the time most of the journals were purchased, prices were based on the cost of the print subscription. In most cases, online-only access was not an option. Now there is a choice, and the library gave it to the departments that had originally requested the journals.

Why was Towson's library willing to gamble on continuing access to electronic journals and offer departments their choice of format? Our mission and location were two major factors. We are not a research university, although we have recently added three applied doctoral programs to our largely undergraduate institution. Our library's mission has never been to collect books and journals comprehensively. We buy specifically to meet the curricular needs of current students and consider the needs of scholars in the future to be of secondary importance. Furthermore, major research universities, such as Johns Hopkins University, are located not far from Towson, and those libraries buy journals in both paper and electronic formats to support their mission as research universities. In a pinch, our faculty and students can go to there to use paper journals. And there is always interlibrary loan and document delivery!

So what did Towson's departments choose—electronic or paper? At Towson University the 24/7 availability, faster access to new issues, and desktop delivery of articles have become the norm, and our statistics show that the old way of searching the journal stacks for articles has become the exception.

The difference between the cost for print and electronic did not seem to be a factor in the selection of format by faculty. Most departments chose the online journal format over print whether the cost for print-only and electronic-only is the same (as it is for publishers like the Cambridge University Press, Kluwer, Erlbaum, and Wiley), or print is less expensive than the electronic (as it is for a few publishers like the National Research Council in Canada), or publishers charge less for the electronic-only format (as do the Blackwell, ASM, the American Physiological Society, and Oxford University Press).

Two departments chose paper over electronic, even though in some cases the statistics showed that electronic use far exceeded paper use. In those departments, journals that the faculty consider core were kept in paper because there were no firm assurances that electronic access would be permanent—forever and ever—and that Towson users would have access to the electronic archives even after a subscription was cancelled.

Following are questions that were asked by faculty on the Towson campus when considering electronic-only access to journals:

- What if that publisher sells the journal to another publisher or if a society moves its journal from one publisher to another? Who will guarantee that we will still get access to those journal backfiles? Will the previous publisher hand us a CD-ROM and say, that is your archive? That CD-ROM will be of little use to our users 50 or 100 years from now.

- If we do continue to have access to the material we have purchased, what will happen if the price is raised or our budget shrinks so we can no longer afford the journal? (This is not an idle question, since there have been half a dozen journal cancellation projects since 1990 when I first arrived at Towson University.)

- What if the publisher goes out of business altogether or merges with another company?

Responses to these issues include the following:

1. Archiving with the publisher seems like the easiest and most cost-effective way to archive electronic journals. But investigation shows that the archiving provisions by publisher vary and do not seem equally secure.

    For example, the Blackwell Synergy Web site promises ongoing access to archived journal issues "as long as Blackwell continues to publish the journal."

    Looking at another example, according to the FAQ at http://journals.kluweronline.com, "Kluwer has made several provisions for archiving its content: all articles are deposited at OCLC; local hosting options are available for licensees; and Kluwer is actively working with third parties to find a mutually agreeable solution." In May 2003, Kluwer announced that it had signed an agreement with the National Library of the Netherlands on long-term digital archiving. Under the terms of this agreement, the National Library will receive digital copies of all Kluwer journals and books made available on its Web platform, Kluwer Online. The Kluwer FAQ adds, "Kluwer guarantees access through their site for four years after the conclusion of a subscription and will continue to provide access to all [their] journals via either [their] Web site or a comparable searchable medium (such as a CD-ROM). Subscribing institutions may make one copy of licensed material electronically, as well as in print, for backup and archival purposes."

    CD-ROM is not an archival solution. If a library cannot rely on a publisher to provide ongoing access to electronic journal archives, what other alternatives are there?

2. The alternative most like the archiving of paper journals is to archive materials in an institutional repository. Software for LOCKSS (Lots of Copies Keep Stuff Safe) is being beta-tested right now. This Web caching program for electronic journals was designed and is being implemented at Stanford University with funding from the National Science Foundation, Sun Microsystems, and the Andrew Mellon Foundation. According to the LOCKSS Web site, "LOCKSS provides tools which use local, library controlled computers to safeguard reader's long-term access to web based journals. LOCKSS is intended to demonstrate to librarians that it is safe for them to subscribe to the web edition of journals and to cancel the paper edition."

However, LOCKSS does not solve the digital library problem completely. LOCKSS requires that URLs be mostly static; that the Web site have a logical structure; and that the HTTP headers permit caching. It works only for HTTP/HTML and related formats such as GIF and JPEG.

Another example of universities providing their own archiving systems is DSpace. MIT, in collaboration with Hewlett Packard, pioneered a system that implements an institutional repository service. What can be found in DSpace? According to the DSpace Web site, it includes, "MIT Research in digital form, including preprints, technical reports, working papers, conference papers, images and more."

Clifford Lynch, in an interview in *Ubiquity: An ACM IT Magazine and Forum* (July–August 2003), described DSpace this way:

It is a place—a system, technically, but it's important to recognize that it's really a service that will be manifest in a series of evolving systems over time—where faculty can deposit content and the institution will commit to both continued dissemination and preservation of that content, thereby making it less at risk than if it were running on a machine in some faculty office. And an institutional commitment to support the service on a continuing basis. I think that's a very important step. DSpace has been open-sourced, and the Andrew Mellon Foundation and other sources have made funds available for a number of additional institutions to replicate it both in the US and abroad. So there are some reasons to believe that we will see the growth of institutional repositories to provide an institutional stewardship safety Net for this new genre scholarship work.

3. The alternative that we are specifically considering today is archiving with a trusted third party. If we cannot get all publishers to commit to archiving journals in perpetuity and the library can preserve only a portion of its electronic-only resources, how will future generations get access to these materials? Is archiving with a trusted third party the answer? If libraries choose to archive with a trusted third party, what kind of costs should they anticipate?

The following chapters cover two models for archiving electronic journals with a trusted third party. Chuck Costakos, director of content services at OCLC, describes the OCLC model, Electronic Collections Online. Eileen Fenton, the executive director of the Electronic Archiving Initiative launched by JSTOR this year, follows with a chapter on JSTOR's E-Archive.

ARCHIVING WITH A TRUSTED THIRD PARTY: OCLC'S DIGITAL JOURNAL ARCHIVE SERVICE

Chuck Costakos, Director, Content Services, OCLC Online Computer Library Center, Inc.

(Adapted from a PowerPoint™ presentation)

1. OCLC Electronic Collections Online (ECO)

OCLC's digital journal archive service now contains 4,750 journals and 1.6 million full-text articles from 70 publishers. It has been in service for more than 10 years and continues to grow in numbers of full-text articles, journal titles, and publishers.

2. Electronic Collections Online Titles by Subject

Subject	Titles	Subject	Titles
Science	1,610	Geography/anthropology	255
Medicine	1,291	Education	229
Business/finance	799	Political science	201
Technology	629	Law	171
Social sciences	527	Agriculture	161
Psychology/philosophy	320	Religion	85
Language and literature	293	Music/fine Arts	88
History	292	Library science	85

Note that some journals cover more than one subject.

3. Content Fee Options

The price for the content can be affected by whether the institution subscribes to the printed edition of a particular journal. The three types of options are shown below. Some journals are available in an online-only edition, with no connection to print subscriptions, and also may offer a discount for the online edition if the institution subscribes to the print edition of a particular journal.

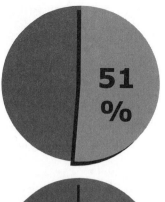

Online Only
The price is *not affected* by whether the library subscribes to the print edition. 51% of the journals fall in this category.

Add Online to Print
If the institution subscribes to the print edition of the journal, there is a discount off the price of the online edition. 38% of the journals offer such a discount.

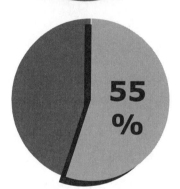

Print Subscriber Program
For 55% of the journals, there is *no additional charge* for the institution to get the electronic edition.

4. OCLC Fees and Terms

- Libraries choose title by title.

- The OCLC access and archiving fee is $12–$20 per title, depending on number of titles.

5. Access Rights

Rights

The library has ongoing rights to access every year/volume paid for even if

- there is no subscription to current issues,

- the journal is sold or discontinued, or

- the publisher agreement with OCLC is terminated.

Access

Access is managed by subscription profile on the OCLC FirstSearch service.

6. Access to Titles

- Access to full Electronic Collections Online Bibliographic Database (all 4,750 titles) is included with a subscription to any journal, and also is included in the OCLC FirstSearch Base Package.

- All journals can be accessed by interlibrary loan, using the library holdings shown in WorldCat.

- Search results are linked to full text within FirstSearch *and* other full text that the library subscribes to via partner information services.

- Per-article access is available for 1,657 current Electronic Collections Online titles:

  ○ Fees average $17.67 for publisher royalty and

  ○ $5 for OCLC costs.

7. Electronic Collections Online Profile: Access

All articles are loaded in OCLC's digital journal archive system, although about 5% of the articles are actually accessed at other sites, such as the publisher's Web site.

8. Electronic Collections Online Profile: Formats

- *Articles* are always either in PDF or HTML. Some include multiple formats as options, such as GIF, PostScript, DVI, SVC, TEX, and RealPage.

- *Metadata* for the articles (author, title, etc.) is principally in SGML tagged format. A small but growing number are coded in XML format.

9. OCLC Digital Archive initiatives

The preceding points deal mainly with accessing content from OCLC's digital journal archive. Now we turn our attention to preservation of the digital content:

- OCLC's digital archive encompasses much more than digital journals. State libraries, federal agencies, academic libraries, and museum libraries can use Web archiving for item-by-item harvesting and submission of Web pages and Web-based documents, or batch archiving to submit their collections on various storage media for ingest and auto-mated metadata creation at OCLC. The OCLC Digital Archive has been developed em-ploying industry standards, including Dublin Core, Open Archival Information System (OAIS), and the emerging Metadata Encoding and Transmission Standard (METS), to name some of the well-known efforts in this field.

- OCLC has developed tools for such archiving functions as

    - harvesting and archiving HTML pages and PDFs from the Web,

    - batch ingest processing of digital information,

    - collecting preservation metadata, and

    - administration of digital resources.

- In addition, OCLC is conducting research into preservation options for various commonly used file types, such as HTML, PDF, TXT, TIFF, JPEG, GIF, and BMP.

10. OCLC Digital Archive Protection

Bit preservation actions include the following:

- off-site storage of both journal content *and* subscription profiles,

- disaster recovery methodologies,

- refreshment of the data on storage media, and

- ongoing virus and fixity checks. (A *fixity check* is a method of verifying that an archived stream of binary digits in a digital object has not been corrupted.)

11. OCLC Digital Archive Protection

This includes

- periodic inventory of file types in each digital journal and

- actions based on risk assessment, the properties of each of the file types, and on input from the library community.

Preservation options include

- migration to a new version or a new format,

- emulation, and

- as a last resort, distribution for local mounting.

12. Electronic Collections Online Future Enhancements

Additional features for libraries will include

- simplified pricing;

- simplified ordering;

- packages of e-journals, packages with e-books; and

- continued commitment to the e-journal archive.

13. Partnership with Publishers

Additional features being considered for publishers are

• archive protection by a trusted third party,

• options for a dark archive, and

• backup online access and other services.

More information on OCLC Electronic Collections Online is available at http://www.oclc.org/electroniccollections/default.htm. More information on OCLC Digital Archiving is available at http://www.oclc.org/digitalpreservation/.

ARCHIVING WITH A TRUSTED THIRD PARTY

Eileen Gifford Fenton, JSTOR

Elements of a Trusted Archive

Available Resources

- Report of the Task Force on Archiving of Digital Information

    ◦ 1996, sponsored by the Commission on Preservation and Access and the Research Libraries Group (www.rlg.org/ArchTF/)

- Trusted Digital Repositories: Attributes, and Responsibilities

    ◦ 2002, sponsored by the Research Libraries Group and OCLC (www.rlg.org/longterm/repositories.pdf)

Mission

The mission is absolutely critical:

- It drives resource allocation,

- guides decision making, and

- shapes routine priorities and activities.

If archiving is the mission, preservation is no longer the poor cousin competing for resources.

Business Model

- The revenue stream must be sufficient to cover the cost of the archive's work.

- The source(s) of revenue must be evaluated for reliability and predictability.

- Sustainability of the model must be assessed.

Technological Infrastructure

The infrastructure must

- support the diversity of content entrusted to the archive,

- support the necessary range of functions,

- comply with accepted models and best practice, and

- be maintained over time.

Relationships with Libraries

Libraries

- traditionally charged with the work of preservation and

- represent the needs of scholars—today and for generations to come.

Relationships with Publishers

- The archive must secure the rights necessary to carry out its preservation work.

- The archive must establish the agreements necessary for the secure and timely deposit of content.

- Deposits may need to be ongoing.

What Is Not an Archive?

- Eileen's voice mail collection

- A collection of digital materials

- A mirror site

JSTOR's Electronic-Archiving Initiative

- The goal is to establish a credible, sustainable operation for archiving electronic scholarly resources.

- The approach must include all key components required for an ongoing archiving enterprise.

- It builds on JSTOR's ongoing work as an archive of digitized print journals.

At the 2003 Conference, the focus of electronic publishing concerns seemed to revert back to journals after the extended focus on e-books. This discussion on electronic publishing covers a wide range of issues including resource management, purchasing decisions, migration management, linking, vanishing articles, and deep log analysis.

Electronic Publishing

ELECTRONIC RESOURCE MANAGEMENT: VALUE OF IN-HOUSE DEVELOPMENT VERSUS VENDED APPROACH

Robert Alan, Head, Serials Department, Pennsylvania State University Libraries

Introduction

During the past 10 years there has been a significant increase in the number of electronic resources available for purchase. Library users are now expecting 24/7 desktop access to resources formerly only available in print. The growth of electronic resources in libraries, combined with the challenges associated with keeping track of electronic resources, has resulted in the development of in-house electronic resource management systems. But library vendors have also responded to market demand by developing vended approaches to electronic resource management. This chapter focuses on the in-house approach to electronic resource management.

In-House View of Electronic Resource Management

In response to the need to improve management of electronic resources, Penn State developed an in-house electronic resource management system in 1999. The Electronic Resources Licensing Center (ERLIC) database was originally created as a stand-alone ACCESS database to manage information relating to electronic resources that could not be maintained in the University Libraries in-house–developed Library Information Access System (LIAS) library management system.[1] The original intent of ERLIC was to track orders and subscription renewals, but the database quickly expanded into much more. ERLIC provided budgetary support, access and authentication information, status of current and pending orders, licensing terms, reports, and a data file for document delivery blocking, and supported the generation of Penn State's A–Z list.

Development of the original in-house ERLIC database required a significant staff commitment. But why develop an in-house electronic resource management system in the first place? There were several factors that led to the development of ERLIC. First of all, the dynamic, even unpredictable growth of electronic resources at Penn State and lack of an acceptable vendor solution in 1999 required some action. Penn State also had a culture of in-house development and sufficient staff and system resources to devote to such a project. Penn State's LIAS system supported ordering and payment functions but was not designed at that time to accommodate electronic resource management. Penn State was also in the process of planning for a future migration to a new integrated library management system.

As an ACCESS database, ERLIC quickly became very large and required more staff time to maintain. Information needs of the primary stakeholders (collection development) were not being met due to access limitations. In 2002/2003 a new Web version of ERLIC called ERLIC[2] was developed and implemented. ERLIC[2]'s goals included enhancing access to the full content of ERLIC, access to critical documentation such as licenses not previously available in ERLIC, and the reports function. Additional data elements were added to bring ERLIC[2] into closer compliance with the data model being developed by the Digital Library Federation Electronic Resource Management Initiative (ERMI).[2]

ERLIC[2] required a considerable commitment of staff time. An estimated 300 hours were devoted to the coding. This estimate did not include time devoted to the planning phase of the project. It is important to note that while much of the data migrated from ERLIC to ERLIC[2], an additional 300 hours of keying, updating, review, and data cleanup were required. Ongoing maintenance of ERLIC[2] will require approximately .5 FTE of staff (20 hours per week) to ensure the database is up-to-date and data are accurately maintained.

The current configuration of electronic resource management at Penn State includes several components (Figure 1). The ERLIC[2] database includes order, payment, access, and authentication data. The A–Z list is generated from ERLIC[2] and updated in real time. An optical imaging database of critical documentation (e.g., licenses, invoices, etc.) is under development, and the images will be linked to ERLIC[2]. Staff will be able to search ERLIC[2] for detailed information on electronic resources and eventually view images of critical documentation. ERLIC[2] is a more integrated database than the original ERLIC database, as data formerly maintained in separate EXCEL and ACCESS databases were integrated into the ERLIC[2] design.

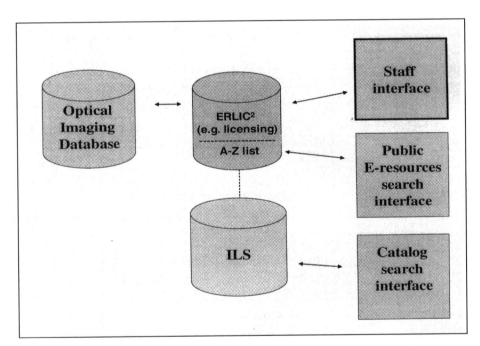

Figure 1. Current Configuration.

While ERLIC[2] has improved integration and access, there are also limitations that need to be addressed. There continues to be a need to better leverage data maintained in the library management system and reduce redundancy resulting from the need to maintain some data in both ERLIC[2] and the library management system. Journal aggregators are accessible via the A–Z list generated from ERLIC[2], but in most cases title level records do not appear in the online catalog. And there is a need to support more effective linking to the title and article level.

Given the success and limitations of ERLIC and ERLIC[2], what is to be gained from developing an in-house electronic resource management system? Based on Penn State's experience, there is much greater knowledge of the data and how the data can be used. This knowledge can be put to work to customize ERLIC[2] to better meet stakeholders' information needs. Development of an in-house database led to an increased awareness of the need for standards. However, it can also be concluded that the development of ERLIC and ERLIC^2 required a significant commitment of staff time.

Library vendors are responding to demand for new products and services that support various aspects of electronic resource management. Penn State now has the ability to acquire specialized capabilities beyond ERLIC^2 that would add value to existing service. There is also a willingness on the part of the Libraries to work collaboratively with outside vendors.

In 2002 the University Libraries Linking Task Force was charged to examine technological alternatives to the time-intensive processing and access work currently managed by library staff and to provide "one-stop shopping" for users to fulfill research and teaching needs. The task force's final recommendation was to continue ERLIC^2 for management of the order, access, supplier, and payment information and to contract out other services such as the A–Z list, linking, and purchase of MARC records for journal aggregators. The vendor solutions will hopefully be implemented in 2004.

Penn State continues to monitor the marketplace and is also encouraging its library management system vendor to support management of electronic resources. Penn State fully supports the development of standards that would eventually facilitate importing of data (e.g., licensing data) directly into either ERLIC^2 and/or the library management system. While ERLIC and ERLIC^2 databases have provided and continue to provide excellent support for management of electronic resources at Penn State, there are now viable alternatives to the in-house approach to be considered.

Notes

1. For additional information on ERLIC, see the summary of the 1999 NASIG Workshop presented by Nancy Stanley, Betty Nirnberger, and Angelina Holden; Donnice Cochenour, "Taming the Octopus: Getting a Grip on Electronic Resources," *Serials Librarian* 38 nos. 3/4 (2000): 363–68.

2. For a description of the Digital Library Federation Electronic Resource Initiative (ERMI), see *A Web Hub for Developing Administrative Metadata for Electronic Resource Management*, maintained by Adam Chandler, Cornell University, and Tim Jewell, University of Washington [Online], available: http://www.library.cornell.edu/cts/elicensestudy/home.html (accessed June 18, 2004).

CONVERTING TO E-JOURNALS? WHEN DO WE NEED TO KEEP PRINT?

Sandy Campbell, Science and Technology Library, University of Alberta, Edmonton

Abstract

As we move to an environment in which all of our periodicals and many of our serials are available in electronic format, and our buying power is shrinking in spite of budget increases, it makes sense to cancel the print subscriptions that duplicate the electronic. In many cases this saves us the cost of the duplicate subscriptions, and even when the print "comes with" the electronic at no additional charge, canceling the print saves us the cost of receiving, processing, binding, shelving, and circulating the print copies of serials. As we move to an increasingly electronic environment, we need to establish criteria that will guide us in selecting those titles that we must maintain in both print and electronic format.

Background

In 2000, through the Canadian National Site Licensing Project (CNSLP), the University of Alberta Library received access to more than 700 titles in electronic format. These included journals from the following publishers: Academic Press (199 titles), American Chemical Society (33 titles), Institute of Physics (39 titles), Royal Society of Chemistry (28 titles), and Springer Verlag (402 titles). New titles have also been added over the life of the project. The abundance of electronic titles allowed faculty, staff, and students to become familiar with this format and to realize its advantages.

By the fall of 2001, recognizing that we could not continue to maintain both electronic and print subscriptions, cancellation of the print equivalents of electronic journals became the clear direction of the University of Alberta Library. With the knowledge that maintaining print duplicates would be an exception, selectors needed to understand the conditions under which print journals would still be required.

There is little in the literature that discusses the issue of maintaining print as well as electronic subscriptions. In 1999, Frazer and Morgan at Old Dominion University identified a series of factors that they had hoped would be "formulated into criteria which could be applied to electronic-for-print substitution questions." These included adequacy of hardware both inside the library and elsewhere, software support, adequacy of the electronic versions, long-term accessibility, solutions to cataloging and bibliographic control, faculty input, and consideration of "areas of excellence." In their analysis they noted that they needed to add a print subscription for one title because "much of its research value lay in the illustrations (photomicrographs and halftones) that are far better for research as originals than as photocopies."[1] However, no other criteria for preferring print to electronic journals were described.

Many of the problems that the Old Dominion University study identified still exist; however, there have been solutions found to some of these, particularly in the area of print and delivery technology. We can expect that over the next five years the issues of unstable software, hardware, adequacy of the copy, and bibliographic control will be largely solved. If we assume that the technical problems will be solved, and e-journals are the preferred choice for delivery, we are still left with a final question: Are there any journals for which we will always need to maintain both a print and electronic copy?

To begin answering this question, the Science and Technology Library Selectors Team developed its preliminary list of criteria for maintenance of print in addition to electronic titles by reviewing sample issues looking for potential problems and by consulting with faculty in scientific and technical departments on specific points of functionality.

The Collection Development Committee, a librarywide committee, then reviewed the list. This group recognized the value of having criteria that could be applied to e-publications beyond those licensed through CNSLP. The criteria were broadened so that they could be applied to serials as well as periodicals and could be used to evaluate publications outside the CNSLP license. The result is a list of criteria against which we can test any new continuing electronic product to determine whether print should be maintained in conjunction with the electronic format.

Applying the Criteria

Many of these criteria, such as the right to copy articles for interlibrary loan and the issue of perpetual access, are answered by reviewing the vendor contract, or in our initial case, the CNSLP contract. Others, such as Web site stability and the monographic nature of some journals, require selector and user knowledge of the title or site. Still others, such as the issue of collections of excellence and geographic specialization, require local policy decisions.

The first criterion, involving the determination of content equivalency, is the most time-consuming to apply. In the case of the CNSLP titles, student workers compared the most current print and electronic issues page-by-page. A comparison checklist (see Appendix A of this chapter) was developed, based in part on the 2001 work of Henebry and Safley.[2]

To test the second criterion, printability, the students printed from each journal the image that they thought would be the most complex or difficult to reproduce.

Criteria for Maintaining Print Copies of Electronic Journals

Preamble

These criteria are meant to be starting points for the consideration of the issues involved. Not all will apply to every title. Sometimes several will apply, but one will outweigh others.

The criteria need to be applied with discretion. Selectors deciding if the print is required need to consider the extent to which the usability of the content is limited by any of the issues raised by the electronic format. Is the Web site down consistently or rarely? Is a single article missing or a year's worth of issues? Is the problem one that has been corrected over time?

Selectors also need to be open to other potential criteria. For example, there may be user requirements for print that we have simply not anticipated. There may also be good political reasons for maintaining the print copies of certain journals.

Making the decision to cancel print subscriptions takes us into a realm of collection building where there are uncertainties. We have to recognize that we may make errors and that some print subscriptions may need to be reinstated. However, making the decision to duplicate electronic subscriptions in print involves a cost burden and often means that another title cannot be purchased, so the decision must be made thoughtfully.

Criteria

1. Substantial Content Is Missing from the E-Journal

The most obvious reason for keeping the print copy of a journal is that the electronic version does not contain all of the content of the print. Most journals received through aggregated services fall into this category. Individual selectors must decide whether the omissions are "substantial." If the instructions to authors have been moved from the individual issues to the main page of the journal, that is probably not a "substantial" omission. The information is still accessible. If, however, articles, whole issues, supplements, or images were routinely missing, maintenance of the print would probably be indicated. For example *Canadian Geographic* as presented in *Academic Search Premiere* contains no images, so that title would need to be maintained in print. Our review of the titles acquired through CNSLP did not reveal "substantial" omissions.

2. Content Not Reproducible in Electronic Format

If a journal contains materials meant to be touched or smelled or have other qualities not reproducible in the electronic environment, then the print must be maintained. For example a publication containing samples of textiles or wallpaper, meant to be touched, would have to be maintained in paper format. In our tests of the CNSLP titles, we did not find irreproducible materials. We were particularly concerned with the quality of color images, but found that using a standard office color printer (Hewlett Packard Desk Jet 1120 C), we were able to reproduce images in which the color was indistinguishable from the original. Faculty members reviewing the prints and the originals found them adequate for scientific purposes. In some cases, faculty found the ability to "zoom" on an image made the electronic image more useful than the one in print. However, we are aware that the reproduction of color images on a standard computer screen or from most printers will not be exactly the same as the original image. For some users, only the original will be adequate. For example, fine arts students studying painting techniques rely on images of paintings in journals to be as close to the original work as possible.

3. Oversize Inserts

Our review of current issues of CNSLP journals did not reveal any examples of oversized inserts. However, we are aware of journals that routinely contain large foldout maps or posters. While these might be available in electronic format, they cannot be viewed at full size on a standard monitor. For example, a geologic map might show a formation that extends half a meter on paper and is not comprehensible when viewed on a screen in sections or at a less-detailed scale.

4. Requires Special Equipment

Our review of current issues of CNSLP journals did not reveal any examples of this. However, we are aware of journals that contain material that would require special equipment for reproduction. In the example of the geologic map in criterion 3, a plotter would be required to make a print of the map.

5. Monographic Journals and "Read Much" Journals

Work by Summerfield, Mandel, and Kantor on e-books at Columbia University identified "read much" books as being more usable in print than in electronic format.[3] "Read much" materials are those that are studied closely and intensively. They are works that the user might read cover to cover, such as literary works, or may use intensively, flipping from part to part. Length of the publication, by itself, does not define a "read much" work; rather it is the need to work intensively with the entire text. Extreme examples of "read much" journals are those issued as monographs. For example, *Lecture Notes in Mathematics*, a CNSLP title, is published in monograph format.

6. Restricted Access

If access to a journal is restricted to individual stations or buildings, or a user must have a password to read the journal, then the use of the e-journal is more restricted than the use of the print journal. Print journals do not require the user to sit in a particular place to use them, nor do they require the user to remember a password. If the e-journal is more cumbersome to use than the print, then libraries will want to maintain print. None of the CNSLP titles has access restrictions. However, other journals available in electronic format, such as *Polymer Engineering and Science,* do have such restrictions.

7. Interlibrary Loan Not Permitted

If the library has a mandate to supply interlibrary loan services to other libraries and the contract forbids the printing and mailing of copies of articles, then the library will have to decide whether it is a priority to maintain a print copy of the journal to continue supplying interlibrary loans. The CNSLP contract permits interlibrary loans.

8. Web Site Is Unstable

Although the CNSLP publishers are all fairly large and stable organizations, other e-journal publishers, particularly small association publications and some government departments, may have difficulty maintaining a stable Web site. If libraries cannot be confident that they will have access to the journal when their users need it, then the print will have to be maintained.

9. No Alternate Site

Most large publishers, such as those whose journals are licensed through CNSLP, have mirror sites and will be able to reroute traffic from one to another if a server fails. However, many small publishers do not have this backup. If the publisher has no alternative site, libraries may wish to maintain a print copy.

10. No Permanent/Safe Archive

If the library has a mandate to maintain an archive of the material that it collects, continued access to the content is an important consideration. This information can only be determined through discussion with the publisher—usually in the context of licensing. The CNSLP license includes a "perpetual access" clause, which guarantees that libraries will continue to be able to use the electronic journals to which they have subscribed. However, some e-journal publishers make no attempt to archive their publications. Some simply have a "rolling wall" and maintain only the most recent issues. For example, *Northern Miner*, like many newspapers, currently maintains only the current material online.

11. Collections of Excellence

If the library has "collections of excellence," this may be a consideration for maintaining the print copies of journals. There is no reason to believe that a "collection of excellence" could not be entirely in electronic format, so the library may not choose to buy the current duplicate subscription. However, if the "collection of excellence" includes an archival or historical function, the library might choose to keep the "comes with print" issues and might accept donations of journal backruns.

12. Geographic Specialization

When searching for regional or local publications, there is an expectation that large libraries in the specific region will hold them. For this reason, the maintenance of print copies of locally or regionally produced e-publications may be desirable. Archiving of geographically specialized publications may be something that can be shared among libraries. There are no publications specific to Alberta in the CNSLP journals.

13. Paper Retained by Agreement/Contract

Although this is not a part of the CNSLP agreement, other contracts or agreements may require the library to keep a paper copy. Depository agreements would be an example. This situation should be distinguished from agreements in which the library is required to buy the print and electronic together. In this case, if the library decides that the electronic copy is adequate, the print can be discarded.

14. Judicial Requirement for Paper Copies

In many jurisdictions, legislative materials and law reports, which are presented in a court of law, must be copies from "official sources." Databases are not considered "official sources." In this case, the library must maintain the print copy. This criterion applies to serial materials rather than journals and does not apply to any titles under the CNSLP agreement.

15. Faculty Need

Faculty may come up with some criteria that we cannot imagine at the moment, although our many discussions have not revealed any to this point.

Notes

1. Stuart L. Frazer and Pamela Morgan, "Electronic-for-Print Journal Substitutions: A Case Study," *Serials Review* 25, no. 2 (1999): 1–7.

2. Carolyn Henebry and Ellen Safley, "Before You Cancel the Paper, Beware—All Electronic Journals in 2002 Are Not Created Equal" (paper presented at North American Serials Interest Group, 16th Annual Conference, May 23–26, 2001).

3. Mary Summerfield, Carol Mandel, and Paul Kantor, *The Potential of Online Books in the Scholarly World—From the Columbia University Online Books Evaluation Project*, December 1999, 17 [Online], available: http://www.columbia. edu/cu/libraries/digital/olbdocs/potential.doc (accessed June 18, 2004).

Appendix A: University of Alberta, Science and Technology Library: Project to Compare Print and Electronic Journal Content Non-CNSLP Titles

Title of Journal _____ Publisher _____

We will then compare the issues with the e-issues looking for:

1. Completeness of the issue including:

    ___ All articles present

    ___ Are the articles available in: ☐ PDF ☐ HTML ☐ other (e.g., postscript)

    ___ Supplements present

    Advertisements (print missing ads for such things as invitations to review papers)

    ___ Calls for papers

    ___ Letters to editor

    ___ Are color images, color in the online version?

    ___ Any other differences?

    ___ Is there something in the e-copy not available in the paper copy?

2. Speed of publication: Is the most current issue on the shelf available electronically? It should be, but we need to ask the question.

3. Legibility: Can you see on the screen all of the things you can see on the printed page, paying particular attention to the graphics-like material listed above, and including color to black-and-white conversion?

    If there are color images, please print a color page (preferably from the PDF version.) If there are PDF and HTML versions of the colour images, compare both. Are there differences?

4. Printability: When you print the page, can you still read the content?

5. Completeness of the volume: Are all issues of the journal year-to-date available online?

VALUE FOR MONEY IN THE ONLINE ENVIRONMENT

John Cox, Managing Director, John Cox Associates, Ltd.

Introduction

Measuring use and assessing what constitutes "value for money" in scholarly journal publishing has always been difficult. In the print environment, usage has been measured by reshelving statistics and by analyses of cost per article or cost per published page. Neither really measures the number of times an article is "used." The rapidly growing use of online content has extended the use of even the most specialized and esoteric journals.

This chapter is based on a paper that I wrote early in 2003, published in *Serials Review*. I want to review various methods of establishing "value," including a comparison of journal prices, not only at the journal but also at the article level, and other measures that are relevant to the online environment. From the publisher's viewpoint, this may be seen as a simple arithmetical calculation of the price charged divided by the number of uses made of the journal. From the library's perspective, there are indirect costs of space, staff, and other overhead to add to the direct cost of the acquisitions budget of the title concerned.

The first step was to bring together some empirical data from two contrasting publishers:

- Emerald: a commercial journal publisher with 116 primary journals in management, engineering, applied science, and technology.

- Institute of Physics Publishing: a non-profit society publishing 34 research journals in physics as well as a range of encyclopedias, textbooks, and proceedings. It also publishes magazines and other resources for schools. IOPP is digitizing all its journals back to 1874.

I have compared the data supplied by these two publishers with other evidence in the published literature to evaluate and compare alternative methods of measuring "value" and validating pricing online journals.

The Environment

Academic libraries in the United States get their funding from the university of which they are a part. Within the overall library budget, some 46% represents staff costs, while other operating costs account for 13%. Of the remaining 41% spent on materials, some 63% is spent on serials, 26% of the total library expenditure. Although these figures are based on U.S. academic libraries, there is no reason to think that funding and expenditure patterns are significantly different in Europe or elsewhere. Libraries spend approximately US$1.50 on staff and operating costs for every $1.00 spent on materials.

Emerald

Emerald provides a dramatic contrast between print (plus online) and electronic-only pricing. The aggregate 2002 UK institutional subscription price for all of these titles, for print plus online access, was $750,000. The Emerald Full Text Database provides access to over

40,000 full text articles from the Emerald journals back to 1994 and is priced at not much more than $42,000.

The contrast between Emerald's print plus online and online prices per journal, per article, and per page is striking (see Table 1).

Table 1. Emerald Journal Pricing per Title, per Article, and per Page

Type	Median Price per Title (US$)	Average Price per Article (US$)	Average Price per Page (US$)
Individual journals: print + electronic	3,849	108.50	7.66
Emerald Full Text Database: electronic only	218	6.14	0.43

This can be explained by Emerald's decision to shift its publishing output from print to electronic. It has taken a risk—that its electronic databases will not generate revenue sufficient to replace its income from its individual journal subscriptions. It is encouraging libraries to replace their Emerald print subscriptions with the Emerald Full Text Database. It is reengineering its business model to meet the requirements of the current market.

IOPP

Institute of Physics Publishing (IOPP) presents less of a contrast between print and electronic pricing, if only because it has not experienced the same sort of criticism of its pricing policy as Emerald did in the early to mid-1990s. Consequently, it has not faced the need to reinvent the way it does business. (See Table 2.)

Table 2. IOPP Journal Pricing per Title, per Article, and per Page

Type	Median Price per Title (US$)	Average Price per Article (US$)	Average Price per Page (US$)
Individual journals: print + electronic	1,270	4.79	0.51

IOPP does not offer a full text database that is comparable with Emerald Full Text. Its pricing is generally based around the institutional subscription price. It should be noted that this table does not illustrate the price per article or price per page advantage to be gained from negotiating a consortium license.

Price Per Use

It is self-evident that an expensive journal that is well used may be better value for money than a low-priced title that is read infrequently. In its 2002 report on scientific publishing, Morgan Stanley provided some data to illustrate this point on a selection of STM titles (see Table 3).

Table 3. Journal Cost per Use

Journal	Publisher	Cost (US$)	Number of Uses	$ per Use
Brain Research Bulletin	ANKHO [now Elsevier]	2,385	187	12.75
Hospital Medicine	Mark Allen Publishing	398	6	66.33
Advances in Clinical Chemistry	Academic Press [now Elsevier]	98	3	32.67
International Journal of Neuroscience	Gordon & Breach [now Taylor & Francis]	5,922	183	32.36
Archives of Physiology and Biochemistry	Swets & Zeitlinger	496	18	27.56
Brain Behaviour and Evolution	Karger	1,389	52	26.71
Journal of Neuroscience Research	Wiley-Liss	5,095	483	10.56
Brain Research	Elsevier	14,669	1,777	8.25

Source: Morgan Stanley, *Scientific Publishing: Knowledge Is Power,* 2002 [Online], available: www.alpsp.org/MorgStan300902.pdf.

A high-priced ($14,669) title like *Brain Research* yielded a cost per use of $8.25, while a journal like *Hospital Medicine*, with a subscription price of $398, yielded a cost per use of $66.33. There is more to value than the headline subscription rate.

Don't Overstate "Use"

Online usage provides absolutely rigorous data on access but creates a host of difficulties of definition and interpretation. I asked both Emerald and IOPP to exclude all free access to table of contents information, abstracts, or any free access to full text material, and to define full text access as a download or printout of the article. Browsing was excluded. Both organizations were requested to provide information on the following basis:

- Number of paid-for article downloads or prints; articles accessed free of charge either on free trial or, in the case of Emerald, free as part of its "Journal of the Week" facility were explicitly excluded.

- Number of articles available online by month throughout 2002.

- Revenue generated by the online journal.

The last measure caused some debate. Online-only subscriptions, revenue from licensing online access to consortia, and pay-per-view sales made online are clearly wholly generated by the electronic journal. But the most difficult—and largest—portion of electronic revenue is that generated by individual journal subscriptions for both print and electronic access. Most journals continue to have high fixed costs and a low number of subscribers, whether delivered in print or online. In the event, a purely subjective judgment had to be made, and it was agreed that 50% of the subscription revenue should be attributed to the electronic version.

The average cost per use in 2002 of each publisher was calculated, and the result was as shown in Table 4.

Table 4. Cost per Use (US$): January–December 2002

Publisher	Number of Articles Available			Total Downloads	Price per article	Average price per use
	January	December	Average			
Emerald	117,226	154,882	136,054	3,093,655	6.14	4.58
IOPP	32,091	39,934	36,012	3,062,502	4.79	5.46

Calculating Operational Cost Savings in the Library: The Drexel Study

The first systematic analysis of the organizational impact of the migration to electronic journals is a case study by Montgomery and King at Drexel University, which identified changes in staff, resources, equipment, and space needed, and the impact on the library's operational costs.[1] Drexel was early in moving to a journal collection that is now predominantly electronic: 8,600 electronic and 370 print journal titles in 2002.

The study examined all costs, including all attributable overhead and fixed costs: Space, systems, services, supplies, and staff were allocated separately to unbound print journals (current issues), bound journal volumes, and electronic journals. It addressed the complexity of assessing electronic journal costs by looking at different e-journal categories: individual subscriptions, publishers' packages (whether or not they were part of a consortium "deal"), and packages of journals from different publishers (e.g., Muse, JSTOR).

The study clearly demonstrated that the perception of value changes if cost per use is used as a measure of a journal's "worth." Montgomery and King included aggregators' databases of full text, which I considered somewhat different and therefore excluded. In summary, their data can be consolidated and restated in summary form as shown in Table 5.

Table 5. Operational Costs for Journals

Journal Type	Subscription Cost	Cost per Title	Recorded Use	Subscription Cost/Use	Operational Cost per Use	Total Cost per Use
Electronic journals						
Individual subscriptions	$ 73,000	$432	23,000	$3.20	$0.45	$4.00
Publishers' packages	$304,000	$134	134,000	$2.25	$0.45	$3.00
Multipublisher packages	$ 27,000	$ 60	20,000	$1.35	$0.45	$2.00
Total	$404,000	$626	177,000	$6.80	$1.35	$9.00
Print journals						
Current journals	$ 38,000	$100	15,000	$2.50	$6.00	$8.50
Bound journals	N/A	N/A	8,800	N/A	$30.00	$30.00
Total	$ 38,000	$100	23,800	$2.50	$36.00	$38.50

Interpreting these figures is fraught with difficulty. The study acknowledges that the print and electronic use data are not directly comparable. The Drexel study was undertaken in the absence of agreed standards on how usage data should be defined and measured. This is fully acknowledged by the authors, who, nevertheless, maintain that, in spite of the difficulties, large differences in operational costs are meaningful:

- The operational costs per use of $30.00 for bound print titles—where 80% of this cost is attributable to the space they occupy—and $6.00 for current print subscriptions are striking compared with $0.45 per use for electronic journals.

- Publisher and vendor packages are cost-effective, though the titles in these packages are not selected individually.

The Need for Standards

Measuring the use of online information should be done in a more agreed-upon and consistent way. Both publishers and their customers want to know how information is being used. But to be meaningful, the recording and reporting of online usage data must be done to agreed-upon international standards. Counting Online Usage of NeTworked Electronic Resources (COUNTER) released a Code of Practice on January 14, 2003, that specifies and defines the data elements involved, and the format, delivery, frequency, and granularity of output reports in respect of journals and databases. It defines how remote usage of institutionally licensed products can be measured. The significance of COUNTER is that it is a genuinely international effort, widely supported by librarians, subscription agents and other intermediaries, and publishers, as well as their professional organizations. It is with COUNTER that we can begin some more rigorous analysis of usage and cost data.

Notes

1. C. H. Montgomery and D. W. King, "Comparing Library and User Related Costs of Print and Electronic Journal Collections—A First Step Towards a Comprehensive Analysis," *D-Lib Magazine* 8, no. 10, 2002 [Online], available: www.dlib.org/dlib/december02/king/12king.html (accessed June 18, 2004).

"A SLICE OF THE LIFE OF AN ELECTRONIC RESOURCES MAVEN": OR—HOW DATABASE PURCHASE DECISIONS ARE REALLY MADE IN LIBRARIES

Eleanor Cook, Appalachian State University
Stefanie DuBose, East Carolina University
Wes Daughtry, East Carolina University
John Abbott, Appalachian State University

Background and Introduction

This skit was conceived during the 2002 Charleston Conference after Barbara Meyers and her colleagues devoted some time to something similar from the publishers' point of view. In fact, Barbara had led humorous skits at several past Charleston Conferences

Katina asked Eleanor Cook and Stefanie DuBose to work on something—and Eleanor asked John Abbott, her colleague at Appalachian State University—to collaborate with us. The resulting script, drafted primarily by John but added to by Stefanie, Wes Daughtry, and Lauren Corbett, reflects a lighthearted yet frighteningly real slice of the life of a librarian working with electronic resources. The main character, "Silky Searyals" was certainly drawn by John with Appalachian State University's environment in mind, but anyone who works with the acquisitions of electronic products will recognize and identify with these situations. We had dozens of people come up to us afterwards throughout the 2003 Conference, telling us how funny the skit was, and also how real-to-life it was—it hit home with many, even the publishers and vendors!

It is our hope to bring another skit to the podium in 2004.

John Abbott
Eleanor Cook
Lauren Corbett
Wes Daughtry
Stefanie Dubose

> The Script: John Abbott, Appalachian State University
>
> The Players:
>
>> Silky Searyals: Eleanor Cook, Appalachian State University
>>
>> Female Voice: Stefanie DuBose, East Carolina University
>>
>> Male Voice: Wes Daughtry, East Carolina University
>>
>> Sign Master: Lauren Corbett, Emory University

The "schtick" is a day-in-the-life, as suggested, done sort of "Greater Tuna" style with minimal cast, props, etc.

Set:

Desk, piled high with paper (any table from the Lightsey will do)

Chair

Phone set that looks like it would have an answering machine

Wastepaper basket

Cardboard box to simulate a computer (or a real laptop would work)

Cast:

Silky Searyals, serials librarian extraordinaire

The Voices (dressed in black, seated with backs to the audience)

Sign Master out front

Time: 8:13 A.M. Tuesday (Sign Master)

Silky Searyals (SS) arrives at her office, dragging two or three large canvas bags stuffed with junk from conference exhibits. Talking to unseen people offstage.

A Voice (V): How was the conference?

SS: Yeah, the conference was great. What was that? (*Pause*) Oh, how nice. Everyone needs a 27th cat . . . (*Drops the bags on the floor*)

SS sits down at her desk, roots through some piles saying she is looking for her to-do list. She finds some of this and that in her search (an old banana, shoe, etc.). Finds the to-do list.

SS: Ah, Now back to work.

V picks up a hand bell and rings it. The phone is ringing. SS picks up the phone.

SS: Hello, this is Silky. . . . Oh, good morning Madame Director . . . we finally have the budget figures for 03/04? . . . only a 15% one-time reduction this year combined with last year's 12% permanent reduction. Isn't that special? (*Hangs up*)

On the table is a basket labeled "Mail," and it is overflowing.

SS turns to the mail and begins sorting business mail from catalogs, flyers, etc.

SS: Why don't these vendors target the library markets better?(*Holds up a Victoria's Secret catalog*)

SS: Here is some interesting realia.(*Holds up another oddball catalog/mailing illustrating the off-target junk we receive*)

V rings the bell. SS answers the phone.

SS: This is Silky, may I help you?

V (*in chipper British accent*): Yes, good morning, this is Jack with Top Inflation Publishers calling from the U.K. I am calling in regards to the e-mail I sent you 15 seconds ago about our extensive new product line. Have you had a chance to read it yet?

SS (*turning to her computer*): No, Jack—I was too busy responding to the quick money-making opportunity from Nigeria. If all goes well, I will be a millionaire by next week- and I plan to donate all the money to the serials budget, of course.

V: Well, let me tell you about our offer and upcoming big sale. For this month only we . . . .

SS: Excuse me, but I just got in from the Librarians Without Funding conference . . . . we're modeled after Doctors without Borders, you know. . . . My inbox, mailbox, and brain are simply too full to listen right now. Let me read your e-mail later and if I think we might be interested, I'll call you back.

V: May I call you back in a few days after you have chance to read my e-mail?

SS: No, I will call you. Thanks. Take care. Goodbye.

> *SS flips through some papers. Phone rings.*

SS: Hi, this is Silky. . . . Oh, hi Claude, how are things in Collection Development? (*Listens for a minute*) So you need a report of all the active journal titles sorted in ascending order by the average number of words in each issue. . . . When do you need it? . . . Tomorrow by noon? . . . for the Provost? . . . Oh sure, fine, no problem. (*Hangs up*).

> *SS types at the computer.*

SS: Damn!! Payroll is due today. Where are those forms? (*Shouting off stage*) Hey everyone! I need signed timesheets by 4:00 today! Are you listening, people?

> *Phone rings.*

SS: This is Silky.

V: Ms. Silkwood, this is Pippy Longtalker, your rep from Way Behind Publishing. I just got off the phone with our legal department. I regret to inform you that they will not allow that change of governing law from Tajikistan to North Carolina. Sorry it took three months to get back to you on this. However, if you're OK with our totally inflexible attitude concerning these changes, we could turn on your account today.

SS: Gosh, that's too bad. I'll have to talk to our university attorney before agreeing. Let me check with him and I'll call you back.

> *Phone rings.*

SS: Hi, it's Silky.

V: Hi! it's Jack from Top Inflation. I know it has only been 10 minutes since we last talked, but I wonder if you had a chance to preview our omnibus microfilm set on the history of grass composting yet?

SS: No, Jack. Remember, I said I'll e-mail you if we are interested? I will—I promise. Bye.

SS: (*Looks up as if at a wall clock*) "Damn, it's 10:00. Maybe I can skip that 28-person committee meeting revising yet *again* the Mission Impossible form and flowchart for "The Investigation, Vetting, Usability, Negotiating, Pricing, and Training of New Electronic

Products." Where *is* that flowchart anyway? (*Holds up a mock spaghettilike flow chart*) No one uses this silly thing. Gosh, I better check my voice mail. (*Presses at the phone set*)

V (*in a stilted voice mail tone*): You have 164 new messages.

V: Beep. Hi, Silky, this is Bob from Reference calling. While you were at the conference, this guy from YouGottaHaveIt Databases called me and I went ahead and set up a trial for us for their new database package. He said you wouldn't mind. If we don't like it, we just write "drop dead" on the first invoice which, by the way, they are having sent to your home address. If we like it, we do nothing and the invoices come with a non-cancelable term of five years. I didn't get a firm pricing estimate, but he said it was a great deal. I think the rep's name was Dave something. It'll be on the invoice. Hope this is okay. Oh yes, and Judy has already assigned this database to some of her classes so we hope you can get it turned on tomorrow.

V: Beep. Err, yes, Ms. Searyals, this is Professor Hiram Lofty in Biomedical Engineering. For months I have been using an online journal, but now I can't get to it on the library Web site anymore. Since you were out, I went ahead and called the publisher. They said the journal was only offered as free online with the print for a period just long enough so you would spend hours setting this title up. Now, since that time has elapsed, they decided to change the pricing model and now it's not free online anymore. Of course you will *have* to continue it. It is essential to my research and any "real university" *must* have this title. Oh, and I am on the editorial board. Thank you so much Silky, you always are *So* helpful. Please call me when access is restored.

SS: Hmmm . . . . I think I'll save the rest of these messages for after lunch. (*Looking over her shoulder and shouting off stage*) No, I don't know how to fix the photocopier.

> *She types at the computer.*

SS: Now here's an interesting e-mail. Olga, the head of monographic acquisitions writes:

"Silk-meister, I just read in the *Chronicle of Higher Ed* that profs are now taking kick-backs from publishers for requiring books for their classes. So what the heck, since the basketball coach gets a shoe contract for having players wear certain shoes, starting this week, I am notifying our book jobbers that I want an honoraria for each book I order with them and I am making the suggestion that I could do my job better with a few weeks in Aruba. Forget those Principles & Standards of Acquisitions Practice I swore to uphold! Guess this won't work for you since your serials vendor tanked. I was surprised that even Divine intervention couldn't save them this time. I'll send you a postcard from the beach."

> *Phone rings again.*

SS: Hello, this is Silky. . . . Yes, Madame Director and Vice-Chancellor of All She Cares to See. . . . Allocate the new materials budget for the Faculty Senate Library Committee meeting next week? . . . Sure—I'll get with Olga and Claude . . . we'll use the usual allocation formula based on rational factors and then completely undo it based on how afraid we are of the faculty in the various departments. Yes ma'am—Can do.

> *She picks up the phone and dials.*

SS: Hi, Doris, this is Silky over at the Library. Is Larry, the campus attorney, in? Oh, too bad . . . when he gets back from Aruba, will you have him call me? I have another licensing problem to go over with him. Yeah, a change of governing law question and a database vendor who insists that when their product is on the screen that no other patron should be able to view it. I told them that was impossible with our floor plan in Reference. He suggested issuing patrons a sheet to drape over themselves and the terminal or to use a Pier One room screen behind them. Thanks—you too.

Sign Master: WAY BEHIND PUBLISHING LICENSE IS COMPLETED 6 MONTHS LATER.

> *Phone rings.*

SS: This is Silky.

V: Ms. Sulky, this is LaDonna NoBrainer from Parsley Publishing. Our records show that a number of your subscriptions with us were canceled this past year. Would you mind taking a few minutes to explain why?

SS: Sure. We did cancel some of your print titles, but we are still getting them online through a special deal with consortia. You are aware of that, aren't you?

V: Uh, well . . . actually, no. Which consortia is that? The state deal, the regional deal or the universal deal?

SS: Actually, none of the above. We have a deal with the Libraries Without Funding Organization—have you heard of them? We had to cancel over $100,000 in subscriptions last year, due to the state budget freeze, and your titles were just a drop in the bucket—but at least we still have the online for yours.

V: Oh gosh, you know, our arrangement with that group is up for renegotiation and we have decided to make some subtle, market-driven changes in continuing it. If you act now you could sign up for our special offer of print plus 55% extra for online with the added feature of tables of contents and abstracts transliterated in your choice of Latin or Middle German for an additional 2.5% or an FTE formula based on 1.5%, whichever is less. The service will also now only be available from our new division and its new URLs.

SS (*Rolls her eyes*): Wow, that sounds so complicated. Are you sure we couldn't just get the online? We just finished changing all our catalog records to reflect the print cancellations, and if we change the access provider too, then all the URLs in the catalog records have to be corrected.

Sign Master: CANCELLATION OF OVER 700 PRINT TITLES TOOK 10 MONTHS TO COMPLETE IN THE LIBRARY'S ONLINE CATALOG.

V: Oh really? Well, let me keep you posted on that and I'll let you know. But our special will be over at the end of this month, so you'll really need to act pretty soon.

SS (*Sarcastically*): "Oh yeah, I'll be right on it." (*Hangs up*)

> *She sniffs the air.*

SS: What the devil is that smell? Where did these flies come from?

> *She stands up and looks offstage. Picks up fly swatter and swats imaginary flies.*

SS: Hey—Doug, what's in those boxes you just put outside my office?

V: A gift.

SS: But what?

V: Dr. Buzzoff, dropped a gift collection of 20 boxes of his journals at the loading dock.

SS: But what is it with the smell and the flies?

V: Oh, he packed the volumes in boxes that once had raw chicken parts in them. I guess the flies are a bonus.

SS: Well, you are gonna have to take them right back out to the loading dock! This is ridiculous!!

Sign Master: THIS ACTUALLY HAPPENED.

> *SS moves some paper on the desk.*

SS: I've had it! Before I completely lose my appetite, I am going to lunch. I might come back if those boxes are gone!

> *As she is walking away from the desk, the phone rings. The answering machine answers.*

V: Beep. Hi, again. This is Jack at Top Inflation Publishers. I know you said not to call but I thought you might have a few questions . . . .

The End

MANAGING THE MIGRATION

Pinar Erzin, General Manager, Extenza Marketing Solutions

In this chapter I would like to share some results we obtained regarding lapsed print subscriptions, reasons for cancellations, and migration to online. Extenza Marketing Solutions provides marketing and promotion services for publishers. Over a 12-month period we conducted 30,000 interviews with librarians on behalf of publisher clients. Around 60% of these calls were made to lapsed subscribers. Table 1 shows the results of these interviews and compares these figures with results from 11,000 calls made to lapsed subscribers in 2002.

Table 1. Renewal Responses

	2003	*2002*	*Variance*
Subscriptions			
Renewed	35%	29%	+6%
Pending	10%	11%	-1%
Cancelled	24%	24%	0%
Status unknown	31%	36%	-5%
Total	100%	100%	0%
Cancel reasons			
Lack of budget	33%	35%	-2%
Migration online	12%	8%	+4%
Subject not relevant	11%	10%	+1%
Subscriber left	6%	4%	+2%
Price	2%	5%	-3%
Other	36%	38%	-2%
Total	100%	100%	0%

"Other" includes sales to consortia, the library closing, or duplicate subscriptions.

Analyzing the results of calls to lapsed subscribers (i.e., subscribers who had gone through the publishers' printed renewal process without renewing), we found that

- 35% of lapsed subscribers actually renewed;
- 10% had not yet made up their minds; and
- the main reason that subscribers cancel remains a lack of budget, but migration to online products is accounting for a greater proportion.

Reasons for Cancellation

There is a wide range of reasons why subscribers cancel. The greatest of these is a lack of budget, which accounts for 33% of all cancellations. Twelve percent have moved to some form of online subscription—a trend that is likely to continue given the proliferation of electronic delivery. Eleven percent of subscribers have changed either position or assignment and find that the subject is no longer relevant. And 6% cancel due to the subscriber leaving the company. Surprisingly only 2% cancel due to price.

Comparing with the Previous Year

Although lack of budget remained the main reason for not renewing or subscribing in 2003, fewer publications were being dropped than in the previous year, which may point toward a slight recovery for the media industry. In 2003, 35% of lapsed subscribers renewed, while the figure was only 29% the previous year.

The other significant trend is the growth of electronic, something that will come as little surprise to those involved in the industry. During 2003, 12% of cancellations were due to a migration to online, compared with 8% the previous year. Given the proliferation of electronic delivery, this trend is expected to continue, and publishers are urged to consider how they can best take advantage of the growth.

The Migration Process

There are strong reasons for librarians to move to online. The ability to increase and measure usage, married with the proliferation of consortia deals, particularly in the United States, is pushing many to electronic delivery. Indeed, some librarians we have spoken to only take electronic products now. Yet feedback from librarians suggests that the online activation process does not always happen without pain. On the contrary, we see that there is a major lack of communication between librarians and publishers.

In recent online activation campaigns we contacted 800 institutions that had not activated their free online access and found that 52% were not even aware of it! And 13% were either too busy to talk at the time or had experienced language problems that meant that they could not take advantage of the offer. This is an incredible missed opportunity.

Thoughts for Solutions

It is very costly for a publisher to establish local offices around the world and serve each client in its own language. Most publishers therefore keep their customer service to one language, follow traditional means of communication when it comes to announcing new electronic services, and somehow expect librarians to chase them to access information via the Internet.

Although these issues seem obvious, they have a massive impact on the relationships between a publisher and its library clients. If publishers would become more market-driven, listen to their librarian clients, and find cost-efficient ways to communicate better with libraries, the process would be much smoother. Likewise, librarians should articulate their needs more openly and become true partners to publishers. In this way there would be an increased usage of electronic information, a drastic decrease in lost business, and a lot fewer headaches for all.

ELECTRONIC RESOURCE MANAGEMENT: A VENDED APPROACH

Tony Harvell, Head of Acquisitions, UCSD Libraries

UCSD Libraries, an ARL library, subscribes to over 400 paid electronic resources (including e-journal packages, aggregators, databases, and CD-ROMs). About 60% are purchased consortially through California Digital Library, a "co-library" of the University of California, which manages the shared digital content for UC Libraries. In addition, our library has been an Innovative Interfaces (III) user since 1987. Historically, our library has maintained a high level of bibliographic control over electronic resources. Full-level cataloging is done on nearly all e-journals (both for UCSD and the California Digital Library), and these records are then redistributed to other UC Libraries through the Shared Cataloging Program of the California Digital Library, housed at UCSD Libraries.

Like most libraries, we have long felt a need to better manage e-resources. This is the result of a number of trends:

- There has been a shift to e-only journal access (over 8,000 paid e-journals, more than five times the number five years ago).

- The e-resource budget as a share of the overall materials budget continues to grow (in excess of 15% currently) and is twice what it was only five years ago.

- We have long felt a need to track resources from trial through licensing negotiation and payment. Our integrated library system had no means for monitoring all activities, so many separate files were being maintained, many in paper; some license records were scanned and redacted on the Web. These were not easily accessible to the users of the information (other library staff and users).

In looking for a solution we faced a number of considerations. We first identified all potential users of an electronic resources management (ERM) system, then identified the potential uses of the system. It readily became apparent that the system was not needed for technical services staff but rather for our collection managers (bibliographers) and other library staff, as well as our patrons in some cases. We also did an analysis of the human and computer resources needed to develop and maintain the system in-house. Given the limited resources and competing priorities in our Information Technology Department, any solution would have to be carefully negotiated with them. In addition, it would have to be both scaleable and sustainable. Because of our large commitment to resource sharing within the University of California and in other consortia, it would have to incorporate nationally and internationally accepted standards, if they exist. Public universities in California (as in most states) are in the midst of a financial crisis. Will there be financial support available for future developments and enhancements? Our experience has show that any product developed in-house would have to be supported, developed, and enhanced, and there was no guarantee we would have the funding or staff to do so in the future.

In early 2003 there were only a few options available:

- Develop a system in-house: Initial estimates indicated that the costs would be prohibitive and that this would be unlikely to happen for a period of time. Our information technology staff was already committed to digital library initiatives and work on a scholar's portal.

- Adopt (purchase?) a system from another library: We looked at the system developed by our sister campus, UCLA, but found that it would be difficult to rewrite the code to work with our integrated library system and would simply be another stand-alone system, perhaps with wider access.

- Purchase a vended system: At that time, only Innovative Interfaces had a product in development. Other vendors (notably ExLibris) are currently electronic resource management systems.

Our library has historically been a "beta test" library for other III products. We believed the ERM would require little or no local programming or development. We hoped it could be fully integrated into our existing integrated library system. However, library staff had only seen demonstrations at professional conferences and Innovative User Group meetings. We also had worked with Innovative for a number of years and understood their pricing model for maintenance and the model of issuing future upgrades (new releases), which was predictable, along with the option to purchase some features. This model was one we felt could better be accommodated by a budget with some uncertainty.

The software was installed in Installation in October 2003. We had WebEx (a Web-based conference call) training from Innovative. Because of our familiarity with other Innovative Millennium products, the learning curve was fairly short. A working group was created to evaluate the product, provide feedback to Innovative, and develop local standards for implementation. It included representatives from technical services, public services, and information technology. Currently there are 12 libraries using Innovative Interfaces Electronic Resources Module.

There is an e-discussion list, and we regularly have Web-Ex conference calls with other users to discuss implementation issues. Other libraries have been very generous in sharing their codes used in records.

Generally, our experience to date with the ERM system from Innovative has been very positive. It uses the same platform as our existing Web-based technical services components, requiring little staff training in terms of the interface. Most important, it allows us to build a database using existing records for orders and holdings that have been created in the ordering and serials control modules. It offers quite a bit of local customization ability and locally defined fields and labels. Generally the license record structure and definitions follow the Digital Library Foundation's Electronic Resource Management Initiative standards and practices. This is very important, as we are looking at future consortial use, thereby requiring use of nationally accepted standards for creating records, in order to facilitate sharing of information. It has also been advantageous not being the only library using the system. We can share information with our colleagues and work as a group to push for enhancements. We can also learn from their experience.

Because the ERM is in beta, there is currently no written documentation for some parts, and "kinks" are continuously being worked out. The vendor appears to be making changes weekly, so there is some fluidity in how the system appears from one week to the next. Ideally, an electronic resources management product would conform to our current workflow and local practices. However, because the system is structured in certain ways to permit rapid updating, batch loading, etc., it may require us to rethink how we currently catalog electronic resources. Though these are not great departures from current practice, it has required us to re-examine how we structure records within our existing ILS, in order to take full advantage of all the features of the ERM.

The OPAC display has just been developed, so we may have to redesign OPAC screens to incorporate information drawn from the ERM system. We are looking to see how it can be used with our e-resources portal (SAGE), which includes both licensed and open access resources. Using the ERM to manage this resource would require us to restructure how the portal resources are created. The ability to batch load e-holdings information is of great benefit to many libraries, but we are unsure how it could benefit us, given our current cataloging practices.

We have identified a number of priorities we would like to address fairly soon. We want to experiment with e-holdings loads from a publisher to see if the data can be brought easily into the system. We have begun to work with public services staff to redesign OPAC displays to incorporate ERM data such as permissions/restrictions and resource availability and downtime messages. We would like to see the system be able to monitor resource vendor performance and track usage statistics. Finally, we have also begun exploration of using the ERM in a consortial setting. As other vendors develop electronic resources management systems, we are optimistic that the competition will result in better products for all users.

JOURNAL LINKING AND BEYOND

Carol A. Meyer, Maxwell Publishing Consultants, Winchester, Massachusetts, on Behalf of CrossRef

Overview

This chapter focuses on journal linking as facilitated by CrossRef. It briefly reviews DOIs and how they are used in scholarly online publishing, then discusses CrossRef's role. Next, the chapter provides some statistics on CrossRef's relative size and then concentrates on how CrossRef works with various parts of the scholarly community, emphasizing libraries. The first section discusses the benefits to libraries in working with CrossRef, describing library affiliates. The relationship of CrossRef and local link servers and the OpenURL is introduced. The chapter closes with a discussion of linking enhancements on the horizon for journals and beyond.

What Is a DOI?

A digital object identifier (DOI) is an alphanumeric string created both to uniquely identify or name a piece of electronic intellectual content and to serve as a stable, persistent link to that content's location on the Web. Think of a DOI as analogous to a UPC code; it doesn't mean anything just to look at, but it is a standard that holds information (or metadata) about an object.

The DOI is the only widely adopted, persistent, actionable identifier for online scholarly works. A DOI persists throughout changes in copyright ownership or location because it is just a name used to look up an address in an easily updatable directory. The core functionality of the DOI system is to resolve the DOI to the registered, updatable uniform resource locator (URL).

The DOI directory comes into play when a user clicks a DOI link. The DOI system automatically resolves the DOI to the URL deposited by the publishers. This happens as an automatic redirect in the user's browser, and the user isn't even aware of it. Adding this level of indirection through a central DOI directory helps ensure that DOIs are persistent. While the location of content may change, and the ownership of content may change, the DOI itself does not change. Of course, publishers have an obligation to keep the URL up-to-date; their commitment to do so makes the whole system work.

A DOI might look like this:

```
http://dx.doi.org/10.1038/nature01566
```

The first part, "dx.doi.org" is called the DOI directory. The next part, "10.1038" is called the prefix and indicates the original publisher. Finally, "nature01566" is the suffix and is a unique document identifier assigned by the publisher. The URL for this DOI might be:

```
http://www.nature.com/cgi-taf/DynaPage.taf?file=/nature/
journal/v422/n6932/full/nature01566_fs.html
```

DOIs are increasingly being used to cite scholarly literature. For example, *Nature* now prints DOIs on each article and also displays the DOIs in online tables of contents and at the top of each online article. In addition, the references in *Nature* articles display the traditional bibliographic metadata as well as a DOI when available.

PloS Biology, another CrossRef participant, displays a DOI locator on its home page (www.plosbiology.org), allowing users to search PLoS articles by DOI.

Another way to locate an article if the DOI is available is to simply to type the DOI into Google. The results list may contain links to the actual article or links to other articles that cite that item by DOI.

Here is an example of a search results list in Google using this approach:

```
http://www.google.com/search?hl=en&lr=&ie=UTF-8&oe=UTF-8&
newwindow=1&q=10.1038%2F425107a&btnG=Google+Search
```

PubMed uses DOIs to link to articles, although the actual DOIs are not actually displayed. Here is an example:

```
http://www.ncbi.nlm.nih.gov/entrez/query.fcgi?cmd=Retrieve&
db=PubMed&list_uids=12968173&dopt=Abstract
```

Another important use of DOIs is to identify articles that are published online before they are published in print. When a publisher chooses to publish online first, an article may appear online individually before volume, issue, and page number are issued. DOIs can be used to cite the article even before traditional bibliographic information is available. Later, when volume, issue, and page are assigned, those can be used to cite the article as usual. *Nature's* Advanced Online Publication (AOP) system uses the DOI for advance online publication, as the following example shows:

```
http://www.nature.com/cgi-taf/DynaPage.taf?file=/nature/
journal/vaop/ncurrent/toc_r.html
```

CrossRef's Role in Making Linking Work

CrossRef is an independent, not-for-profit membership association of scholarly publishers. It is also a cross-publisher citation linking network that uses the DOI. CrossRef is one of seven official DOI registration agencies worldwide. The organization's mission is to provide services that bring the scholar to authoritative primary content, focusing on methods that are best achieved through collective agreement by publishers.

To accomplish this mission, CrossRef provides the technology infrastructure that makes linking possible. CrossRef's reliance on the DOI ensures that users do not encounter broken links in citations or database records. Why is this so important? According to Michael Lesk, the average half-life of a URL is 44 days.[1] CrossRef publishers can update URLs that have changed in just one location rather than having to notify multiple partners about new locations. About 50% of the records in CrossRef have already been updated at least once. The system reduces maintenance effort for librarians and others who are linking to the scholarly literature.

CrossRef also provides the business infrastructure for linking. CrossRef members simply sign one agreement that allows them to link to more than 250 publishers. No bilateral agreements are needed; one agreement with CrossRef is a linking agreement with all CrossRef publishers.

Membership is business model neutral, which allows commercial publishers, scholarly societies, and alternative publishers alike to join. As examples, Elsevier, the American Institute of Physics, and the Public Library of Science (PLoS) are all CrossRef members. The membership agreement required of all members sets the rules and creates a level playing field among participating content providers.[2]

How CrossRef Is Used

CrossRef is used in different ways by its different constituencies: librarians, end-users, publishers, and secondary and A&I publishers.

Libraries

Libraries can take advantage of CrossRef services to submit metadata to obtain DOIs to link to full text. They can also send DOIs to CrossRef from local link servers to look up metadata. Some administrative issues with libraries remain; more automation is needed.

Anyone, including librarians, can use the free DOI resolver available on the CrossRef Web site: http://crossref.org/05researchers/58doi_resolver.html.

Librarians must sign up to become library affiliates to take advantage of CrossRef's ability to submit DOI queries in batches.

End Users

As already seen, end-users can use CrossRef to click on DOI links in online resources (in which case, CrossRef is invisible to the user). Researchers may also find DOIs using the free DOI Lookup form on the CrossRef Web site: http://crossref.org/04intermediaries/37guest_query.html.

Publishers

Publishers deposit XML metadata for their articles' content into the CrossRef metadata database. They also parse references (dividing them up into parts such as author, title, publication name, volume, issue, page number, etc.) and then send this metadata to CrossRef to obtain DOIs to embed in their online references. Finally, publishers make reference links by sending the DOI to http://dx.doi.org/, where it is resolved to the correct URL. Secondary and A&I publishers can also take advantage of CrossRef by linking from bibliographic records to the full text.

CrossRef Scorecard

CrossRef has seen very healthy growth, with 250 member publishers, 162 library and library consortia affiliates, and 36 agents and affiliates. CrossRef contains metadata records for 9.2 millions items (up from 5 million in 2002), including records for 8,500 journals (up from 6,500 the year before).[3]

The number of publishers who have digitized their backfiles and made them linkable through CrossRef is larger than originally expected. For example, the American Physical Society has made all of its legacy content published since 1893 linkable through CrossRef. The award for the oldest metadata in CrossRef goes to the University of Chicago Press—records from the *Astronomical Journal* dating from 1849 can be linked through CrossRef.

A very important statistic is the number of DOI resolutions per month, which roughly indicates the number of DOIs that actually get clicked by users. The average number of monthly resolutions to all CrossRef publishers is now 3.9 million per month and growing.

CrossRef membership represents an international and multidisciplinary body of scholarly literature. Publishers represent more than just journals and more than just American research. Recently added library affiliates include

- Harvard University

- Sandia National Laboratories

- Swarthmore College

- Czech Technical University

- Danish Library of Science & Medicine

New members include

- Walter de Gruyter

- *American Scientist*

- *International Journal of Psychoanalysis*

- Human Factors & Ergonomics Society

- Guilford Publications

- ASTM International

- Society for Neuroscience

Affiliates and agents include secondary publishers and aggregators that use CrossRef to retrieve DOIs and link their records to primary content. This category also includes technology partners who host journals for publishers and/or provide linking platforms. The newest affiliates include Innovative Interfaces, Serials Solutions, and SIRSI.[4]

While CrossRef has a strong history in scientific, technical, and medical (STM) journal articles, fields now include social sciences, humanities, and business. In additional to journal articles, publishers now deposit records for journal titles, conference proceedings, and books. For an example of a DOI for a Wiley journal title, see `dx.doi.org/10.1002/`
`(ISSN)1521-3862`. Oxford University Press has recently deposited over 700 records for books, which include separate DOIs for chapters.

CrossRef and Libraries

So what does all this mean for libraries? Jim Mouw mentioned in his remarks four main goals for linking in libraries: increased access to resources for users, valid and robust links, links that are appropriate and in the proper context, and increased provider participation in linking. Outlined below are the ways CrossRef is contributing to these needs.

User navigation at the article level leads to increased usage of electronic resources, improving access. Another way CrossRef can aid in the quest for better access to research materials is by providing DOI-facilitated links to content that the library doesn't own, opening an awareness of the resource and a path to obtain it.

As discussed, one of the primary objectives of CrossRef is to provide persistent DOI links, leading to validity and robustness. Finally, in conjunction with local link resolvers (from library systems vendors or built by internal library systems organizations), CrossRef helps find the appropriate copy of a document, supporting the goal of links that are appropriate and in context. Article-level metadata lookup makes CrossRef publishers OpenURL-compliant. Finally, CrossRef has a dedicated business development function to continue to increase the numbers of participants in the system and organization.

Library Fees Eliminated

In support of libraries and to promote the use of the DOI, the CrossRef Board of Directors waived library affiliate fees (which allow batch DOI lookup) beginning May 2003. (Libraries who wish to deposit metadata to link to their own published content must still join at the regular member rates.) The result has been a rush of new library affiliates and link resolution server implementations over the past few months. This change to the fees is part of a larger fee structure revision that made DOI retrieval free for everyone starting in January 2004. The goal of this fee restructuring is for DOIs to be adopted everywhere in the scholarly process that they can be useful.

CrossRef and the OpenURL

Jenny Walker's presentation discussed localized linking in more depth, but I want to briefly mention that CrossRef supports localized linking through DOI redirection. Here's a very high-level view of how it works.

First, a library installs a local link server. A user in the library clicks on a DOI link, and a cookie on the user's machine alerts the DOI proxy server to redirect this DOI to the local link server. The article-level metadata that is needed for local resolution can come from the source of the link, or it can come from CrossRef via the OpenURL. In some cases, the metadata from CrossRef may be more reliable or more complete, depending on the source of the original metadata.

Thus, the OpenURL and CrossRef are compatible, not competitors. The OpenURL is not an alternative to CrossRef and DOIs—they work together. The DOI system and CrossRef are OpenURL-aware; therefore publishers that are members of CrossRef are OpenURL-enabled through the use of CrossRef and DOIs.[5]

What's Coming?

CrossRef staff and members continue to work on "enhanced linking," incorporating such ideas as multiple resolution, forward linking, parameter passing, and full text search.

Multiple Resolution

Multiple resolution is the ability to assign more than one URL to a single DOI. What applications could that serve? It would allow metadata labels to be associated with URLs, and have the relationships between DOIs captured in metadata. Other applications could be to link to services associated with a DOI. Such services could include mirror copies, rights clearing, and ordering print document delivery or interlibrary loan copies. Clearly, local linking servers must be able to take advantage of DOI multiple resolution services.[6] CrossRef is currently implementing the first phase of its multiple resolution functionality.

Forward Linking

The type of reference linking that CrossRef has supported until now can be considered "backwards linking." References in articles generally point *back* to articles published earlier. Forward linking, on the other hand, will allow users who are viewing a particular article to see articles published later that cite the article they are reading. CrossRef implemented cross-publisher forward linking in 2004. Users will soon have access to complete citation pathways and be able to link to content that cites, as well as is cited by, a given document.

Parameter Passing

Parameter passing will allow publishers to use the OpenURL to pass additional information with the links. One application of parameter passing would to implement a toll-free linking agreement, which might enable a publisher to grant limited full text access to users linking from a partner publisher's content.

Full Text Search

Finally, CrossRef has also begun to explore cross-publisher full text search functionality, which could allow users to search the full content of all participating publishers' sites.

Summary: How CrossRef Is Meeting Libraries' Linking Needs

To conclude, again using the parameters that Jim laid out, CrossRef is contributing to the scholarly landscape by making links valid and robust, appropriate, and in context; encouraging content providers to participate; and expanding the types of resources available. Publishers who elect to join CrossRef commit to updating URLs so DOI links don't break. The fact that CrossRef maintains a central database repository for metadata and DOIs makes the system much more efficient to maintain than individual bilateral linking agreements between publishers, which is what was required before CrossRef was available.

The OpenURL and the variety of link resolvers available from libraries and library systems vendors in collaboration with the CrossRef system is beginning to send users to the right copy, whether locally hosted or at a publisher's site. Publishers of all sizes continue to join CrossRef, representing subjects from physics to philosophy, medicine to medieval studies. And the coverage in those subjects is international; while primarily in English, CrossRef publishers come from countries throughout the Americas and Europe.

The types of resources assigned DOIs and linkable through CrossRef currently extend beyond journal articles to journal title records, books and book chapters, and conference proceedings. At its current rate, CrossRef will continue to expand along these dimensions.

Vision

As far as CrossRef has come, a vision remains of a much broader linking landscape, where the breadth of content contains critical material in every scholarly discipline, and where expanded content types include a wide variety of useful material, including, just for starters, grey literature such as patents, technical reports, and government documents; learning objects; datasets; and images. Another dimension of linkable material is that of time, as more content providers consider digitizing and linking their legacy content, ensuring that older research doesn't "disappear" from the record. Likewise, publishers can make their documents more granular, assigning DOIs to meaningful parts of documents. Finally, much more work can be done on the problem of context-sensitive resolution so that a user links to the instance of a document that best meets his or her needs.

Notes

Acknowledgments: My appreciation goes to Amy Brand, director of business development for CrossRef, for her careful review of the presentation and chapter. Ed Pentz, CrossRef's executive director, and Amy both contributed essential information. Any errors or omissions are mine alone.

1. Michael Lesk, *Mad Library Disease: Holes in the Stacks* [Online], available: http://www.lesk.com/mlesk/ucla/ucla.html (accessed June 18, 2004).

2. A complete list of participants can be found on the CrossRef Web site, http://crossref.org/01company/06publishers.html.

3. These figures were current as of November 7, 2003, when the presentation this chapter is drawn from was delivered. An updated summary of statistics is available in the most recent CrossRef newsletter, available on the CrossRef Web site, http://crossref.org/01company/10newsletter.html.

4. A complete listing of library affiliates may be found on the CrossRef Web site, http://crossref.org/01company/07libraries.html. A listing of current agents and affiliates is also available at http://crossref.org/01company/08intermediaries.html.

5. A more complete discussion of the relationship of CrossRef and the OpenURL can be found on the CrossRef Web site, http://crossref.org/03libraries/16openurl.html.

6. A demonstration of multiple resolution through DOIs is available at http://crossref.org/mr/index.html.

OPENING UP THE DIGITAL BOX: WHAT DEEP LOG ANALYSIS CAN TELL US ABOUT OUR DIGITAL JOURNAL USERS

David Nicholas, City University, London
Paul Huntington, City University, London
Ian Rowlands, City University, London
Bill Russell, Emerald

Jill Cousins of Blackwell Publishing also participated in the presentation.

Abstract

This two-part chapter considers the implications of log data for publishers and librarians. In this connection it reports on ongoing research into the use of two digital journal libraries, those of Emerald, a business and information studies publisher, and Blackwell, a scientific journal publisher. Employing deep log analysis techniques and adopting a strong consumer perspective, the first part of the chapter examines the information seeking behavior and background characteristics of the users of these two systems. Among the information traits examined are "site penetration," repeat use (perhaps, signs of current awareness and loyalty), and number of journals consulted. Users are characterized, among other things, according to their type of subscription, the type of university they come from, and the nature of their job. The concept of information promiscuity in the age of massive consumer choice is raised and reflected upon. A small case study is also included highlighting the relationship between log and citation data. The second part of the chapter features the publishers telling us what this all means to them, and what actions they propose to take.

Introduction

In 2002 in Charleston at The Ingenta Institute pre-meeting we showed some "data snapshots" of information seeking in a digital library that we had compiled from the usage logs of the Emerald Web site and suggested that there were some very interesting—and unexpected—findings[1] and that we would return to Charleston with more robust data and more provoking ideas. We came back, this time with some publisher friends, to see what they make of the data we supplied them with.

This chapter has two prime purposes: (1) to show what deep log analysis can tell publishers (and librarians) about the information seeking behavior of their users and to suggest ways by which they can learn even more and (2) to hear from publishers their reaction to the log findings. While we allude to some of the technical problems inherent in log analysis, this is not our main purpose, which is to demonstrate the utility and significance of the data. City University researchers are currently working with the logs of two publishers, Blackwell and Emerald, as part of the Virtual Scholar research project,[2] which is investigating the use and impact of digital scholarly journals. Many of the ideas and methods presented here were developed as part of the work we have done in helping the UK government map and evaluate the rollout of digital health services to the consumer. Our future goal is to do the same in the scholarly journal field.

Part 1

Log Analysis and Its Benefits

All digital information platforms have a facility by which logs are generated that provide an automatic and real-time record of use by everyone who accesses information services on these platforms. They represent the digital information footprints of the users, and by analyzing them we can track and map their information seeking behavior; when enhanced, they can tell us something about the kinds of people that use the services. These data have traditionally been extremely difficult for publishers (and librarians) to obtain, but not any longer.

The attraction of logs is that they provide abundant and fairly robust evidence of use. With log analysis it is possible to monitor the use of a system by millions of people, around the country. Logs record use by everyone who happens to engage with the system—there is no need to take a sample. The great advantage of the logs is not simply their size and reach, although the dividend here is indeed a rich and unparalleled one. More important, they are a direct and immediately available record of what people have done: not what they say they might, or would, do; not what they were prompted to say; not what they thought they did. The data are unfiltered and speak for themselves, providing a reality check that both represents the users and complements important contextual data obtained by engaging with real users and exploring their experiences and concerns.

Publishers and Logs

Not surprisingly then, albeit rather belatedly, publishers are showing a growing interest in what logs can tell them. This is an interest driven, no doubt, by the enormous costs associated with maintaining Web sites/digital libraries, some of the worrying rumors that are going around about what logs are saying, and the fact that most publishers are seriously in the dark when it comes to their users.

Publishers usually contract out a lot of the log analysis to third parties (e.g., Catch Word/Ingenta, Atypon) or rely on proprietary software, like WebTrends, Net tracker, etc. Notwithstanding the undoubted technical expertise of the third parties and the software suppliers, the analyses performed are very limited, and the dangers inherent in this are that publishers are at one remove, and in an information dust storm kicked up by the log data. This means that they do not always have the time to fully understand what the log data mean, do not always get the data they need, and do not always know what their limitations are. In consequence huge opportunities are missed. Thus, in many cases, instead of this enormous data-gathering exercise being powered by the big policy questions that are confronting publishers these days, too often the enormity of the data actually overwhelms policy makers. Therefore, to no one's surprise, after the initial euphoria that greeted Web log data a general frustration has crept in as publishers, with one eye on the costs, realize that they are still without critical intelligence on the user, which only deep log analysis can give them.

Deep Log Analysis

The ubiquitous metric "hits" can only get publishers, or any other service provider, so far —not very far in fact, competitively speaking, when everyone is quoting such enormous figures. It is also clear that logs alone are not the magic bullet but rather the essential methodological first step. Logs map the digital environment and raise the questions that *really* need to be asked by questionnaires and interviews (powerful triangulation). Clearly if publishers are to obtain really rich and accurate data from log files that will inform both them and their paymasters, they will have to go beyond proprietary logging software and start triangulating the data with other datasets and data collection methods. What is really needed is what we at Ciber call "deep log" analysis techniques—the magic bullet as far as policy makers are concerned. Deep log analysis refers not simply to mining the data more deeply than proprietary software can achieve but also to our method of relating "usage" data with "user" data.

Deep log analysis involves three steps. First, the assumptions about how the data are defined and recorded (for instance, who is a user, what is a hit, what represents success, etc.) are questioned and realigned as necessary, and their statistical significance is assessed. This is important, as skewed data are a real problem. This ensures both that incorrect, over-inflated readings that give a false sense of achievement or progress are avoided and, in the wider sense, that data gathering is better aligned to organizational goals. Second, the usage logs are enriched by attaching user demographic data (e.g., age, gender, ethnicity, occupation, specialty, organizational affiliation, and postal code) to them, either with data obtained from a subscriber database or online questionnaires. Where outcome or impact data are available, regarding, for instance, promotion, job performance, or formal course assessment, that can be related, too.

Finally, equipped with a detailed picture of the digital environment, much will have to be explained and a whole range of questions will have to be asked through qualitative work—questions about personal experiences, outcomes, and impacts. Observation also often plays an important part in our analysis, as issues concerned with usability, engagement, and exploitation of materials may be examined.

During the whole of the evaluation period, the researchers attempt to provide a visualization, interpretation of the data, and their implications as a coherent picture emerges. This will be for policy makers, managers, and other interested stakeholders. We are aware of no publishers that have gone beyond step 1, and some have yet to get on the first step. We are hoping to take Emerald and Blackwell the full distance, although we only chronicle some of their moves toward step 3 in this chapter.

Methods

One year's worth of Emerald's logs (2002) were evaluated, long enough so that we could pick up on return visits, a key deep log analysis. In the case of Blackwell, where we were still at the "testing stage" and wished to experiment with relating log data to the user characteristic database, we based our studies on a day's worth of data (September 17, 2003),[3] a little over half a million user transactions in all. All the data were obtained in "raw" form from the publishers and their agents and were processed using deep log techniques developed at City University.[4] Given the sheer scope of the study and the limited space available for presentation, we have chosen a selection of analyses that show what is possible using deep log techniques. What we show here are the two sophisticated and meaningful use metrics—site penetration and return visitors, and a breakdown of users by a number of characteristics

Logs differ in structure and content, so a few words about the working definitions used are in order:

- **User.** In the case of Emerald, user identification was based on the "Unq" number—the unique identification number used by the server to write and read cookies. A user is effectively a computer; sometimes that computer represents an individual, in other cases a number of people. For Blackwell, for the purposes of the pilot users we used sessions as the user metric in all general counts.

- **Sessions**. Sessions are identified in the logs by a session identification number. Both Emerald and Blackwell had session identification numbers.

- **Items viewed/requests made**. These are "complete" items returned by the server to the client in response to a user action. Typically this might include an abstract, an article, or a table of contents. A complete item might be all the pages, charts, etc., from an article, and this is recorded as a single item and hence is quite different from traditional server log files that record pictures and text documents separately. The Blackwell logs also recorded views to the home page and a returned search screen.

Results

Sophisticated Use Metrics: Site Penetration

Research we have conducted in health and media[5] shows that many Web users do not dwell; they examine just a few items before they leave and go and search for information elsewhere. In some cases only a home page or introductory page is visited—in other words, no substantial content is consumed. We call these people bouncers or checkers. Table 1 shows this is true of scholarly journals as well; with well over two-thirds of Blackwell and Emerald users consulting between one and three items; in the case of Emerald, 42% of users consulted just one item. Ten percent of Blackwell users and 8% of Emerald users consulted more than 10 items. How deeply a person investigates a site is clearly an interesting metric, showing perhaps interest, relevance, and "busyness." Of course, it might also tell us something about searching style, digital visibility, and the structure and nature of the Web site. A number of hypotheses may be postulated to explain this distribution. Users might access the site just to see what is there but return later to pick up their material. Alternatively, a user (student) may be given the exact Internet reference of an item, say, in a bibliography, like an article, and might go directly to view the item without investigating other pages. A further reason relates to the nature of the Internet itself. In many cases users will use a search engine to find information on the Internet. These engines return a number of clickable links that users will cycle through. They may click on the first link, viewing maybe a page or two to see what's there, and then go on, if their search has not been satisfied or only partially satisfied, to the next link.

Table 1. Sessions and Users Classified by the Number of Items Viewed (Site Penetration)

		Emerald	Blackwell
Type of User/Session	*Number of Items Viewed*	%	%
Bouncer/checker	1 to 3	70	68
Moderately engaged	4 to 10	20	24
Engaged	11 to 20	6	5
Seriously engaged	Over 21	4	3
	Total	100	100

The question we need to ask about a digital journal Web site is whether there is anything about it that would make it different, in site penetration terms, from other consumer Web sites. In a sense we might expect a natural level of busyness as a result of 1) the bibliographic and full text mix that gives a natural movement, 2) the massive choice of data on offer, 3) the investigative nature of some information seeking, or the 4) presence of a search engine and other retrieval aids. But this does not seem to have made a difference; classic Web consumer searching behavior holds.

Return Visitors

Another aspect we discovered about the bouncing behavior referred to previously is that not only are people not very active when they are at a site, they also rarely or never come back. We put this down to a promiscuity that has arisen out of massive digital choice. There was a feeling that this might not occur so much in the more restricted and purposive environment of a digital library. Table 2, which shows the number of times Emerald users returned to the site during 2002,[6] however, tells us otherwise. It shows that the large majority of people (69.9%) just visited the site once. Just under a quarter of the users visited the site between 2 and 5 times, about 5% of users visited the site between 6 and 15 times, and just 1.5% visited the site more than 15 times. Given that in some cases the user is in fact a multi-user, the numbers of people returning are an overestimation.

Table 2. Users Grouped by Number of Visits Made During 2002 (Emerald)

Type of user	*Number of Visits in 2002*	*Percent*
Bouncer	Once	69.6
Infrequent visitor	2 to 5	23.6
Frequent visitor	6 to 15	5.2
Very frequent visitor	Over 15 times	1.6
	Total	100.0

There are plainly significant implications here for publishers who might be considering moving to a pay-by-level-of-activity (however that is defined) model and for education policy makers who might be concerned about what is going on in terms of current awareness activities by academics. Current awareness is surely a major performance metric, and perhaps academics are not pursuing it online.

Categorizing Users

When dealing with two million global users, as we were in the case of Emerald, there is a need to burrow down and discover whether there are any significant differences between the various subgroups of user, to determine, for instance, whether students behave differently in a digital journal environment than do professors, whether physicists behave differently than economists, practitioners than academics, Americans differently than the British and those from research-led universities differently than those from teaching-led ones. In the following discussion we highlight some of the differences.

User Status

Figures 1–4 show the impact of user status on digital information seeking behavior for Blackwell Synergy, where this analysis proved possible thanks to the existence of a user database. This database enabled us to determine whether it was an undergraduate, postgraduate, researcher, professor/teacher, or practitioner who undertook the search.

Figure 1 shows the number of items requested in a session. Undergraduate students made the most use of this metric: Nearly half of undergraduate sessions saw 21 or more items being requested. Researchers were least likely to request 21 or more items; only 29% did so. This might be because researchers are much more likely to know what they are looking for and might have greater system familiarity. Researchers and university teachers/professors seemed to be the most likely to view between 4 and 10 items; 37% and 38% did so, respectively.

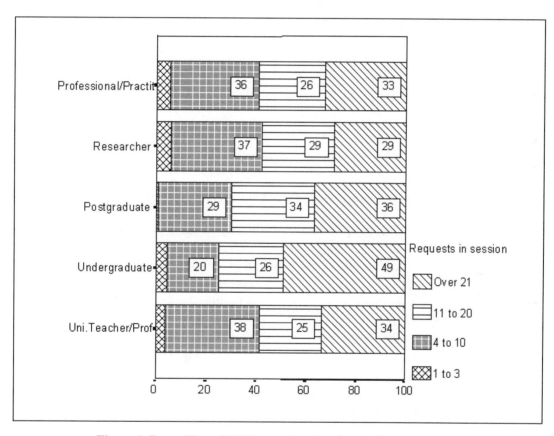

Figure 1. Items Viewed (All Items) in a Session by Status of User.

Whereas Figure 1 is all about site penetration or busyness, Figure 2 tells us about the "width" of the search, showing how many different journals were consulted in a session. Perhaps surprisingly with so much choice, 91% of people just viewed one title in a session. Undergraduates were most likely to view two or more titles in a session (35% had done so), while professionals/practitioners were least likely to (only 16% had done so). Both researchers (18%) and university teachers and professors (17%) were less likely to view two or more titles in a session, compared to both undergraduates (35%) and postgraduates (27%). Thus the undergraduates "busyness" also saw them searching more journals.

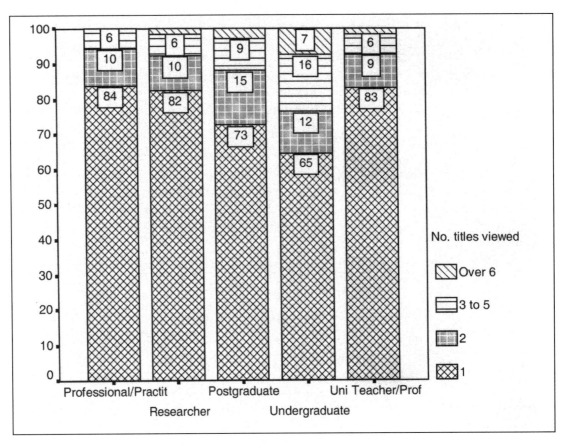

Figure 2. Number of Journal Titles Viewed in a Session (Blackwell).

Figures 3 and 4 show what people take from the site in the way of type of item (TOCs, abstracts, and articles) and how they navigate around the site. The figures should be looked at together. Figure 3 shows that university teachers and professors made the greatest use of PDF-formatted articles: 42% of teachers or professors viewed articles in this format and a relatively high 36% of researchers did so, as compared to only 27% of undergraduates. Undergraduates were most likely to view articles in an HTML format: 31% did so as compared to 20% of teachers and professors and 15% of researchers. Perhaps researchers, teachers, and professors have faster machines and find it relatively easy to access the PDF format compared to undergraduates. Or alternatively researchers, teachers, and professors prefer a "journal" type format, while students might prefer an HTML format, which is easier to import into their Word files. This may also reflect on the age of the user; users farther up the academic tree are more likely to prefer a journal formatted paper, and researchers may like to collect papers and prefer the journal format for their collection. Tables of contents are plainly used to navigate, browse around the site, and for current awareness purposes, so it is interesting to note their high use by practitioners (accounting for 27% of items requested) and lower use by undergraduates (14% of items viewed).

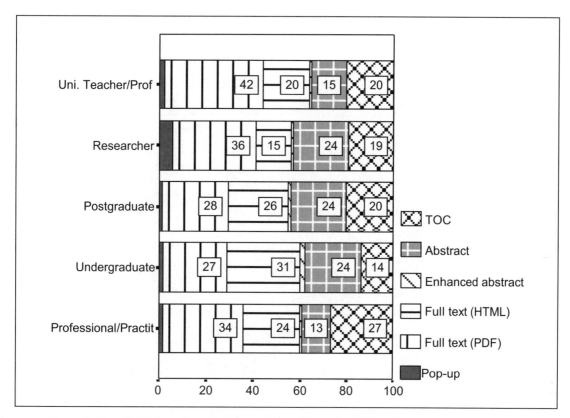

Figure 3. Type of Subscriber by Type of Item Viewed (TOCs, Abstracts, and Articles).

Figure 4 examines the use of the search engine on the site, in particular if a user session involved using the engine, and how many searches took place in the session. Most sessions did not involve a search session, which is interesting in its own right, but those that did involve a search were more likely to be conducted by undergraduates. While 46% of undergraduates used the search engine (with 10% of sessions involving 10 or more searches), researchers (19%) were the least likely to use it. Note that undergraduates were least likely to use the tables of contents.

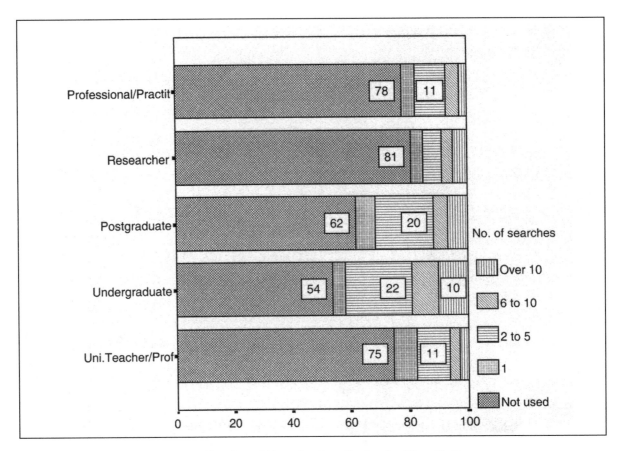

Figure 4. Number of Searches in a Session by User Status.

Broad Subject Background of User

For the Blackwell data it proved possible to define users by subject according to the broad subject field of the journal they searched. Figures 5 and 6 show analyses using this characteristic. Figure 5 looks first at the number of requests (TOCs, abstracts, and articles only) made in a session. Those viewing academic titles (a descriptor used by Blackwell to describe social science and humanities titles) recorded the highest number of requests in a session. Over half of this group (55%) viewed 11 or more items in a session, compared to 33% for those viewing medical journals, 45% viewing professional titles, and 35% viewing science publications.

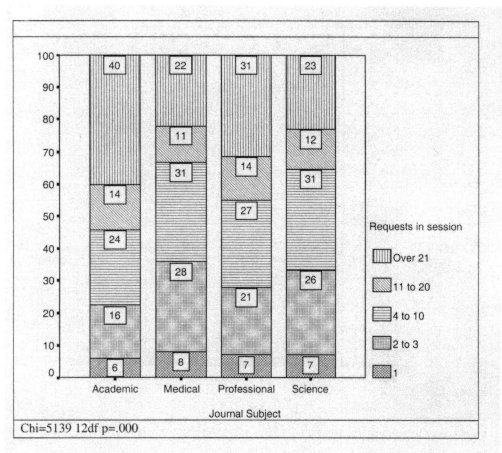

Chi=5139 12df p=.000

Figure 5. Number of Requests (TOCs, Abstracts, Articles) in a Session by Journal Subject Group.

Figure 6 provides information on the type of item requested. The most significant difference in type of request is between academic journals and the rest. A little over a third of accesses to academic journals were to table of contents pages, compared to about 19% for other subject groups. Further views of academic journals were least likely to be made up of views of full text HTML-formatted articles: only 8% compared to about 25% for other subject classifications. Although accesses to abstracts were about the same (30%), those using academic journals were far more likely to make use of enhanced abstracts. Science journal users were more likely to make use of pop-ups (4%) and full text PDF-formatted files (24%). Readers of professional journals were more likely to make use of full text HTML-formatted articles (29%) and least likely to make use of PDF-formatted articles (19%).

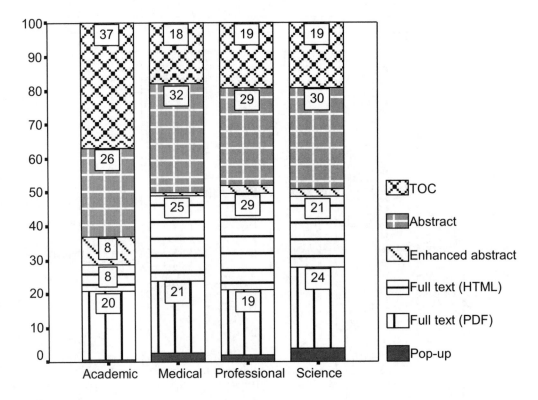

Figure 6. Journal Subject Group by Type of Journal Item Viewed (TOCs, Abstracts, and Articles).

Other log analyses reported at the Charleston Conference can be found at the Ciber Web site (www.soi.soi.city.ac.uk/organisation/is/research/ciber).

Citation Substudy

Deep log analysis seeks to associate log data with other datasets, and there is no better set to relate them to than citation data. This substudy shows what can be done.

In the traditional print world of journal publishing, we have a pretty good idea of what "authority" means and how it can be measured, however imperfectly, using journal impact factors and other citation-based measures. Critics of impact factors, and of the quantification of journal "influence" more generally, have set forward a series of arguments that acts of citation are at best a partial indicator of a journal's quality (whatever that means) and, at worst, may be highly misleading when applied in practice.

For all the caveats, impact factors do provide a useful summary of the way that articles become incorporated into the documentary fabric; moreover, they yield rankings of journals that are reasonably acceptable for most evaluation purposes.

The question raised from a deep log perspective is whether the stamp of authority conveyed by acts of citation might in any way be related to the decisions that readers make in the apparently more democratic, free-for-all environment of electronic journals platforms, like Blackwell Synergy. On the face of it, any such correlation would be quite surprising. Citations, by definition, can only be made and recorded by authors. While authors are simultaneously also readers, they represent a very small proportion of the reading constituency, perhaps on the order of around 5%. Not only that, they are likely to be senior researchers and professors; readers will include teachers, students, industrial users, and perhaps administrators and other professionals.

There have been many studies of the citation characteristics of the kinds of peer-reviewed journals that are the subject of this study; and there have been quite a few studies of the readership and usage patterns of journals, based on data such as reshelving statistics. Before the advent of electronic platforms like Synergy, it was naturally a far from easy task to establish incidences of journal use. It is still surprising that few studies have tried to explore connections between citations (votes by authors) on the one hand and readership (votes by users) on the other, and the orientation of these studies has largely been to explore whether the declining intensity of citations over time can be used to inform library shelf management: If a time comes when an issue of a journal has exhausted its citation yield, can that be used as an indicator that its natural reading life is similarly drawing to a close?

Method

The raw data for this small-scale experiment take the form of an analysis of the most highly downloaded papers recorded by Blackwell Synergy servers over a 24-hour period. These were subsequently screened to identify the top 50 most downloaded papers published before 1998. (Older papers were chosen to make it possible to calculate five-year impact factors.) Citations were captured using standard ISI tools: the Science Citation Index (SCI) and the Social Sciences Citation Index (SSCI) in their online form on Dialog Classic.

The total number of citations (c_a) that *each article* attracted during the first five years of its life was calculated. On its own, this is a pretty slippery and meaningless number. A paper may have attracted relatively few citations because it was on a minority topic with few active researchers, for example in children's librarianship. The converse is obviously possible: Papers on the immunological aspects of the HIV virus will attract the attention of thousands of active researchers. Hence, raw citation numbers are not comparable across disciplines, or even across specialties within the same discipline.

The second indicator calculated is a five-year journal impact factor (I_a) for the journal in which each article in the sample was published. If two articles in the same journal from two different years, say 1996 and 1997, occurred in our sample, then impact factors were calculated for each publication year. This impact factor expresses the number of times that the *average* paper in, say *Physiologia Plantarum*, was cited during the first five years of its life. We used the diachronic method for estimating impact factors online recommended by Ingwersen, Larsen, and Wormall.[7]

If we compare c_a, the number of times that our highly downloaded papers were actually cited, with I_a, the average number of times that papers in that year of the same journal were cited, then we have a measure that is to some extent independent of field effects.

In this chapter we introduce a new indicator, the article citation rate a_c, as the ratio:

$$a_c = c_a \text{ (times actually cited—observed) } / I_a \text{ (expected number of citations)}$$

Thus, a paper that has been cited five times, published in a journal whose impact factor is 2, has clearly "done better" than an article cited 10 times in a journal whose impact factor is 10. In the former case, the article has been cited more often than those around it have been; it could be said to have outperformed its peers in the same journal.

Results

The results of this small-scale pilot experiment are set out in Table 3.

Table 3. Citation Characteristics of High Download Synergy Papers

Total citations (Σc_a)	587
Mean citations/paper	11.74
Total expected number of citations (ΣI_a)	1,009
Expected citations/paper	20.18
Ratio Observed: Expected citations	1.72

It is striking that high download papers, at least those drawn from older publications, seem to exhibit much higher citation rates than might be expected: 72% higher across the whole sample. This effect is not due to the presence of a single very highly cited "superclassic" pushing up the average; the majority of papers in the study were cited more often than were their peers. More work needs to be done to establish whether there are indeed persistent relationships between reads and cites across Synergy and other full text journal platforms, and if there are, why this is.

Conventionally, citations are regarded as a form of currency through which authors express the usefulness of items in the literature. The emphasis here is on utility rather than "quality," since information only has value in the context of its application to a given task. If citations measure usefulness (at least to authors), they ought, in principle, to be able to say something indirect about use. They may be a very indirect measure of use, though, since the very act of citation raises the visibility of a document in the literature, whatever the platform, thus confounding the effect.

The results of this small-scale pilot could easily be disregarded on account of the tiny sample size employed. However, in a paper submitted to *JASIST* by Michael Kurtz,[8] compelling evidence of a constant reads–cites relationship is demonstrated on a much larger scale in the case of the NASA Astrophysics Data System (ADS). Kurtz and his coworkers estimate that an average paper is read about 20 times for every time it is cited. The implication of this paper and the work reported in full in *JASIST* in 2004 is that we may need to rethink our views on the ways that citations seem to attract readings.

Part 2. The Publishers' Response

Blackwell

During 2003 Blackwell Synergy had already introduced analytical tools to provide information on their users, what they were using, and how often, and also to determine the most visited parts of the Web site. These tools included more reports on most accessed content; most-searched keywords, created by Atypon, Blackwell's software partner; and the use of Net tracker to be able to see where people were coming from and where they entered or exited the site. However, the Ciber analysis of Synergy's log files and multidimensional databases has revealed some very exciting patterns and types of use. It also seems to have posed at this stage as many questions as it has answered.

The Data

As we have seen, Blackwell Synergy's users are classified into five types: professor/teacher, researcher, professional/practitioner, postgraduate, and undergraduate. The Ciber analysis shows us that these end-users, one of the major types of stakeholder for the site besides the librarian, the author, and the editor, really do have different needs and preferences according to their status, possibly their age, and definitely their subject.

We can categorize these users by their preferences:

- Professors use a community or .net address; they like quite recent tables of contents. The most frequent professor/teacher users of Blackwell Synergy are in the science arena; they tend to only look at one title; they browse; they much prefer the PDF format; and they have only average site penetration, looking at between 4 and 10 items per visit.

- Researchers, while also browsers, prefer older TOCs and tend to be researching in the professional journals such as veterinary science or addiction. However, they are similar to the professors in their preference for the PDF format and site penetration.

- Professionals or practitioners (e.g., nurses, dentists, vets) have similar usage and preferences to researchers.

- Students are searchers rather than browsers; they use the library more than .net or .com access, use the site heavily in each session, and mostly use academic journals. They also prefer HTML over PDF because they like to read on screen. We partly discovered this via a focus group with some Oxford students who read on screen and download because they are charged per page they print in the library.

In some ways these conclusions may have been predicted. Librarians know who uses the library most. One might also assume that the younger generation has been searching the Internet since childhood or adolescence and hence has searched rather than browsed. It is also well known that the Internet has become the primary research tool for many students and that they have to dig deeper because they know the subject less well than their teachers or specialists in the area. This observation may be the proof of the article economy: Students focus on articles, and they appear not to care about the journal.

But all this received wisdom, thanks to the Ciber log file analysis, has been given a quantitative basis. Blackwell Publishing now knows the percentages of types of user and use, the value of each customer to the company, and the beginnings of the value of each customer to the library. From this analysis customer usage ratios can be garnered, indicating where the most need is, where resources should be focused, or where and how efforts should be targeted.

The other seriously useful and directly applicable information that comes out of the analysis is the origin of the user, as this will tell both the publisher and the librarian where and how to market the resources contained within the site that have been purchased by the library.

Remembering that this pilot study represents a single day of log files, in September 2003, before the majority of the European universities were back in session, some of the statistics could be skewed. However, we recorded that 8% of total use of the site appeared to come from the library. While this is small in percentage terms, the analysis shows that the majority of these users were students and that this 8% of total site usage accounted for the heaviest penetration of the site, by far: 57% of the 8% undertook four or more views in any session. Conversely, 35% of usage came from Google, but 82% of the usage sessions from this group were effectively "bouncers." Another reason the library percentage may be low is that only libraries that had entered "lib" or "biblio" in their domain name server could be associated on the log files as coming directly from the library.

Another area of interest, particularly for libraries trying to facilitate the use of their resources, is the remote access user. Remote access provided by the library (e.g., Athens in the United Kingdom) had a low percentage of total traffic, but 94% of the users were heavy users.

Finally, a statistic that may have particular meaning to the publishers is the heavy country bias in the use of that country's journals. There was heavy country bias in journal usage, with 21% of use from Australia being from journals published in Melbourne, and in the United States 19% of use is of journals published in Boston. A further breakdown of this area would be useful to discover whether only the professional/practitioner journals were affected or this occurred across all subjects and user categories.

We have been given some significant insights into users' needs and desires, which will help develop the Web site to meet those needs in the short term, but which also poses more questions for the future

Short-Term Benefits for Blackwell Synergy

The disparate needs of users should encourage Blackwell Synergy to look at greater personalization of the site. This does not mean making users create favorites and taking more ETOCS, but that different views be shown according to what is known about the users' predilections for PDF over HTML and searching over browsing. This will mean providing more individualized home pages—"as a professor I want to browse"—so that, for example, professors are presented with a page that pushes browsing into prominence, which may mean the application of technology, such as Vivisimo, to encourage more browsing than is currently available. For students, however, the need is to create a page where search has prominence or which has the air of Google and where more options for their areas of interest are created on the fly and the article economy is facilitated. The beauty is that Synergy can also use these data to prioritize what should be done first, that is, cater to the best users before the more reticent ones. Presenting different views of the information contained within the site according to type of user has been used to good effect in the travel industry and in language presentation. It is more than feasible to do this technically and should serve to increase usage.

The knowledge of what users are using and where they are coming from will serve to create much tighter and more targeted marketing. Blackwell Publishing can market to faculty, telling them about the journal that is available electronically, but Blackwell knows it is more likely to get at students via viral marketing, promotion on the search engines, and helping librarians to incorporate the site within their library portals. There is also some obvious editorial impact to be gained in knowing the readers and what they do, much more powerfully than via a reader survey.

Benefits for Libraries

Through the sharing of these data libraries should obtain greater insights into what their users are using and how or where from, such as via Google, the library portal, or remote access. This should give the libraries hard proof of use by students. The insights this information will give on how to promote the use of the library might include the adoption of an Athens remote access protocol and knowledge of how to target use by academics.

What Questions Still Need to Be Addressed?

- How should we cater for the article user versus the journal user?
- Do we swap search to prominence if the majority of users are browsers?
- Will the current generation of searchers become browsers?
- Are they browsers because of the way the site is laid out?
- Is HTML the future?
- Will time take care of penetration?
- Can I turn the "bouncers" into users?
- How many "home" pages can we cope with?
- Is "internationalization" in certain fields false?
- Should we spend more of our efforts on getting the medium-use students to use more resources?
- What does increasing use do to my budget?
- What influence does price have on usage?
- If usage is increased, is the Big Deal more attractive?
- What is the return rate of users?
- What other reports does the library need to influence decision making?
- What does this mean for open access?
- What does this mean for usage-based pricing?
- Can we predict the future from the current situation?

So there is more work for Ciber, some triangulation of the data for us, and some advice from librarians on what is useful to know or to change.

Emerald

Since Emerald first moved to Ingenta in 2001 and usage statistics became more detailed, great emphasis has been put on analyzing and interpreting them. Just as Blackwell had set up certain analysis criteria, so had Emerald.

The areas that were analyzed on a monthly basis during 2003 included

- Total events per month
- Contents pages viewed
- Abstracts viewed
- Full text downloads

- Full text turnaways

- Ratio of database size to average daily usage

- Comparison with previous year

- Top user organizations

- Financial Times Top 100 Business School use

- Overall usage trend

- Customer usage trend

- Usage by country/region—with ratios

- Customer usage by sector (academic/public sector/corporate)

- Customer value for money

- Number of automated free trials

- Top requested articles

- Top journals/average position/monthly average

- Usage by subject group, e.g., strategy, human resources

- Article usage decay

Even before the Ciber results had come through, we had committed to COUNTER-compliant usage statistics. Over and above COUNTER, we had resolved to add the following reports for 2004:

- Article/abstract/TOC/Fulltext turnaways per journal

- Total searches run

- Total sessions run

- Facility to create usage reports for a consortium and on different levels

- E-mail alert when statistics have been updated

Deep Web log analysis gives publishers, information professionals, and subject faculty members the opportunity to assess, in a quantitative way, how users actually carry out many of their research and learning tasks. Through working together in a collaborative way, Ciber, Emerald, and Blackwell have managed to rapidly improve the analysis techniques applied to the Web logs. We have also taken advantage of our different skill sets and experiences to interpret the findings together.

Ciber has extensive experience in analyzing the use of digital media, while at Emerald we also have extensive experience in analyzing the transactional buying patterns of consumers within supermarkets, and in analyzing consumer loyalty to product and company brands. This wide experience has accelerated the development of our understanding of the digital user, as research angles and theories can be applied from other disciplines beyond both the digital media and library environments.

Another benefit of this open research approach has been the emphasis on discovering and interpreting what users actually do within the digital environment. None of the research partners had any fixed ideas about the outcomes of the research. At Emerald, our data are not structured so that we break down usage by user group, and now we can see the benefits of this analysis.

Access to Emerald content occurs in three main ways: through access to individual journals, typically using the library e-resource lists; through access to a version of the Emerald Fulltext database; or through access on a free trial to an Emerald journal or database. In 2002, Emerald had 992 database subscribers, out of a total of 8,456 customers—11.7% of all customers. The data showed that for the full 2002 annual period, 44% of visitors were authorized (paid for) database users. Therefore 44% of all visitors came from 11.7% of the customer base. However, authorized database users generated 65% of all usage. The truth is that 11.7% of all customers generated 65% of usage.

Table 2 (page 122) demonstrates that most visitors are "bouncers" or "infrequent visitors." Only 6.8% of visitors visited more than six times in 2002, but of these, 1.6% visited 15 times. For publishers, these frequent or very frequent visitors are the most important group, because we aim to convert regular visitors into heavy users, and then advocates. Publishers want to make their content part of the "world" of key researchers and teachers, who will in time become advocates for the journals and databases that they use on a regular basis.

This is all very similar to the way that both retailers (both physical shops, e.g. Wal-Mart, and Web-based services, e.g., Amazon.com) and brands (e.g., HP) and product brands (e.g., iPAQ) look to develop loyalty. Hallmark is expert at building relationships with customers, looking to win customers for life.[9] Their experience is that repeat customers who have built up a feeling of brand loyalty toward Hallmark visit Hallmark outlets (Gold Crown stores and branded shops) more often, buy more, and respond better to promotional activities. The same story can be told in many other product areas.

The Ciber research analyzing Emerald's 2002 logs demonstrated that the more users visit the Emerald site, the more they come back, and the more material they access during each visit. Of those who visited more than 15 times (only 1.6% of all visitors), 56% downloaded more than four articles. Of the 5.2% of all visitors who came to the site between 6 and 15 times, 52% downloaded more than four articles. What we are seeing here is classic consumer loyalty behavior. The more individuals come back, the more features they use.

However, consumer loyalty is not a simple subject. An extremely useful review of the brand loyalty literature[10] prises apart the differences between product involvement and brand loyalty. A simple relationship does not exist between the two. In the future, Emerald will be looking to analyze loyalty to certain products—both journals and databases.

Emerald employs a problem-solving approach to electronic product development. We look for the activities that cause headaches for key user groups, and then look to provide solutions that take the headaches away. Up until now we have taken a qualitative approach to identifying headache areas, but the opportunity to use quantitative research to see how individuals actually use electronic resources—particularly through job function and considering user return behavior—really does open up the digital box.

While the research on Emerald shows that repeat visitors download more articles, the Blackwell data show that professors, researchers, and professionals/practitioners are less "busy" than students, taking a more circumspect approach to journal content. This is probably due to the users knowing—more or less—the types of material that they are looking for. This links once again to the brand and product loyalty literature, in which a central premise is that consumers who are more involved with a particular brand are more committed and hence more loyal to that brand. Journals should be considered more as products than as brands in themselves. However, the academic community that groups itself around a subject area will tend to be very involved with the journal literature focusing on that subject. It would seem that subject specialists tend to become very involved with the journals that they see as valuable, frequently writing for them, and meeting at the conferences focusing on the subject. Further Web log analysis, linked with additional qualitative work, will give publishers such as Emerald and Blackwell more insight into how users build up their product involvement (e.g., at the journal level) and how this can be translated—if it can—into building loyalty at the database level.

Implications for Future Research

We are currently working to understand whether the type of institution (e.g., doctoral awarding, teaching) has any bearing on the type of usage patterns within databases and journals. It would also be interesting to contrast total usage levels with the total number of FTEs—ideally broken down by subgroup (e.g., researchers)—at an institution. Other areas for research include examining whether the amount of material published from an institution (possibly including EAB and editor involvement as well) has any correlation with usage levels. Another way to check loyalty is to establish whether users at institutions who read a certain set of journals heavily also have a strong article submission rate to those same journals. The impact of language, where English is a second language at best, also needs investigation.

Implications for Ongoing Librarian–Publisher Working Relations

This Charleston Conference showed that an increasing number of people from the publisher and library communities are now working to analyze usage and to draw meaning from the statistics. While COUNTER has gone a long way toward creating standardized terminology for user statistics, it is also clear that in the area of deep Web log analysis we are now developing research techniques and potentially a new research vocabulary. Some librarians and publishers are fascinated by what they can learn from usage statistics and seeing how this analysis compares with from citation analysis.

A very positive trend is that through concentrating on usage analysis, publishers and librarians are forging a new area for cooperation. The digital world is a rapidly evolving one, and many of those involved want to understand how the scholarly research process is really evolving.

Publishers know that their future will be built on their ability to supply relevant, high-quality research to faculty and students, and that librarians are their partners in providing this material in the format that best meets the needs of librarians and the wider academic community. Librarians have also always striven to meet the needs of their users, with a strong service mentality. Through analyzing usage, publishers and librarians can now have a fresh and objective view of how both parties are serving faculty members and students. There are many similarities to the approach that many suppliers take to working with retailers—it is not enough to just supply the product and put it on the shelf. Through joint category management suppliers and buyers at leading retail outlets look to increase the sales (usage) performance of certain products (e.g., Coca Cola), as well as increasing the performance, for example, of the overall nonalcoholic drinks category. Through joint work with libraries, Emerald is keen to understand how subject librarians are meeting the needs of the business department overall, while also understanding the performance of Emerald journals within the business area.

All of this is leading both librarians and publishers to develop new skills and to have new and different conversations. Importantly, discussions between publishers and librarians are now becoming more evidence-based as usage analysis comes to the fore.

New Skills to Be Developed: Library Marketing, Data Analysis

Usage data analysis is all very well, but if all this analysis does not lead to some positive change for users, librarians, and publishers, this is not a very fruitful activity. From Emerald's perspective, in-depth usage analysis has changed some—not all!!—of the conversations that we have with librarians.

Hannelore Rader (dean and university librarian of the University of Louisville, Kentucky) exhorts all of us to, "Put the library at the centre of the university." Usage analysis can demonstrate the vital role that paid-for library resources play in the intellectual health of an institution. However, where usage is low—by subject for example—librarians will look to market their resources even more professionally to professors, teaching staff, researchers, postgraduates, and undergraduates than before. After all, maybe 25% of the user community is new with the turn of every academic year.

Librarianship seems to be developing in two key and divergent areas. On one side, the technical demands are becoming more IT driven. On the other, data analysis and library marketing are growing in importance. The one constant is the focus on meeting the needs of the increasingly digital consumer, with a need to demonstrate the importance and utility of quality-stamped, peer-reviewed material to the growing ranks of "Google-satisfied" users.

Drawing Conclusions—But Not Extrapolating Too Far

Through the Virtual Scholar program, members of City University and staff at Emerald and Blackwell have learned a great deal. We also know that we have a great deal more to learn. It is important to recognize that while this study has taken us all into new territory, we are still only seeing snapshots and partial slices of user behavior. Digital fingerprints don't tell the full story. To return to the retail analogy, just because we can start to understand how a shopper selects greeting cards (a high involvement, slow selection process) does not mean that we understand how the same shopper selects other products or services such as pet food or hair care. Many factors influence behavior (e.g., age, education, assignment, language, time/deadlines), but how all the variables mix together is a complex jigsaw puzzle. While usage data may help us find our way through a digital dust storm, there will be different types of digital dust storms subject category by subject category.

Those involved in the Virtual Scholar program are keen to access data at a full institutional level, or ideally wider than this, so that differences and similarities in user behavior can be analyzed by subject, academic role (e.g., Ph.D. student), etc.

Conclusion

We hope that in this chapter we have shown how deep log analysis can help librarians and publishers better understand the challenges and information flows that they manage together.

Through learning these new skills, librarians and publishers have the opportunity to share information and work together to serve user communities even better than before. A particular benefit of using deep log analysis is that it identifies opportunities to support heavy users better, with these heavy users having a disproportionate influence on the information seeking behaviors of other user subcommunities. The cross-disciplinary approach taken by the Virtual Scholar program has brought together publishers, librarians, and information scientists, with some consumer behavior experience thrown in. This is an unusual mix, but together we are collectively learning how to build a better service through understanding the digital box.

Notes

1. D. Nicholas, P. Huntington, P. Williams, and T. Dobrowolski, "Re-appraising Information Seeking Behaviour in a Digital Environment: Bouncers, Checkers, Returnees and the Like," *Journal of Documentation* 60, no. 1 (2004): 24–39.

2. The Virtual Scholar research program was supported by Blackwell, Emerald, Thompson Scientific, Elsevier, and The British Library, 2003–2004.

3. This was extended to three months.

4. For more details see D. Nicholas and P. Huntington, "Micro-mining and Segmented Log File Analysis: A Method for Enriching the Data Yield from Internet Log Files," *Journal of Information Science* 29, no. 5 (2003): 391–404.

5. D. Nicholas, P. Huntington, and A. Watkinson, "Digital Journals, Big Deals and Online Searching Behaviour: A Pilot Study," *Aslib Proceedings* 55, nos. 1/2 (2003): 84–109.

6. We could not conduct this analysis for Blackwell as we only had one day's data.

7. P. Ingwersen, B. Larsen, and I. Wormall, "Applying Diachronic Citation Analysis to Ongoing Research Program Evaluations," in *The Web of Knowledge: A Festschrift in Honor of Eugene Garfield,* ed. B. Cronin and H. B. Atkins (Medford, N.J. American Society for Information Science, 2000), 373–87.

8. M. Kurtz et al., "The NASA Astrophysics Data System: Sociology, Bibliometrics and Impact," *Journal of the American Society for Information Science and Technology* (2003) [Online], available: http://cfa-www.harvard.edu/~kurtz/jasist-submitted.pdf (accessed December 10, 2003).

9. S. Robinette and C. Brand, *Emotion Marketing: The Hallmark Way of Winning Customers for Life* (New York: McGraw-Hill, 2001), 115–27.

10. P. Quester and A. Lim, "Product Involvement/Brand Loyalty: Is There a Link?" *Journal of Product and Brand Management* 12, no. 1 (2003): 22–38

WHEN ARTICLES VANISH: POLICY AND PRACTICE FOR REMOVING ARTICLES FROM FULL TEXT COLLECTIONS

Anthony Watkinson, Consultant

Introduction

Although Scott Plutchak and Anthony Watkinson shared the conference presentation, this chapter is the responsibility of Anthony Watkinson. It is very similar to the handout given to those attending the session. My role in the presentation was to follow on from Scott. Our division of roles was that Scott framed the issues and presented the results of what he found in terms of current practice, and then I discussed the publisher perspective.

Fortunately this is one of those areas where librarians and publishers share common goals, as set out by Scott in his JMLA article (http://www.pubmedcentral.gov/articlerender. fcgi?artid=100760). However, Scott is both a librarian and a journal editor. I am a publisher but also work in an information science department. There will be differences in our approaches. I would also like to add that the issues at stake in the presentation were not ones that impinged a great deal on the thinking of most publishers and (I suspect) most librarians. Both communities owe a lot to Scott for raising the issues, articulating them clearly, and proposing rational solutions. It is clear to me from my recent investigations that there is a much greater level of awareness of these issues in the publishing community than there was a year ago.

It is easier to prepare a big handout than it is a small handout, and what follows in this chapter may have too much detail in it. However, I defend this approach by arguing that it helped those attending the session and will help those reading this chapter to have some key documents. In the first three sections of this chapter I have included the following documents:

- A proposal to an international publishing body written by Scott at my invitation, which provides (to my mind) a splendid summary of what we discussed in the session.

- The Elsevier policy, which is recognized as an important and impressive construct.

- An internal document from a major STM publisher (adapted to disguise the source), which indicates some of the problems experienced by publishers that attempt to put final versions of articles online before print publication.

In the fourth section of this chapter I begin by giving quotations from the responses of a number of major publishers, who have replied to my request for information about their policies. In the fifth section I give some information about retraction standards, as I suspect that those who are neither medical authors nor publishers will be unfamiliar with this area. I then in the sixth section make some comments about the relationship between take down for legal reasons and archiving. Finally, mindful of the fact that the session was originally billed as covering the "problems of identifying the original version, the relationship between electronic pre-prints and official published versions," I provide some e-references for openly accessible work in this area.

The Vanishing Archive: Best Practice on Article Removal in the Digital Environment—Comments from a Librarian*

T. Scott Plutchak, Editor, Journal of the Medical Library Association; Associate Professor and Director, Lister Hill Library of the Health Sciences, University of Alabama at Birmingham

While librarians today (and in particular those who specialize in STM areas) are primarily concerned with making sure that the members of their primary clientele have ready access to the best current information available, they also have a primary concern for the preservation of the scholarly record. While it may sometimes seem, from the publishing standpoint, that the ability to remove an article from the electronic version of a journal represents an advance over the policies for retraction that have been developed in the print world, many librarians view this possibility with considerable alarm.

I originally framed the issues in an editorial in the *Journal of the Medical Library Association* and further developed them in a presentation at the Charleston Conference in November 2002, followed by discussion on the liblicense-l list during the winter of 2002, and a guest editorial published in *Against the Grain* (see list of sources below).

Briefly put, the two primary reasons for not withdrawing articles follow:

- The experience of the past several decades of dealing with retractions shows that disagreements over whether an article manifests inaccuracies, misconduct, or other inappropriate behaviors are often issues of serious contention. Debating these issues within the scholarly community is essential for that community to come to terms with the underlying issues involved. When an article is removed, no further discussion is possible, unless someone, somewhere, has managed to archive a copy.

- The history of science is a history of stumbles, mistakes, and outright frauds, as well as of brilliant successes and stunning insights. It is essential for the history of science that we maintain a clear and readily accessible record of the published literature, warts and all.

In challenge to this, the argument is made that to allow offending articles to remain in the scientific literature risks perpetuating errors and, in some cases, particularly in the clinical medical literature, putting people's lives at risk if therapeutic decisions are made on the basis of flawed articles. But the very technology that makes it possible to withdraw an article also enables us to ensure that whenever an article is accessed, any errors, challenges, retractions, etc., will also be seen. Digital technology, in other words, makes it unnecessary to remove an article in nearly all of the cases that one might argue that it would be desirable to do so.

There is an urgency to these issues because we are moving quickly into an era in which the electronic article is the article of record. The major commercial publishers are beginning to offer electronic-only subscriptions to libraries, and in the current economic climate, many libraries will take that option. Without guidelines from a respected source, librarians fear that many publishers will either adopt policies that are not sound in the long run or, more likely, fail to develop policies until they are faced with the sort of situation that Elsevier Science faced with the *Human Immunology* situation, and make decisions hastily that they, and the rest of the scholarly community, may later regret. Elsevier Science has recovered from that situation and has developed a policy which, while it may not be completely ideal from a librarian's standpoint, is a considerable advance and demonstrates their concern to come up with a sound policy that protects, as far as possible, the interests of all concerned.

The International STM Association is well positioned to establish a framework that publishers can use in developing their own policies. In my article in *Against The Grain,* I suggested that the following principles (based on policies recommended by the U.S. National Library of Medicine and the International Committee of Medical Journal Editors for handling retractions in print publications) should be used in retracting, rather than removing, offending articles:

- The retraction should appear on a numbered page in a prominent section of the journal.

- The retraction should be listed in the contents page and include in its heading the title of the article.

- The retraction must be signed by one of the following: the author, the author's legal counsel, the author's sponsoring institution, or the editor of the journal.

- The text of the retraction should explain why the article is being retracted.

- The statement of retraction and the original article must be clearly linked in the electronic version so that the retraction will always be apparent to anyone who comes across the original article.

If these principles were followed, I believe that in virtually all cases it would not be necessary to remove a published article from the electronic journal. Such a policy would represent an appropriate balancing of the interests of all parties concerned.

Sources:

Foster, A. L. "Elsevier's Vanishing Act." The Chronicle of Higher Education. January 10, 2003. Available online at: http://chronicle.com/free/v49/i18/18a02701.htm.

Lapelerie, F. "Re: Vanishing Act." [Online posting, posted by A. Okerson]. Licensing Digital Information, January 23, 2003. Available: http://www.library.yale.edu/~llicense/ListArchives/ (accessed June 21, 2004).

Menefee, D. "Article Removal Policy." *LibraryConnect Newsletter* 1, no. 2 (June 2003): 6–7.

———. "Elsevier Policy on Article Removal." [Online posting]. Licensing Digital Information, February 5, 2003. Available: http://www.library.yale.edu/~llicense/ListArchives/ (accessed June 21, 2004).

Plutchak, T. S. "Re: Elsevier Policy on Article Removal." [Online posting]. Licensing Digital Information, February 7, 2003. Available: http://www.library.yale.edu/~llicense/ListArchives/ (accessed June 21, 2004).

———. "Sands Shifting Beneath Our Feet." *Journal of the Medical Library Association* 90, no. 2 (April 2002): 161–63. Available http://www.pubmedcentral.gov/articlerender.fcgi?artid=100760 (accessed June 21, 2004).

———. "Vanishing Act." [Online posting]. Licensing Digital Information, January 7, 2003. Available: http://www.library.yale.edu/~llicense/ListArchives/ (accessed June 21, 2004).

———. "Vanishing Act." *Against the Grain* 15, no. 2 (April 2003): 36, 38.

Elsevier Revised Policy on Article Removal**

It is a general principle of scholarly communication that the Editor of a learned journal is solely and independently responsible for deciding which of the articles submitted to the journal shall be published. In making this decision the Editor is guided by the policies of the journal's editorial board and constrained by such legal requirements as shall then be in force regarding libel, copyright infringement, and plagiarism.

An outcome of this principle is the importance of the scholarly archive as a permanent, historic record of the transactions of scholarship. Articles that have been published shall remain extant, exact, and unaltered as far as is possible. However, very occasionally circumstances may arise where an article is published that must later be retracted or even removed. Such actions must not be undertaken lightly and can only occur under exceptional circumstances, such as

- infringements of professional ethical codes, such as multiple submission, bogus claims of authorship, plagiarism, fraudulent use of data, or the like [see "Article Retraction by the Scholarly Community"];

- legal limitations upon the publisher, copyright holder, or author(s) [see "Article Removal"]; or

- the identification of false or inaccurate data that, if acted upon, would pose a serious health risk [see "Article Removal" or "Article Replacement"].

Each of these instances, together with the Elsevier procedures, is detailed below.

Article Retraction by the Scholarly Community

The retraction of an article by its authors or the editor under the advice of members of the scholarly community has long been an occasional feature of the learned world. Standards for dealing with retractions have been developed by a number of library and scholarly bodies and this best practice is adopted for article retraction by Elsevier:

- A retraction note titled "Retraction: [article title]" signed by the authors and/or the editor is published in the paginated part of a subsequent issue of the journal and listed in the contents list.

- In the electronic version, a link is made to the original article.

- The online article is preceded by a screen containing the retraction note and it is to this screen that the link resolves; the reader can then proceed to the article itself.

- The original article is retained unchanged save for a watermark on the pdf indicating on each page that it is "retracted."

- The html version of the document is removed.

Article Removal

In an extremely limited number of cases, it may unfortunately be necessary to remove an article from the online database. This will only occur where the article is clearly defamatory, or infringes others' legal rights, or where the article is, or we have good reason to expect it will be, the subject of a court order, or where the article, if acted upon, might pose a serious health risk.

In these circumstances, while the metadata (title and authors) will be retained, the text will be replaced with a screen indicating that the article has been removed for legal reasons.

Article Replacement

In cases where the article, if acted upon, might pose a serious health risk, the authors of the original article may wish to retract the flawed original and replace it with a correct version. In these circumstances the procedures for retraction will be followed with the difference that the database retraction notice will publish a link to the corrected re-published article and a history of the document.

In all cases, our official archives at the National Library of the Netherlands will retain all article versions, including retracted or otherwise removed articles.

Elsevier recognises [sic] the importance of the integrity and completeness of the scholarly record to researchers and librarians and attaches the highest importance to maintaining trust in the authority of its electronic archive. This policy has been designed to address these concerns and to take into account the current best practice in the scholarly and library communities.

As standards evolve and change we shall revisit this issue and welcome the input of the scholarly and library communities. We believe that these issues require international standards and we will be active in lobbying the information bodies to establish international standards and best practices which the publishing and information industries can adopt.

Putting Articles Online Before Print Issue Released: Errors and Errata Usage Policy

What happens if the production editor or author finds an error in an article after it has gone live?

It is important that the version of a paper that appears online is considered complete and final. Even though it is theoretically possible to correct an article before it goes to print, there are very good reasons why this should not happen. First, publication online constitutes public disclosure. Although many authorities consider print publication as the definitive version of a work [sic], to our knowledge the distinction (if any) has not been adequately explored in the courts. There are also issues of copyright and precedence, which would become very complex if we allowed changes to articles after online publication. Second, although indexers and aggregators currently only receive article headers etc. on print publication, they will doubtless change this policy in the future to keep pace with the increase in pre-publication services. Once this happens, it would not be possible (or at least it would be extremely complex) to make changes known to the abstracting services if anything was altered. Therefore we emphasize that the online version should be considered by authors to be as final or unchangeable as a page published in print. Our adoption of this errata policy is well in line with the thinking of other publishers and third parties.

Exceptions

We will correct online proofs in cases of a major *technical* error on our part, e.g. if a figure has been published inverted. Bibliographic errors (author name mis-spellings) will also be corrected. Content errors, however minor, will not be exempted.

In any proposed case of technical error, the production editor should discuss the matter with their divisional journal production manager and get approval to proceed before any agreement on action is made with the author.

Use or errata

An article published online should be treated no differently than if it were published on paper. Therefore, if an author does complain that we have made an error and requests alterations they should be informed that the correct solution for this is an erratum (or corrigendum if it is an omission on their part, or they acknowledge that the error is their fault). If the request is subsequently withdrawn because they do not wish to have an erratum published, it may be that the error was not significant and was only brought to light because they assumed simple changes were possible after online publication.

Escalation

If an author still insists on a change being made but is unwilling to publish an erratum, or they request the complete removal of an article from the online database or considerable alteration of an article before its appearance in print, the production editor should escalate the issue with his or her superiors [specified].

Publisher Policies

I presented a number of publishers with the principles set out in the documents above, but in an abbreviated form. Publishers will not read more than a page and hate answering questionnaires. It is clear that the Elsevier policy has been very influential, and in general the publishers I asked followed its general thrust. There is (as far as I know) no formal policy online available in such detail.

For example, the linking between the retraction and the original was specifically mentioned by several.

The devil, however, is in the details. For example, a leading commercial publisher writes, after explaining, as all the publishers did, that they never remove anything without a legal requirement:

I can think of one article that we took down because it had also been published by a competitor and the copyright position was extremely unclear. I think that in this case we removed all references to it.

The rights manager of a major non-profit press writes:

In some cases, it may be necessary to withdraw all or part of an article for legal or safety reasons (and the two are virtually synonymous since we would be open to an action for damages if we were guilty of negligent misstatement).This would never be done lightly, but under such circumstances we would follow Elsevier's policy below in so far as the metadata (title and authors) would be retained and the text replaced with a screen indicating that the article has been removed for legal reasons. *However, we aren't contemplating the deposit of the withdrawn article.* [Emphasis added.]

I return to the questions of "legal requirements" and also of the relationship with archiving and preservation arrangements in section 2 below.

When we look at the relationship between online versions and final online plus print versions, it is clear that the practicalities of each different situation may lead to different solutions and solutions that may be guided by (to some extent) expediency rather than policy

It is clear that the policies set out only scratch the surface. The American Geophysical Union gives a differently nuanced explanation of policy at http://www.agu.org/pubs/ecorrection_policy.html:

In 2002 the electronic article became the version of record for AGU journals. Therefore an article becomes part of the permanent record when it is published online, and it must be preserved in this original format. In order to protect the integrity of the journal literature, it is essential to have a clear record of any changes to the content of published files.

The guiding principles of the AGU electronic corrections policy include the following:

- The original version of an article will remain available to readers. When a modification to the content of a published article is necessary, a formal "Correction to" article will be generated for the electronic and print formats as well as the permanent archive.

- All content-related modifications to a published article require notification that a correction has been made. Format corrections, such as replacing a fuzzy image, correcting corrupted figure labeling, and similar changes not involving intellectual content, can be made without formal notification.

- Formal corrections will be linked to the original article through a labeled button in the navigation bar of the Web display (HTML). In the online PDF version of the original article, notification will be provided through placement of a "corrected date" note at the top of the file. If there is sufficient time before a print issue is assembled at the end of a calendar month, the correction for the printed issue will be placed immediately behind the original article; if there is not sufficient time to process the correction article, a note "[Correction in process]" will be added at the end of the article entry in the table of contents.

In a commentary on the above policy a publisher wonders why, if the print version is not the version of record, one cannot make changes. In practice one wonders how far the policy and the reasons for it are truly understood.

Retraction Standards

Librarians may not be familiar with standards laid down for retraction. For the retraction to have any impact in the medical world (where I would guess that such questions come up to a disproportionate extent), the retraction must be visible when the original article is found through MedLine.

Following are two references on this subject: http://www.nlm.nih.gov/pubs/factsheets/errata.html and http://onlineethics.org/reseth/mod/mod/icmje.html#corrections. The section of the first item cited headed "Retraction" follows:

Articles may be retracted or withdrawn by their authors, academic or institutional sponsor, editor, or publisher, because of pervasive error or unsubstantiated or irreproducible data. For example, an article's conclusions may have been based upon faulty logic or computation, its data may have been obtained by accident from a contaminated cell line or through poor instrumentation, or it may have been derived from falsified or fabricated data. NLM does not differentiate between articles that are retracted because of honest error and those that are retracted because of scientific misconduct or plagiarism. If the notification in the journal is labeled as a retraction or withdrawal, NLM will index it as a retraction.

It is NLM's policy that a retraction will be indexed as a retraction only if it clearly states that the article in question is being retracted or withdrawn, and is signed by an author of the retracted paper or author's legal counsel; by the head of the department, dean, or director of the laboratory where the paper was produced; or by the journal editor. In addition, the retraction must be labeled and published in citable form; that is, the retraction must appear on a numbered page in an issue of the journal that published the retracted article.

NLM does not simply expunge the citation of a retracted article from its indexes or databases, but rather links the original to the notice of retraction, by adding a Retraction statement after the source of the retracted article on the PubMed Summary display. The bibliographic reference for the retraction notice also appears above the title in the Abstract and Citation formats in PubMed. In the MEDLINE format, it appears in the RIN (Retraction in) field. The MEDLINE record of each retracted article will be given an additional Publication Type of RETRACTED PUBLICATION (PT) as well.

NLM makes a reciprocal linkage between the retraction statement and the retracted article. That is, the retraction statement is indexed as RETRACTION OF PUBLICATION (PT). The bibliographic reference(s) for the article(s) being retracted appear above the title in the Abstract and Citations formats in PubMed. In the MEDLINE format, they appear in the ROF (Retraction of) field.

"Legal Reasons" and Archives

There have been a number of statements of principle about the duties of publishers—for example, see postings on liblicense-1@lists.yale.edu for June 19, 2003. My copresenter posted on the same list and on the same topic on January 29, 2003. Librarians want publishers to account for any action taken for "legal reasons." The counsel for a major commercial publisher put a problem to me in this way:

> Any statement of the reason for removal could also be interpreted as an admission of liability so I would always advise the 'for legal reasons' route rather than a full explanation—and as you know disputes between authors are so complex that it is very hard to get to the bottom of them.

As a former intellectual property director I would have found it difficult to advise otherwise. In what circumstances is the publisher justified in removing anything from the electronic database? There is an interesting dialog between Stephen Barr (Sage) and David Goodman on liblicense-1@lists.yale.edu on February 4, 2003. My hope (like that of my copresenter) is that removals will be very rare if the sort of standards we are discussing here are agreed upon—and understood.

The question about independent, trusted archives for preservation "in perpetuity" is a very big one and not for resolution here. However, it seems to me that what is withdrawn must be secured in a proper archive; for the archives being built and to be built there are many issues to be cleared up regarding both access and legal liability (for the library concerned).

Versions

Over the last year I have written extensively on authenticity, including the question of how we can identify the definitive publication that has to be archived for posterity. The title of my rather large work is *Securing Authenticity of Scholarly Paternity and Integrity,* and it is available at http://www.bic.org.uk/securing%20authenticity.pdf. Much of this document is concerned with versions, but in this context chapter 5 is more relevant. There does seem to me a lack of interest in what version is the version of record, and even senior thinkers are constantly proposing new versions, for example, the "vanilla" version favored by Stefan Harnad. (See https://mx2.arl.org/Lists/SPARC-IR/Message/93.html) to see what I am talking about.)

In this study I also make the point repeatedly that very little scholarly material is produced in an electronic-only form (see my chapter 6) and that usually the definitive online version is identical with the print version. We need to act now to make sure that the online-only document or the online-definitive-version-different-from-print is going to be handled properly and archived successfully. This is a big job for the future, but we can set the right standards now.

Notes

*Reprinted with permission of Scott Plutchak.

** Sourced from http://www.library.yale.edu/~llicense/ListArchives/0302/msg00031.html. Reprinted with permission of Daviess Menefee of Elsevier.. This version of the document and any future replacement versions are to be found at http://www.elsevier.com/inca/publications/misc/libraryconnectvol2.pdf.

Each year a significant number of the panels and plenary sessions raise issues that are meaningful to collection development librarians. The 2003 discussions presented here cover virtual reference collections; functional requirements for acquisitions records; communication issues; special concerns of health sciences libraries; collecting comic books; and using circulation, ILL, and collection characteristics for policy development purposes.

VIRTUAL REFERENCE COLLECTIONS FOR VIRTUAL SERVICES

Sandy Campbell, University of Alberta Library, Science and Technology Library
Juliet Nielsen, Saskatchewan Institute of Applied Science and Technology Libraries
Kathy Carter, University of Alberta Library, Bibliographic Services
Susan Dahl, University of Alberta Library, Bibliographic Services

Abstract

Virtual reference bridges the physical gap between reference staff and remote users sitting at their own computers, by allowing a Web page to be displayed simultaneously on both computer screens. Electronic reference tools need to be organized effectively so that reference staff can guide users directly to the appropriate information on their computer screens. Now that "collaborative browsing" has been established as a viable way of supplying reference service, how do we structure electronic reference collections to supply the best service in this environment? Within the University of Alberta Library's Virtual Reference Project, the Science and Technology Library has begun to develop a structure for a virtual reference collection to meet these needs.

Background

Reference service in the virtual environment is evolving rapidly. At the University of Alberta, we now have several years' experience in answering reference questions using Chat Reference. This service is delivered to authenticated University of Alberta users through 24/7 software. The service involves both a synchronous chat function and the ability to cobrowse with users, guiding them to the resources they need to use. Often, the user will be taken to the catalog to locate books or to a database to locate journals and then out to electronic journals. However, standard reference tools are increasingly available in electronic format, allowing reference staff to guide the user to the electronic equivalent of a dictionary, handbook, directory, encyclopedia, or dataset.

Recently the University of Alberta has joined a consortium of 27 North American academic libraries for the shared provision of virtual reference services. In this environment, a staff person at any of the 27 institutions may answer a question posed by a user at another institution. To be able to guide the user to the resources site-licensed at his or her home institution, the reference provider must be able to quickly identify what resources are available at that institution. Within the 24/7 software, "policy pages" for each institution guide the reference providers to library catalogs and Web pages. However, there is little standardization among the ways in which various libraries have organized their electronic reference resources.

Characteristics of a Useful Virtual Reference Collection

In the print reference environment, reference staff frequently answer questions by relying on a classified reference collection. By knowing the broad one- or two-letter classes of the Library of Congress Classification system and the basic function of different kinds of reference tools, reference staff with little knowledge of a subject area will be able to find appropriate reference tools. For example, if the question relates to plant science, simply by knowing that the subject is classified at "SB", most reference staff could easily walk into any reference collection covering that subject and find core reference tools in a predictable order.

When reference providers, particularly those not resident at the student's home institution, need to find electronic reference tools to answer virtual reference questions, they need the same kind of speedy and certain access that they would have had in the print environment. In essence, the virtual reference provider needs to be able to "walk into the virtual reference collection" at the home institution.

To meet this need, a virtual reference collection must have the following identifiable characteristics:

- electronic format

- selected by a subject selector as a good reference tool

- licensed for the user who is requesting it

- up-to-date (weeded frequently)

- identifiable by subject (e.g., plant science or SB)

- browsable

How Have Libraries Organized Virtual Reference Collections?

There are four methods by which libraries have organized electronic reference tools. Each has advantages and disadvantages and works more or less well, depending upon the specific circumstances of the library. These methods are general reference Web pages, subject-specific Web pages, internal databases, and external databases. At the University of Alberta, we have at various times for various purposes used all of these methods. For the purposes of supplying access to a reference collection for use by remote virtual reference suppliers, all have some shortcomings. Because of this, we continued to search for a catalog-based solution.

General Reference Web Pages

General reference Web pages are common at most academic libraries. At the University of Alberta, the reference page does a good job of supplying access to the general resources. However, it does not attempt to guide the user to subject-specific reference tools. (See Figure 1.)

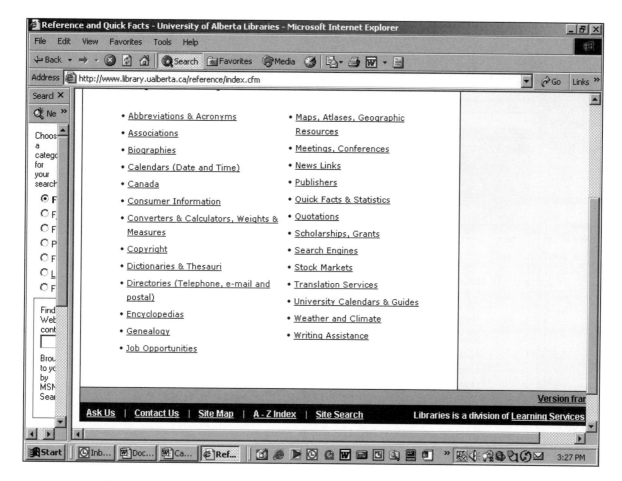

Figure 1. The University of Alberta Library's General Reference Web Page.

Subject Web Pages

Like most academic institutions, the University of Alberta has many excellent subject Web pages. While these have been built to a general standard, they have been built for a variety of purposes, usually not as mirrors of the reference collections. Some have been built as guides to Web resources in the field, some are electronic pathfinders, some are designed to support specific courses. One of the advantages of Web pages is that they allow subject librarians to organize their materials in ways that make sense within their particular discipline, unfettered by the strictures of standard classification systems. While this makes them more useful for people within the discipline, it makes them more difficult to navigate for anyone who is not familiar with the discipline. For example, looking at the University of Alberta's top-level Web page listing by subject, which really reflects faculty groupings, only people familiar with the structure of the faculties at the University of Alberta would know that the "Textiles" subject Web page is a part of "Agriculture". (See Figure 2.)

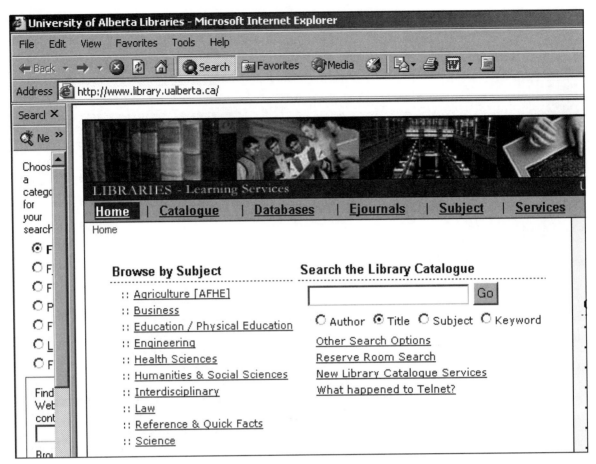

Figure 2. Top Terms in the University of Alberta Library's Subject Web Page List.

Subject Web pages also have two other disadvantages. First, they take considerable time to build and maintain. Second, to avoid becoming unnavigable, they are necessarily selective or many layered. To replicate a strong subject reference collection in a Web page would make it too unwieldy for easy access.

Internal Databases

An internal database is an alternative to static general reference pages and subject pages as methods of supplying access to a selected electronic reference collection. Built with a commonly used database software such as Access, such a database allows for a variety of searchable fields, such as discipline, call number, and keyword, and is easy to build and update.

An internal database has the advantage of being a staff-only resource, which does not require the exacting standards of a database to be delivered as a public service. However, for use with a virtual reference service, an internal database requires the reference staff to work through several steps before leading the user to the resource. The staff member must use the database to identify the appropriate reference tool, then return to the catalog to open the tool with the user. We quickly realized that while the internal database worked well as an identification tool, we needed to have a system that would allow the user to be engaged from the first step.

Internal databases have the added disadvantage of replicating at least some of the work done in the building and maintenance of catalog records for the electronic reference tools.

External Databases

External databases have most of the advantages of internal databases. They are relatively easy to build, populate, and maintain, and they supply a searchable access to a collection of tools specifically selected for virtual reference.

In our prototype database, we used a simple Web form (Figure 3) to add new electronic reference resources to the database. At the user interface, reference staff could query the database by call number, discipline, or resource type (dictionaries, encyclopedias, etc.). Through the cobrowsing function, users could observe the steps to reach the search engine and the search so that they could replicate it later. (See Figure 4.)

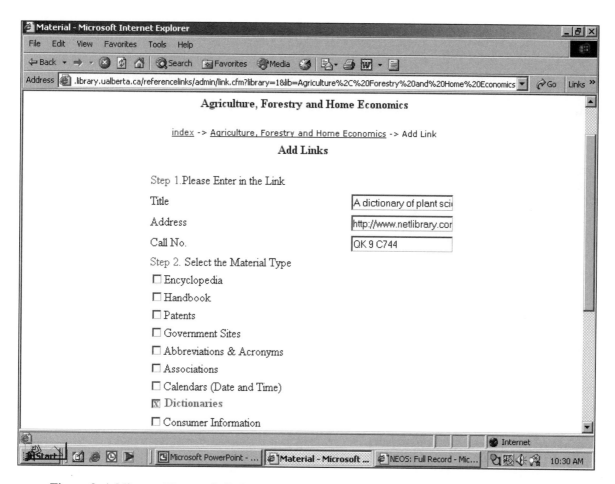

Figure 3. Adding an Electronic Reference Tool to the Virtual Reference Collection Database.

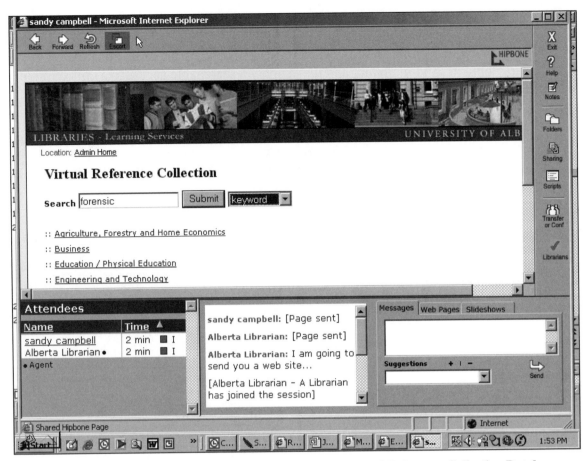

Figure 4. Cobrowsing with a Chat Reference User in the Virtual Reference Collection Database.

The external virtual reference database has the added advantage of having a simple search box design, similar to the many Web search engines with which most users are familiar and comfortable.

However, like the internal database, the external database has the disadvantage of requiring duplication of catalog information and maintenance. However, it is a viable option if a catalog-based solution is not possible.

A Catalog-Based Solution

The limitations of all four methods for the organization of electronic reference tools led us to search for a catalog-based solution. While this had proven impossible in the DRA catalog environment, with the move to the new SIRSI interface in June 2003, we found new possibilities. Focusing on the electronic reference tools offered by the Science and Technology Library, a pilot project was undertaken to develop a catalog-based virtual reference collection.

Within the SIRSI record, Internet resources belonging to the University of Alberta are defined as a "library" and coded as "University of Alberta Internet." Materials receiving this code are available in electronic format and licensed for use by University of Alberta users, meeting two of the search criteria for an electronic reference collection.

A process needed to be created to embed enough information in the catalog record to satisfy the other two criteria: being selected by a subject specialist as a good reference tool and being viewable in browsable call number range. Because the University of Alberta library operates within the NEOS Consortium shared catalog environment, we needed to keep changes to the catalog record within the consortial standards.

A solution was found in the addition of a local call number, prefaced by the code "VREF" (Figure 5). This allowed material selected by subject specialists for inclusion in the virtual reference collection to be uniquely identified and easily searched.

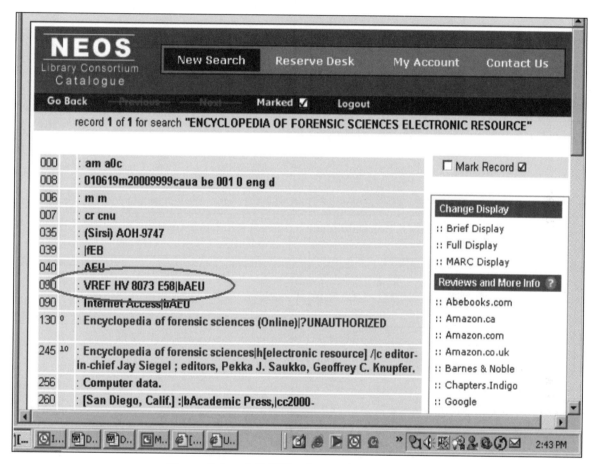

Figure 5. Local Call Number with VREF Code.

By executing a call number search, prefaced by VREF (for example VREF HV in Figure 6) and limiting the search to the University of Alberta Internet library, a searcher is able to produce a browsable classified list of the electronic virtual reference tools. Using this method, a reference staff member at any institution can "walk into" the University of Alberta's virtual reference collection and cobrowse it in a predictable Library of Congress order with their Chat Reference user and guide the user into the resource (see Figure 7).

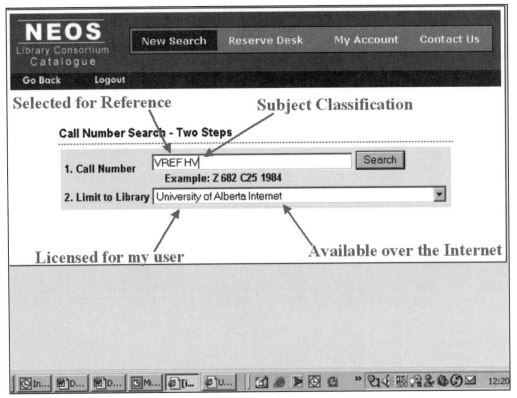

Figure 6. Search to Identify Virtual Reference Tools.

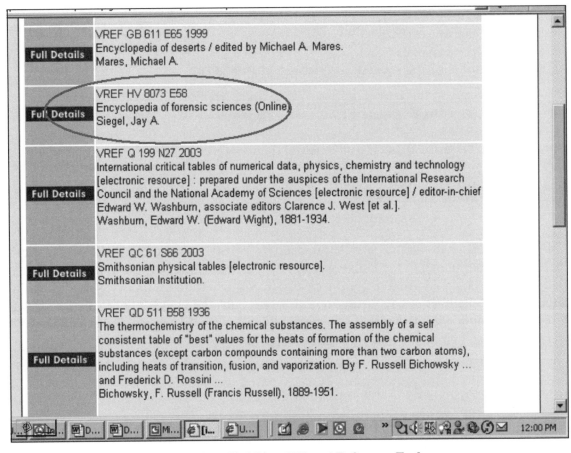

Figure 7. Classified List of Virtual Reference Tools.

Because the primary work involved in creating the virtual reference collection is the addition of a call number, this is an inexpensive solution when compared with the creation and constant maintenance of Web pages or internal or external databases. Many of the electronic resources are already cataloged, or catalog copy is available, and because many are electronic equivalents of print resources that have been classified, call numbers are already available.

Future Directions

While users do use call number searching as an entry point into the library catalog, we know that they are much more familiar with and comfortable with both Web pages and search boxes. We recognize that this function will be primarily used by library staff. However, with the ability to identify a virtual reference collection, it may be possible to create a program that would extract information from the catalog to populate a parallel searchable database, or standardized subject Web pages, based on Library of Congress Classification numbers.

Web Addresses

University of Alberta Library, http://www.library.ualberta.ca

24/7 reference, http://www.247ref.org

DEFINING FUNCTIONAL REQUIREMENTS FOR ACQUISITIONS RECORDS: THE NEXT STEP IN CREATING STANDARDS

Katharine Treptow Farrell, Princeton University Library
Marc Truitt, University of Houston Libraries

Introduction

A couple of weeks ago, we suggested on the AUTOACQ-L discussion list[1] that a major cause of our failure until now to articulate standards for acquisitions data was the lack of a conceptual and intellectual framework for acquisitions processes on which we might hang a standard for acquisitions metadata. By way of analogy, we observed that our colleagues in the cataloging community have various texts that describe the intellectual framework for their work. Among these texts, of course, are the *Anglo-American Cataloguing Rules* (*AACR*). Much of the content of a USMARC record is guided and even determined by *AACR* and the *Library of Congress Rule Interpretations. AACR* is itself the result of over a century of greater and lesser works of cataloging theory, from Panizzi onward. In the context of these rules and this well-established tradition, USMARC as a standard makes perfect sense. We suggested that the community of acquisitions practitioners might do well to learn from this experience, and that perhaps one of our needs was to articulate an analogous intellectual framework for acquisitions work.

Well, you would think that we had waved a red cape before an angry bull. Folks charged out of the electronic woodwork, proclaiming acquisitions to be too specialized for such an effort. One asserted that both *AACR* and MARC were "in trouble" because of their lack of flexibility.[2] Yet another referred to Fred Kilgour's "Is MARC dead?" and argued that the development of analogous structures for acquisitions would take too much time.[3] Finally, one correspondent—who it must be observed later did apologize for his rashness—went so far as to assert that

> Our mantra is "brace yourself" and this is followed by a low dive at the workload. Standards be damned: cataloging is there to clean up the messiness acquisitions makes in getting the materials ordered and the bills paid.[4]

In all of these comments, there was a disturbing "us versus them" quality that we think has traditionally characterized the relations between acquisitions and cataloging practitioners. It needs to be dispelled from the outset of this discussion. We think that the great majority of readers would readily agree with Catherine Nelson's observation that

> The fact of the matter is if there were no MARC format (and there would be no MARC standard if there was no cataloging code) much of what we take for granted in Libraries today would not exist. There would be no OCLC, no RLIN, no OPACs of any kind, no ILL as we know it today. There would be huge backlogs of uncataloged materials and bibliographic discovery would be extremely difficult. *AACR2* and the codes that preceded it made the MARC format possible. Adherence to high standards makes bibliographic records sharable and usable.[5]

The point here is not to compare the relative quality of acquisitions and catalog records, but rather to observe that we can learn something positive and useful from the experience of developing cataloging standards. Although this chapter focuses on modeling approaches to understanding acquisitions processes and data, one of the things we argue is that the lack of an intellectual and conceptual framework for our work has in fact made that effort very difficult. The sooner we do something about it, the sooner we will find ourselves on the road to significant progress in articulating standards for acquisitions metadata.

The question of acquisitions standards has engendered much discussion among practitioners for decades. Most of these discussions have both centered on and resulted in standards movements for specific pieces of acquisitions data: transmission protocols such as EDI, X12, BISAC, and ONIX and industry standards groups such as the Book Industry Study Group and EditEur. At the ALA meetings in 2002 and 2003, the subject of standards—and the problems resulting from the lack of them—was a principal discussion topic at the meetings of the ALCTS/LITA MARC Formats Interest Group (MFIG) and the ALCTS Automated Acquisitions Discussion Group (AADG).

In the wake of these meetings, several individuals, including Linda Lerman of New York University, Wendy Riedel of the Library of Congress, and the authors, have undertaken the first very tentative steps to move the acquisitions standards debate forward. An electronic discussion list, AUTOACQ-L, has been established. Hosted by the University of Notre Dame, AUTOACQ-L's primary purpose is "to provide a forum for discussion of ideas and issues related to automation of library acquisitions and related processes" and especially to "encourage a standards-based approach" to automated acquisitions.[6] The authors received the 2003 ACRL/ISI Samuel Lazerow Fellowship for further research on the topic of acquisitions standards and also presented a paper at the 2003 Timberline Institute on the "Case for Acquisitions Standards in the Integrated Library System."[7] Lerman is now on research leave from her position at New York University to pursue aspects of this topic. NISO has been approached about supporting the work of creating standards for acquisitions records. Clearly there is a great deal of interest in this subject. Continued discussion of these issues on AUTOACQ-L has helped us to gauge the level of interest. It is clear that there is interest, but equally clear that there is no agreed-upon strategy for developing these standards.

What Do We Mean by "Standards"?

When we talk about standards for acquisitions data we mean that we, the library purchasing community, need to define standards for the following:

1. A *conceptual framework* that we call the *acquisitions process*. The framework contains and defines the interrelationships among the activity segments described in item 2).

2. Universally recognized *activity segments*, each of which describes and provides structure for a major tasks and subtasks within the framework.

3. A suite of agreed-upon *data elements*, each of which represents an input or an output of some portion of the subtask described by an activity segment. A data element may be identifiable with multiple activity segments.

4. A suite of *generic interfaces* for inputs and outputs with other systems, standards, and protocols (e.g., MARC, materials vendor transmission protocols, institutional financials, etc.).[8]

Prerequisite for a Data Standard: A Conceptual Framework for Acquisitions Processes?

What we hope to accomplish in this chapter is to move toward what we see as the next step in the standards development process. We believe that there must be a conceptual and functional discussion of acquisitions processes and their relationships to acquisitions metadata. Those of us who are practicing acquisitions librarians probably agree that our preference is for the practical: "Just get it done and move on to the next thing . . . leave the theory to Lubetsky!" This down-to-earth approach may be one reason why there are standards for catalog records and there are no standards for acquisitions records. Another reason, we believe, is that acquisitions data have traditionally been viewed as transitory, of no real use beyond the specific transaction. This focus is also beginning to change.

Comparison to catalog records serves a particular purpose, since the existence of the MARC formats would not have been possible without a preexisting codification of the rules governing what actually comprises a catalog record. MARC is really just a machine-readable *carrier* for metadata encoded according to a set of rules such as *AACR*, which conceptually predates and exists mostly independent of MARC. *AACR2* is only the latest in a long history of various cataloging codes and schema that date back over a century and provide a structure, without which there would be no data elements to encode in MARC or XML or whatever new envelope comes along to contain the data.

We can better understand the importance that cataloging codes have had as a framework for data standards by thinking in terms of metadata and the objects it describes. In the present case, the object is a book (or whatever library material you care to substitute). *AACR* is a framework for adding descriptive bibliographic metadata to the object. *AACR* informs us what bibliographic metadata is required and how we should go about constructing it.

We have the same object—the book—in acquisitions, even if it isn't necessarily yet in hand. Ideally, our conceptual "AAAR" should inform us about the acquisitions metadata to be associated with that object: What metadata is required? How do we go about constructing it? Thus, it comes down to a mere difference of the metadata attributes: bibliographic or acquisitions? In the present instance, our challenge is to conceptualize the problem from a *process-oriented approach,* because none of our seminal acquisitions texts has articulated a *theoretical construct* in the way that the seminal cataloging texts have done with bibliographic metadata. But all we're doing is hanging a different metadata type—or *attribute*—on the same object, and we need some way of informing ourselves exactly of the content and form of the metadata we wish to record.

Acquisitions as a discipline lacks any source comparable to a cataloging code that sets out basic principles. In reviewing the available literature in acquisitions, it is clear that much has been written on many individual aspects of the discipline, but we could find no single universally accepted source. From Wulfekoetter[9] to Schmidt,[10] works on the basics of acquisitions work are episodic and descriptive rather than sequential and prescriptive. Does acquisitions need the analog of a cataloging code to begin to articulate standards? If so, that sounds like a separate research project for a large committee. If it does not, how do we develop robust standards for acquisitions records within the context of an integrated library system?

"Activity Segments"

If we are to continue a dialogue aimed at developing a conceptual framework on which to hang data elements that can be set as standards, where do we begin? In our Timberline Institute presentation we introduced the concept of "activity segments" as a way to describe the various pieces of the acquisitions process. Our first attempt at enumerating "activity segments" included selection, preorder searching, order, order maintenance, receipt, payment, and reporting requirements. Subsequent discussion has broadened these segments to encompass system preparation issues such as the budget process that are the integral underpinnings for any acquisitions activity.[11] Definitions of many of the segments will sound familiar to those who actually remember reading some of the standard texts on library acquisitions. The most recent of these is the second edition of Karen Schmidt's *Understanding the Business of Library Acquisitions*. Schmidt draws on earlier texts, including Magrill's *Acquisitions Management and Collection Development in Libraries*.[12] The descriptions that follow represent our attempt to integrate, update, and augment these generally accepted definitions with our "activity segments" schema:

- *System preparation.* Establish and maintain local system records that serve to support the acquisitions process. These may include, inter alia, budget/fund structures, vendor name/address records, vendor approval/blanket profile data, local collection codes, and staff authorizations.

- *Selection.* Identify, evaluate, and select candidate materials in any physical format for acquisition and possible addition to the collection.

- *Pre-order search.* Verify bibliographic and acquisitions information about a selected item. Examine local catalogs and order records to ascertain if the same or related items are already owned or in-process. Wulfekoetter, Magrill, and Schmidt all refer to this activity as "bibliographic searching";[13] however, under that heading each text delineates the multiple purposes of this activity as stated above.

- *Order.* Assign a vendor, create and authorize an order record in the local and/or remote ordering system, and encumber funds.

- *Order maintenance.* Perform various maintenance functions on an order after it has been created/authorized/sent. Such functions include claiming with the vendor, posting vendor reports about order status, updating an order with information received subsequent to the ordering segment, canceling/closing an order, etc.

- *Receipt.* Receive and/or check in an order. Check for damage, verify against the order and invoice. Update local records to indicate that the item is now "received." Receipt may be physical or virtual. This segment may also include post-receipt searching for catalog copy, editing of order records to agree with the item received, copy catalog processing, etc.

- *Payment.* Record a payment to or a credit received from the vendor. Payment may or may not be attached to a particular order or orders. Payment may be one time or continue over time.

- *Reporting.* Query the system to produce standard or ad hoc reports on a batch or interactive basis. All data elements should be directly available for querying, sorting/limiting, and display. Output may be formatted for direct online or paper display or for export into other systems/software packages.

The remainder of this chapter consists of an examination of two model-based conceptual frameworks that we recently attempted to articulate on AUTOACQ-L. In our preceding comments, we described a possible rules-based framework in our remarks on the relationship between cataloging codes such as *AACR* and the MARC standards for bibliographic metadata. Since, as we've seen, the acquisitions community lacks an accepted, analogous set of formal rules, perhaps we can construct a conceptual framework for acquisitions metadata, based instead on a functional model as a stand-in for rules.

Model-Based Frameworks: Sequential/Linear

Our initial description of activity segments and the tasks that might be included in them was posed in a sequential and linear framework. As we worked with the model, though, it became increasingly obvious that the linear arrangement of both the segments themselves and—especially—the tasks identifiable with each segment seemed far too rigid. This second part—the linearity of the related tasks—was particularly problematic, as some tasks could be identified with more than one particular activity segment.[14] One obvious difficulty for contributors to the standards discussion on AUTOACQ-L has been the institution-specific practices that govern much acquisitions work. Describing activities and tasks in a linear fashion does not serve the idiosyncratic nature of individual acquisitions departments. For example, consider an attempt to identify specific tasks with the "pre-order search" segment. We can readily see that the model is quite rigid and enumerative (Figure 1).

a)   verification (bibliographic, acquisitions, etc.)

    i) bibliographic utilities (OCLC, RLIN, etc.)

    ii) standard online or printed sources (BIP, Ulrich's, etc.)

    iii) vendor online databases

    iv) publishers' catalogues (printed or online)

    v) printed library catalogues (NUC, etc.)

    vi) bookseller catalogues

    vii) miscellaneous online or printed tools

b)   search local holdings/orders

    i) local online catalogue/ILS (incl. integrated acquisitions and/or serials modules)

    ii) local paper-based catalogue (for older/antiquarian materials that may pre-date local online databases)

    iii) local paper-based order or receipt/check-in files

    iv) online vendor order databases (for orders placed via vendor's ordering interface)

Figure 1. Extract from a Model Based on a Sequential/Linear Framework.

The fact is, of course, that the "verification task" (a) in the figure) can actually happen at various stages in the acquisitions process; thus, it can be—depending on exactly what and why we're "verifying"—a task linked to ordering and receipt, in addition to the pre-order segment. Upon reflection, we concluded that this sort of organizational conundrum appears in many facets of acquisitions work and makes the sequential/linear model a relatively poor choice for a framework.

Model-Based Frameworks: Relational

So, we don't have a set of rules on which to base a framework, and the linear model is too rigid. What to do? Figure 2 is another way of looking at the model that may address this problem. Relational database junkies will recognize it immediately.

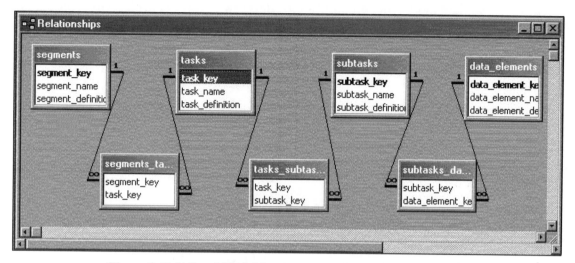

Figure 2. Relational Model for Acquisitions Segments and Tasks.

Consider a table of "activity segments." The table has three columns. The first column represents a key value that uniquely identifies each row of the table. A second column represents the formal name of the activity segment, while the last one is the segment definition. The segments table appears at the top of Figure 3.

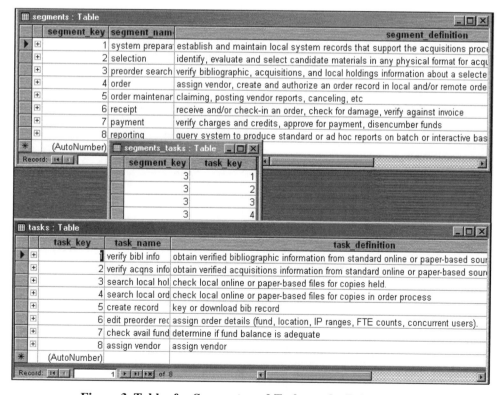

Figure 3. Tables for Segments and Tasks, and a Relator Table.

Similarly, we can imagine another table, this one of generic "tasks" or processes that we all recognize as things that acquisitions practitioners do in the course of their everyday work. The structure of the task table is identical to that of the segment table. It contains a key value, a task name, and a task description. The table, with a few sample "task" entries, is at the bottom of Figure 3.

In a relational data model, the intersection of these two tables is itself a two-column table that relates segments to tasks. An extract of this table might look like the table in the middle of Figure 3, in which segments (represented in the first column by key values from the segments table) are related to tasks (represented in the second column by key values from the tasks table).

As we can see from the example, some tasks might be identifiable with more than one segment, while others will be unique to a particular segment. Similarly, a segment can have any number of associated tasks. Further, while "search local holdings" might stand for a generic task, the specific application and purpose of the task might or might not be the same for all segments.

In other words, as we can see in Figure 4, we can construct *variants* of the "search local holdings" task by creating yet another table—this one of *subtasks*—that describes in detail the individual components of each task. Thus, depending on the needs of the *activity segment*, we can define modularized, customized, and reusable subtasks that can be combined in a variety of ways to help us understand what pieces of metadata are needed at any particular segment.

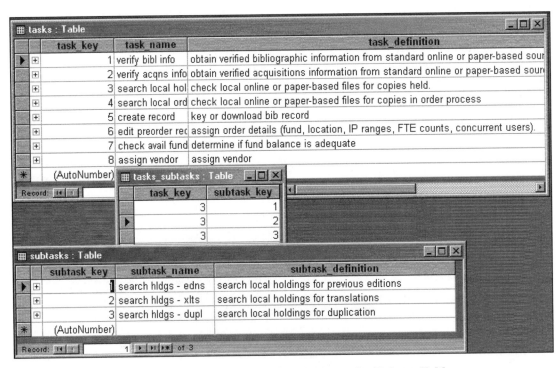

Figure 4. Tables for Tasks and Subtasks, and a Relator Table.

As in the case of the relationship between segments and tasks, the intersection of tasks and subtasks is itself a two-column table, in this case, one that relates task key values with subtask key values. An extract of that table appears in the middle of Figure 4. As before, tasks may be associated with singular or multiple subtasks and vice versa.

We've now mapped acquisitions processes from activity segments to tasks and finally to subtasks. The obvious missing piece in the picture is the metadata elements themselves. It should be clear that the next tables in our model, then, define individual metadata elements and then relate these to subtasks. The technique is precisely that used with segments, tasks and subtasks.

Thus, we can imagine a table of data elements

DATA_ELEMENT_NAME	DATA_ELEMENT_DESCRIPTION
[element1]	[element1 description]
[element2]	[element2 description]
[element3]	[element3 description]

and its relator table, which expresses the intersection of data elements and subtasks:

SUBTASK_NAME	DATA_ELEMENT_NAME
search hldgs—edns	[element1]
search hldgs—edns	[element2]
search hldgs—xlts	[element3]
search hldgs—dupl	[element1]
search hldgs—dupl	[element2]
search hldgs—dupl	[element3]

So, how does this approach help us? To begin with, it suggests questions:

• What exactly do we mean when we speak of "searching," "ordering," and "receipt?"

• What is the *goal* of each of these segments?

• How do segments relate to each other?[15]

Our relational model suggests that acquisitions tasks and metadata elements that relate to the activity segments can be modularized and reused. Figures 5 and 6 illustrate a very simple example of this, by using a database query to relate the segment "pre-order search" to a task called "search local holdings", which itself is composed of three subtasks that define holdings searches for duplication, translations, and editions.

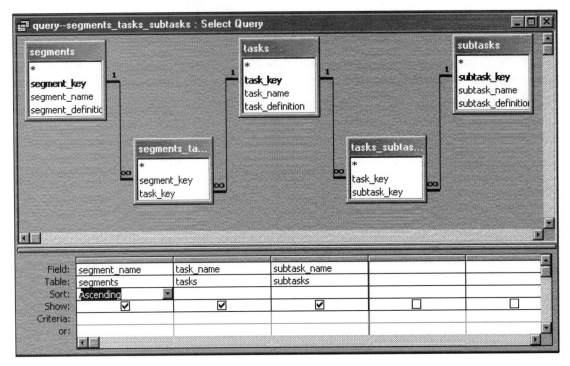

Figure 5. Query Linking Segments, Tasks, and Subtasks.

segment_name	task_name	subtask_name
preorder search	search local holdings	search hldgs - dupl
preorder search	search local holdings	search hldgs - xlts
preorder search	search local holdings	search hldgs - edns

Record: 1 of 3

Figure 6. A Possible Result Table for the Query Illustrated in Figure 5.

This seems to us a helpful way to approach the issues of organization, scalability, and manageability that inevitably will attend any effort more ambitious than "standardization" of the most basic, lowest-common-denominator suite of acquisitions data elements common to many of today's ILSes. As we have argued elsewhere,[16] one of the most conspicuous failures of current generation integrated systems is that they provide for only these basic elements. The increasing need of acquisitions and collections managers to record, extract, manipulate, and analyze a far wider array of metadata elements than are commonly available in our present systems is precisely what has led to the proliferation of labor-intensive, stand-alone local databases of acquisitions metadata. One of the goals of our approach is to provide a structure that would both encourage analysis of the acquisitions metadata needs of today's library managers and at the same time be extensible enough to allow for future needs. A relational approach appears to meet both of these needs.

The relational model also forces us to think about the why of the "tasks" we do every day. Does "search local holdings" imply the same set of specific tasks for each of the selection, pre-order, and receipt segments? Clearly, the answer is no. Can we design a generic task that fits all of these and can be described as "search local holdings?" If so, are we searching the same things in the same ways for each? If not, could we do so, if we rethought the process and the requirements of the segment?

Or should we, as the relational approach suggests, instead work to create modular, reusable subtasks that themselves can be combined in various ways to address the similar but varying metadata needs of acquisitions segments?

Summary

We realize that there are those who will wonder about the relevance of this admittedly conceptual and abstract exercise. We've already seen in some of the AADG meetings and in some responses on the AUTOACQ-L list a tendency to focus on identifying specific data elements and debating the relative merits of this or that specific data format. This approach, in our view, while more satisfying to those who seek quick results, is bound to result in a "standard" that ill-serves our varied needs. In a recent thread on AUTOACQ-L, Michael Kaplan succinctly posed the quandary we face:

> Any standards that the acquisitions world creates need a very different focus from the standards that were created in the late 1960s (MARC) and from the mid-late 1980s on (AACR2). The problem with standards is also their great virtue: they are authoritative and they persist. Then why a problem? They tend to take *too long*to create. Alternatively, they are created quickly and then they require a long time to sort out and refine.[17]

While the quick-fix approach may be more interesting and familiar—in that it focuses on concrete issues with which we grapple every day—it lacks the discipline necessary to ensure that we actually "get it right." Or, as Ted Koppel put it in his response to the same thread

> It's going to take quite a bit of conversation in the acquisitions world before you (collectively) see process patterns and communities of interest and can draw conclusions about best practices. Concentrate on being inclusive and listening to all kinds of libraries. . . . Remember that completeness is a goal, not speed.[18]

Notes

1. M. Truitt, "Needed : An 'AACR for acquisitions'?" AUTOACQ-L electronic discussion list, October 27, 2003, autoacq-l@listserv.nd.edu (accessed October 27, 2003).

2. J. Deeken, "AAAR, relational database, etc.," AUTOACQ-L electronic discussion list, October 28, 2003, autoacq-l@listserv.nd.edu (accessed October 28, 2003).

3. M. Kaplan, "Acquisitions standards in an XML world," AUTOACQ-L electronic discussion list, October 28, 2003, autoacq-l@listserv.nd.edu (accessed October 28, 2003).

4. J. Williams, "Re: Needed : An 'AACR for acquisitions'?" AUTOACQ-L electronic discussion list, October 27, 2003, autoacq-l@listserv.nd.edu (accessed October 27, 2003).

5. C. Nelson, "Re: Needed : An 'AACR for acquisitions'?" AUTOACQ-L electronic discussion list, October 27, 2003, autoacq-l@listserv.nd.edu (accessed October 27, 2003).

6. M. Truitt, "Welcome to autoacq-l!: Or why we're all here . . . ," AUTOACQ-L electronic discussion list, February 8, 2003, autoacq-l@listserv.nd.edu (accessed February 8, 2003).

7. K. Farrell and M. Truitt, "The Case for Acquisitions Standards in the Integrated Library System," *Library Collections, Acquisitions, and Technical Services* 27 (Winter 2003): 483–92.

8. Ibid.

9. G. Wulfekoetter, *Acquisitions Work: Processes Involved in Building Library Collections* (Seattle : University of Washington Press, 1974).

10. K. A. Schmidt, ed., *Understanding the Business of Library Acquisitions*, 2d ed. (Chicago: American Library Association, 1999).

11. Farrell and Truitt, "Case for Acquisitions Standards" ; M. Truitt, "Back to concepts . . . ," AUTOACQ-L electronic discussion list, September 22, 2003; R. Lugg, "Back to concepts (response to Marc Truitt)," AUTOACQ-L electronic discussion list, September 22, 2003; M. Truitt, "Segments with subprocesses . . . cut #01 . . . ," e-mail to K. Farrell, September 23, 2003; K. Farrell, "Re: segments with subprocesses . . . cut #01 . . . ," e-mail to M. Truitt, September 24, 2003; R. Lugg, "Types of acquisitions activities," AUTOACQ-L electronic discussion list, September 26, 2003, AUTOACQ-L messages, autoacq-l@listserv.nd.edu (accessed September 22–26 2003).

12. R. Magrill and J. Corbin, *Acquisitions Management and Collection Development in Libraries*, 2d ed. (Chicago: American Library Association, 1989).

13. Wulfekoetter, *Acquisitions Work*, 45; Magrill and Corbin, *Acquisitions Management*, 90; Schmidt, *Understanding the Business of Library Acquisitions*, 2.

14. M. Truitt, "Activity segments and tasks . . . another approach . . . (LONG)," AUTOACQ-L electronic discussion list, October 15, 2003, autoacq-l@listserv.nd.edu (accessed October 15, 2003).

15. Ibid.

16. Farrell and Truitt, "Case for Acquisitions Standards."

17. Kaplan, "Acquisitions standards in an XML world."

18. T. Koppel, "Acquisitions standards (was AAAR, relational database, etc.)," AUTOACQ-L electronic discussion list, October 28, 2003, autoacq-l@listserv.nd.edu (accessed October 28, 2003).

BIGGER ISN'T BETTER: QUALITY MATTERS, NOT SIZE

Michael Galda, President, Galda Library Services (Berlin, Germany)
Translated by Jan Erik Gjestvang-Lucky, U.S. Marketing Manager, Galda Library Services
(Madison, Wisconsin)

This chapter is essentially a reaction to a talk given at last year's conference. That talk answered the question: "Is the bigger library supplier the better library supplier?" with a resounding "YES!" The main arguments we heard in favor of this point were that the larger supplier has the advantage because it maintains offices in different countries and on different continents, it has better technical knowledge, and, based on its size and experience, it can handle a multitude of tasks that a smaller business can't.

We would like to suggest that these points, although they are certainly important, are not the main criteria on which to judge the efficiency and ability of a library supplier. The current situation of suppliers is best defined by the continually expanding variety of tasks they need to master to best serve their customers. In our opinion, the three most important factors in this situation are those discussed below.

1. The Ever-Increasing Number of Publishers and Publishing Organizations

It is true that the publishing world has been in a "concentration phase" for many years, and several publishing groups have taken over many smaller businesses. This is, however, only one side of the coin. We have heard much talk at this and other conferences about the rapid growth of digital publishing. We find that the growth of "print" publishers is no less explosive. Because acquiring an ISBN prefix is no small effort, and, as a rule, implies the intent of continuous publication, one can assume that only earnest businesses founded with plans for being in business for the long term would go through this process. According to the International ISBN Agency in Berlin, in 1993 there were 267,345 publishers worldwide with an ISBN prefix. Five years later, in 1998, the number of publishers had grown to 424,247, and in 2003 we have 628,795. This is an increase of 135% in 10 years, and that doesn't even include organizations that act outside the ISBN system, or single-title ISBNs. One could get the impression that book publishing is an incredibly profitable business.

Library suppliers are finding it necessary to begin buying from all of these new small publishers, even though very many of them are poorly organized and have only limited understanding of the bookselling business. Don't tell me that the materials from these publishers would rarely be ordered; they are ordered, more than ever before. A typical order that we would receive today from a "normal university library" in the United States follows:

ISBN 8887960291 *Theatre Curtain—The Ring of Transformations*
    published by the Reggio Children International Centre for the Defense and Promotion of the Rights and Potential of All (Italy)

ISBN 2091902233
    Prevelakis: Les Balkans (Paris, Nathan)

ISBN 3922968564
Geber: Ottoman Rule in Jerusalem (Berlin, Schwarz)

ISBN 960490034X
Prevelakis: Ta Valkania (Libro, Athens)

ISBN 8488562314
The Human Genome project—legal aspects 4 Vol. set (Bilbao, Fundacion BBV)

ISBN 9736531619
Prevelakis: Cultura si geopolitica (Balcaniy, Corint)

NO ISBN
Povos indigenas no Brasil (Sao Paulo, Instituto Socioamiental)

Seven titles from seven countries on two continents.

A supplier must be a very internationally focused specialty business to be able to fulfill this order, but is there any indication that a company with 500 employees can do this better than one with 10 or 30 or 50? Hardly, because we can't assume that the larger business places large daily orders with the Centre for the Defense and Promotion of the Rights and Potential of All, for example. It's more likely that this single order would be the only one in many years.

Our example doesn't even include one sample of the "truly" difficult to obtain materials that special collections order. (For example, archeological libraries may request Syrian excavation records, while zoologists happily demand Polish monographs on arachnid research, and ethnological collections seek museum catalogs from India.) Technical knowledge of the publishing business and competence in international purchasing are the deciding factors in being able accomplish this task. Does a larger business have technical tools that will help it get these titles more easily than the smaller business? Not necessarily. The Romanian publisher is not going to be more willing or able to deliver its publications to a company that uses more technology rather than less. Language ability is doubtless important, but it is just as easy for the smaller business to purchase the language services it needs. Financial competence is another matter, because the publishers from the earlier example require payment to their own local banks. There is no competitive advantage related to business size to be found here, either. With the help of modern technology, such as Internet banking and other tools, the smaller business has the same business opportunities as the larger. It is possible that the smaller business has smaller accounts at a smaller bank, but that makes no difference in the end.

2. The Changing Behavior and Standards of Publishing and Publishers

One of the biggest problems for librarians and library suppliers alike is the fact that more and more titles are announced, and then appear either late, or with a different title, or even not at all. This was the subject of one of last year's Charleston Conference presentations. We remember one of the staff at a large library supplier claiming that his company's fulfillment rate was 96%. We must admit we are jealous. Either this company only gets very simple orders, or something is not quite right with the figures. At our small company, the circumstances are a little different. We have about 40,000 suppliers (publishers) in over 100 countries. Ten years ago we were able to deliver about 80% of our orders in a time normal for each publisher. This rate varied greatly depending on the time of year the order was placed. Today our rate, again, depending on the season, has dropped to about 65%. Of course there are significant differences between different countries. Northern Europe is substantially better organized than southern Europe, and North America better than South America. But the number of "out of stock," "not yet published-no due date," "temporarily unavailable," etc., items has no end, and it gets more and more difficult to responsibly handle the flood of backorders, with emphasis on "responsibly." Naturally, we, as a small business, have a computer system that automatically generates claims for unfulfilled orders in different languages. But this only helps in limited circumstances, because publishers are less and less willing or able to announce precise publication dates or respond to a lot of claims from booksellers. Technology alone can't resolve this. The library supplier must decide whether it makes sense to maintain the backorder or give it up as hopeless. This is a job that can only be done by qualified humans, rather than automatically, because it is possible that a backorder can be valid for many years. An example from last month: *Veröffentlichungen des Internationalen Franz Schubert Instituts, Vol. 2* (*Publications of the International Franz Schubert Institute, Vol. 2*), published by a small music publisher in southern Germany, was just released. We *originally* ordered this volume for a library on November 10, 1993. Even though the publication arrived with after a 10-year delay, it didn't matter, because the customer had ordered the preceding volume 1 in 1992, and they needed to have the completed work. Consistency, accuracy, and reliability are the book business virtues needed for all of these tasks. A business with a staff of 500 is not better at these things than one with 10 or 50.

3. Technology and Customer Service

For the supporters of the theory that the bigger supplier is the better supplier, a strong argument is the assumption that the larger supplier can do a better job than smaller businesses of offering technological tools and software products to its customers because it has more capital. This assessment is fundamentally correct, but it is also clear that larger companies have a shrinking technological advantage over smaller companies. Computer technology that was very expensive just a few years ago is now accessible to smaller companies with substantially smaller budgets. Software development has been extremely "democratized" thanks to the Internet, and it is now possible for small companies to do business worldwide and have software developed inexpensively. Our company has had system development done successfully in Moscow for the last 10 years, and at prices that would be unthinkable in Germany. Of course, there are also limits to the use of this technology: A small business couldn't afford to develop a huge database that would require regular maintenance from hundreds of employees. But there are very few of these kinds of limits.

The issue of library suppliers having offices in different countries and continents to provide better customer service works the same as software development. Like other small companies, we also have international offices, in our case in Berlin and Madison. The offices of smaller suppliers are probably also smaller, but this does not mean that they are less effective. Also, communication has been so greatly simplified by the technological possibilities of e-mail and other methods that the day-to-day business advantages of having a physical presence in foreign countries has been greatly reduced, and will continue to be reduced.

As opposed to a large business, a small business generally works more directly with the customer, and can be faster and more flexible in resolving common daily problems. The smaller company has fewer customers than a large business and will regularly and demonstrably be more motivated to respond to individual requests, because its survival depends on the satisfaction of its smaller customer base. A small library supplier can control expenses better and can offer very competitive pricing.

Our assessment of the situation is increasingly shared by libraries in northern Europe. When we founded Galda Library Services in 1985, we met the head of acquisitions of one of the largest libraries in Europe. The library staff thought we were far too small to properly respond to the complex demands of their collection. In the year 2003, this same collection began to cancel many of its subscriptions with very large companies and turned them over to us instead. They were tired of being only one among thousands of customers and dealing with uninterested and constantly changing "experts." In other words, it now appears, for all of these reasons, to be far more advantageous for libraries to switch to smaller suppliers. They will find out that we offer better results for less money than the larger suppliers, which is no surprise to us.

IMPROVING COMMUNICATION BETWEEN PUBLISHERS AND LIBRARIANS

Deanna Graham, Blackwell Publishing

At a Lively Lunch at the conference, we discussed some of the effective and ineffective methods of communication among librarians, publishers, and agents. We started by brainstorming some of the examples, in theory and practice, of effective practices of communication, and came up with the following examples:

- Publishers and agents offering complete information on a Web site, including subscription information, technical upgrades and changes, and contact information

- Vendor databases being up-to-date

- Publisher and vendors being in direct communication with libraries

- Meetings at conferences

- Publisher/vendor visits to libraries

- Post-sale support (posters, template e-mail for circulation to users)

- Librarian and publisher/vendor communication

    ○ Clear communication needed from librarians

    ○ Giving responses and updates (same as expected from publishers and vendors should be practiced by librarians)

- Downloadable presentation provided by publisher/vendor for librarians to familiarize themselves with content and interface

- User training sessions by publisher/vendor

- Contacting agent versus contacting publisher

    ○ Larger/older publishers: direct best communication is generally best

    ○ Smaller/newer publishers: communication through agents/jobbers is generally best

- Phone calls—regularly touching base

- Webex as an effective way to meet, saving time and expense

- Librarian newsletters created by publishers and circulated via e-mail to advise of upcoming changes

- Library Web site providing clear information about contacts

- Advisory boards (It was noted that these are very helpful for all parties and give librarians a chance to have input into policy and process, but that finding librarians willing and able to dedicate time to this can be a challenge.)

- Face to face visits

- Listserv updates being well circulated and effective ways to communicate broadly

It was emphasized that the more communication, the better, as long as it is consistent. When a publisher/vendor uses multiple formats to communicate with libraries, instead of just a few, it is very helpful.

The conversation then went on to identify some less effective areas and methods of communication and problem areas, and tried to identify some solutions:

- Contact information on publisher Web sites is too general. Librarians have a hard time finding an appropriate contact for problem or question. The solution used in some cases is to contact directly the rep with whom they work for help identifying the proper contact. More detail on the publisher's Web site would help this process.

- Response time when using general customer service or help desk contact is sometimes slow. To speed the process, librarians can be more specific about problems; providing as much detail as possible helps the vendor/publisher identify and solve the problem more quickly.

- Sometimes there are bugs in releases of new versions of an interface. The feeling is that sometimes releases are too early and bugs should be better worked out before going live.

- Consortia communication is inconsistent. Lines of communication vary greatly from consortium to consortium. Consortia heads do not always properly communicate new consortia deals and renewals, and librarians are not aware of contract provisions and content available. Publishers and agents can help this by communicating simultaneously with institutions within the consortium.

- After the fact notification; it would help if publishers and vendors could be more proactive with notification of changes and potential problems before they occur. Examples given:

  ◦ Notification of when invoices can be expected

  ◦ In the case of exceptional price increases, notification to libraries as to why this has occurred, posted on the Web site and on invoices and price lists

  ◦ Change of contact; when a staff person is replaced (librarian or rep contact) there should be notification of this via e-mail.

  ◦ Technical changes and possible interruptions.

  ◦ Title migration, volumes/articles missing or removed.

Finally, our group talked about possible ways to continue the discussion about communication, pass on ideas, and help inform sustained improvement. The feeling was that librarians, publishers, and vendors need to continue to create opportunities to talk directly to each other. We do this now at library conferences, the Charleston Conference, and librarian advisory board meetings. Possible suggestions to build on this are for libraries to form publisher advisory boards to discuss and better understand the issues and challenges that face publishers. Also, library groups such as ICOLC should work with publishers/vendors to identify and create best practices guidelines for the standardization of communication.

COLLECTION DEVELOPMENT ISSUES IN HEALTH SCIENCES LIBRARIES: GAMES, RULES, AND PLAYERS

Ramune Kubilius, Galter Health Sciences Library, Northwestern University, Chicago (Moderator)
Jo Anne Boorkman, Carlson Health Sciences Library, University of California, Davis
Beth Jacoby, Health Sciences & Human Services Library, University of Maryland, Baltimore
Elizabeth Lorbeer, Collection Development Manager, Rush University Medical Center, Chicago

About three dozen librarians, publishers, and vendors attended this third annual gathering. Moderator Ramune Kubilius distributed a selected list of trends (since the 2002 Charleston Conference, news items and developments since the second annual Lively Lunch), including the following:

- STM publishing, e-journals, and scholarly publishing: Speculations on the future of archives and repositories, evidenced by journal articles, workshops, symposia, and Web sites.

- Collections: New titles and new formats have been released, particularly in the area of educational software. The respected Brandon/Hill "Print Books and Journals for the Small Medical Library 2003" twentieth edition is now online only at http://www.mssm.edu/library/brandon- hill/small_medical/index.shtml.

- The professional association Web sites of the Medical Library Association and the Special Libraries Association both attempted to support members and provide them with information after serials vendor Faxon RoweCom went out of business. MLA's Collection Development Section also updated its site with health subject collection lists and links.

Three experienced librarians shared observations and facilitated discussions:

1. Jo Anne Boorkman distributed preliminary summarized results from a February 2003 survey she conducted of MEDLIB-L discussion list subscribers on "Reference Collection Development in the Electronic Era." This included survey respondents' feelings on: budgeting, selection tools, access provisions, evaluation criteria, deterrents to licensing, etc. Almost all of the librarians (98%) do want to conduct a trial before selecting an electronic reference resource, and 76% want to be able to provide remote access. The survey and some results will be discussed in an introductory chapter of Boorkman et al.'s forthcoming *Introduction to Reference Sources in the Health Sciences,* fourth edition. More extensive analysis may be done in a future journal article comparing results to those found in a similar survey conducted 10 years ago.

2. Elizabeth Lorbeer shared observations and examples of book and journal supplementary material challenges (print and electronic), questioned the need for some of them, and suggested that publishers could standardize presentation and licensing, especially for supplements destined for institutional, not personal, use. For those interested in pursuing some of these issues, she shared copies of an article she had cowritten in 2001,[1] procedures written at her institution, and a bibliography of articles written between 1997 and 2001.

3. Beth Jacoby talked about roles serials vendors can play. She quoted a 2003 Special Libraries Association conference speaker who had made remarks about the "car dealership pricing" aspect of electronic resource site licensing. Beth noted the "Use of Agents" statements incorporated in the NERL Principles for Electronic Journal Licenses (NorthEast Research Libraries Consortium, http://www.library.yale.edu/NERLpublic/EJrnlPrinciples.html). She also praised Rick Lugg's and Ruth Fischer's timely October 2003 white paper, "Agents in Place: Intermediaries in E-Journal Management," which was prepared with support from Harrassowitz and was included in all 2003 Charleston Conference attendee packets. Discussion points explored issues related to and expanded beyond the serials vendor theme. This included licensing access versus content (often the case with aggregated full text databases), recommendations on how to guarantee continued access while in the process of renewing electronic resources' licenses and payment, and the increasing roles for librarians on publisher user advisory boards.

Medical journal publishers are getting to know not only their readers, but also libraries and third-party archives, better. One medical journal representative expressed clinical medical publishers' concerns about trustworthy archive and mirror sites; he felt that his publication staff has to be vigilant about the integrity of content. In one instance they found inappropriate or irresponsible links to their journal content, advertising a medically unproven or unsound product.

Verbal consensus was expressed that Lively Lunches focusing on health sciences collection development issues should continue to be a feature of Charleston Conferences. During these gatherings, it has been possible to discuss products and issues that may be of particular concern or unique to health sciences resources and collections. Some of these concerns are subject specific and may not be of interest or relevant to the all other Charleston Conference attendees in a general session venue.

Notes

1. Elizabeth R. Lorbeer, Judith Dzierba, William P. Fleming, Christine Frank, Toby Gibson, and William F. Karnoscak, "One Work in Two Places: A 'Mixed Media' Policy for Accompanying Media Dilemmas," *Collection Management* 26, no. 1 (2001): 77–90.

COLLECTING COMIC BOOKS AT THE UNIVERSITY OF MEMPHIS: A BEGINNING

Chris Matz, Collection Development Library, University of Memphis

Abstract

Comic books—also known as graphic novels—are drawing increased attention on college campuses as a scholarly medium in literature, art, history, and popular culture, among other fields of study. In general, however, academic libraries have not demonstrated support for this emerging curriculum in their collections. Librarians face philosophical and practical challenges to acquiring comic books, but it is both possible and desirable to do so. The University of Memphis Libraries examined their efforts in the inaugural attempt at building a comic book collection, collaborating with English faculty for intellectual assistance and the Friends of the Library for financial help.

In this era of cuts, drops, and discontinuations, it is both possible and desirable for academic librarians to incorporate new resources into their collections. One possibility is to support the emerging scholarly interest in comic books, both as popular culture icons and as supplements to established curriculum. Yet academic libraries have been slow to support their inclusion, lagging far behind their peers in public library settings. Why might this be?

The fact that many of you are scrunching up your faces (presuming you've stuck with the chapter this far) at the very notion of spending valuable professional energy on comic books contributes greatly to this gap in collections. The challenge to alter the conventional perception of comic books as trashy and juvenile is considerable. This perception is codified within narrow collection development policies and the limited range of experience in technical services departments.

The faculty doesn't want comic books, it's hard to know which ones to buy and from where, it's too difficult to process them and keep them from being stolen once processed—if these arguments sound familiar, they're the same ones librarians utter every time we're faced with something new. Replace *comic books* with *CD-ROMs* or *electronic journals* in the previous sentence, and you'll recognize the pattern. It may very well be that your library isn't interested in comic books for perfectly valid reasons, and that's fine, but to dismiss an entire resource format based on an unwillingness to learn more about it is the behavior we associate with IT or administrators or patrons. As librarians, we can do better. Consider this exercise a renewal of the critical thinking we used to rave about in library school research papers, if you will.

Comic books are very much worthy of consideration on scholarly grounds. Marshall McLuhan identified them as cool because readers must imagine the action between panels, and so comic books can be seen as sequential art narratives that enhance cognition and perception like no other medium. As critiqued more recently by Scott McCloud, comic books are innovative semiotic expressions with a broad appeal to humanities scholarship at the very least. Faculty from a vast cross-section of academic disciplines would find such a medium scholarly and valid.

Academic value alone is not enough, of course; it is crucial to consider specific collection development concerns for any comic book collection. Any academic library that does not at present include comic books within its development policies must first carefully assess itself before seeking to incorporate the medium into its collections. As acquisition budgets diminish, librarians must be able to articulate the value of comic books to the library, and as with other learning resources, this is best done in conjunction with faculty already engaged in their use. The most meaningful development policies have always come when librarians and faculty work together.

Presuming strong faculty relations to drive or inform the collection process, librarians must identify adequate tools for evaluation of comic books to meet research needs. Just as there is a review serial for every academic discipline, *The Comics Journal* has provided criticism and evaluation of titles (mostly non-superhero comic books, the genres more likely to be collected in academic libraries) since the 1970s. Library science journals and reference sources are beginning to include comic books in their review sections. Many of the titles evaluated there tend to be geared toward the young adult collections of public libraries; this does create a baseline acceptance for the medium, but it can perpetuate the marginalization of comic books as juvenile fare.

However, in its 1998 series "Comic Books and Libraries," *Serials Review* published extensive guides for all libraries to the four largest American publishers, all of which now offer comprehensive lines of library-friendly formats like graphic novels (original work under one cover) and trade paperbacks (republished collections of periodical titles). The *New York Times Book Review* and *Entertainment Weekly* now regularly devote evaluative coverage to comic books from many different publishers, often promoting the growing number of academic titles studying comic books and comic art (led by the University Press of Mississippi) as well as histories of the medium, though to be sure, the latter have mostly tended to be general interest rather than scholarly in their scope.

The recent boom of graphic novels and trade paperbacks has created a format for reprints of rare and expensive primary comic books, available within almost any budgetary limits. DC Comics is producing prestige "archive editions" of historic titles such as 1950s-era *MAD Magazine,* Will Eisner's *The Spirit*, and Joe Kubert's *Sgt. Rock.* DC also publishes more contemporary trade paperbacks like Neil Gaiman's *Sandman* series, Frank Miller's *The Dark Knight Returns,* and Alan Moore's *Watchmen*, still in print almost 20 years after they first appeared. Fantagraphics publishes collections by notable creators such as Daniel Clowes (*Eightball, Ghost World*), Robert Crumb (*Fritz the Cat, Self Loathing Comics*), and the Hernandez brothers (*Love & Rockets*). Nearly all comic book publishers now offer their contemporary periodicals as loss leaders for planned trade paperbacks, with narrative arcs matching up to the 90–120 pages that fit comfortably between two covers. AIT/PlanetLar is remarkable for eschewing periodicals altogether in favor of original graphic novels, as with their *Astronauts In Trouble* series; this may soon become the business model for publishers without the financial resources to sustain both formats.

At the University of Memphis, cultivation of a comic book collection began in earnest in September 2002. The collection development librarian had already performed a cursory review of comic books and other comics-related materials, but it was not until he was approached by the Department of English's faculty chair that a serious evaluation took place. The long-range goal of attracting Ph.D.-level research would necessitate a vast upgrade in resources. The holdings to that point reflected a variety of academic studies of the medium along with several of the standard texts for the chair's Visual and Verbal Texts: The Graphic

Novel graduate course—or more precisely, the library catalog reflected those holdings. In fact, many of the titles listed were not found and later declared lost, requiring replacement copies. Budgetary restrictions prevented the Department of English or Collection Development from immediately plugging these holes.

The Friends of the Library organization for the University of Memphis Libraries, though, was responsive to a solicitation for a $500 monthly purchasing stipend for six consecutive months. This infusion provided the financial means to supplement missing holdings while other related titles (such as original works by Lynda Barry, George Herriman, and Lynd Ward, along with academic studies by David Carrier, Ron Goulart, and Trina Robbins) already in the collection were pulled from general circulation and placed on reserve, creating a greatly expanded "recommended" reading list for the Visual and Verbal Texts course.

Serving the access needs of patrons is a task tempered by the high rate of missing and lost comic book titles. Selected original works remained on "permanent reserve" at the conclusion of the semester, though the reserve holdings themselves were expanded for the entire library in August 2003, and those comic book titles were shelved in an area of the reserves room that can be browsed without the assistance of library staff. The retention results of this experiment will be examined closely.

While the comic book collection will probably not achieve the remarkable growth of 2002–2003 every year, there will be a modest and steady stream of requests coming from the Department of English as its faculty begins to tap the scholarly potential of the medium. Participation in collection building will be expanded to include fine arts and any number of disciplines within the social sciences; individual instructors are already using Art Spiegelman's *Maus* series and Joe Sacco's *Palestine* and *Safe Area Gorazde* for history and political science classes, respectively; while the University's Special Collections archive was eager to add the third volume of Ho Che Anderson's *KING* to the first two they already owned. Promotion of existing holdings will help reorient outstanding biases against comic books in an academic setting. A display of featured titles all throughout the summer of 2003 highlighted the aesthetic qualities of the medium, and the effort received a positive write-up in the Memphis *Commercial Appeal*. Consideration will be given to inviting comic book creators for campus events like the Department of English's "River City Writers Series" for formal presentations and readings.

A recognizable context for comic books as a serious scholarly interest is beginning to emerge, and the University of Memphis Libraries intend to support that aspect of the curriculum. (See Tables 1 and 2, pages 182–86.) Their development policy for collecting comic books will not only inform the libraries' selections but also serve as hard evidence of synergy between faculty and librarians. Scholars understand comic books can represent a form of literacy unique from text or art by themselves, and many of them predict that the distinction will become increasingly important in our culture. One or two of these "radical" instructors surely reside on every college campus, and allied with the power of critical thinking practiced by development librarians, academic collections can be on the brink of a remarkable transformation; that is, if faculty and librarians together desire such a transformation.

Table 1. University of Memphis Libraries Comic Books and Related Acquisitions, 2002–2003

Adult manga/Kinsella, Sharon
Aesthetics of comics/Carrier, David
All in color for a dime/Lupoff, Dick and Don Thompson
Amazing adventures of Kavalier and Clay/Chabon, Michael
B. Krigstein/Sadowski, Greg
Bad language, naked ladies, and other threats to the nation/Rubenstein, Anne
Below critical radar: fanzines and alternative comics from 1976 to now/Sabin, Roger
Bizarro comics/Abel, Jessica, et al
Black superheroes, Milestone Comics, and their fans/Brown, Jeffrey
Classics illustrated: a cultural history with illustrations/Jones Jr., William B.
Comic book confidential/Mann, Ron
Comic book culture/Goulart, Ron
Comic book culture/Pustz, Matthew
Comic book nation/Wright, Bradford
Comic books as history/Witek, Joseph
Comics between the panels/Duin, Steve, and Mike Richardson
Complete E. C. Segar: Popeye 1937-1938/Segar, E.C.
Completely MAD/Reidelbach, Maria
Enigma of Al Capp/Theroux, Alexander
European comics in English translation/Scott, Randall
From girls to grrrlz: a history of women's comics from teens to zines/Robbins, Trina
From hell/Moore, Alan; Campbell, Eddie
Ghost world/Zwigoff, Terry
Graphic storytelling and visual narrative/Eisner, Will
Hal Foster: prince of illustrators, father of the adventure strip/Kane, Brian M.
How to read superhero comics and why/Klock, Geoff
Illustrating Asia/Lent, John A.
Introducing Kafka/Mairowitz, David and Robert Crumb
Jack Cole and Plastic Man/Spiegelman, Art and Chip Kidd
Jimmy Corrigan: smartest kid on earth/Ware, Chris

Krazy & Ignatz: 1925-1926/Herriman, George
Krazy & Ignatz: 1927-1928/Herriman, George
Krazy Kat: the comic art of George Herriman/McDonnell, Patrick
Last day in Vietnam/Eisner, Will
Love & rockets X/Hernandez, Gilbert
Love & rockets: blood of Palomar/Hernandez, Gilbert
Love & rockets: Chelo's burden/Los Bros Hernandez
Love & rockets: duck feet/Los Bros Hernandez
Love & rockets: flies on the ceiling/Los Bros Hernandez
Love & rockets: Hernandez satyricon/Los Bros Hernandez
Love & rockets: las mujeres perdidas/Los Bros Hernandez
Love & rockets: Luba conquers the world/Hernandez, Gilbert
Love & rockets: music for mechanics/Los Bros Hernandez
Love & rockets: poison river/Hernandez, Gilbert
Love & rockets: tears from heaven/Los Bros Hernandez
Love & rockets: the death of Speedy/Hernandez, Jaime
Love & rockets: wigwam bam/Hernandez, Jaime
Many lives of the Batman/Pearson, Roberta
Milton Caniff: conversations/Harvey, Robert C.
New American splendor anthology/Pekar, Harvey
One hundred demons/Barry, Lynda
Rebel visions: the underground commix revolution 1963-1975/Rosenkranz, Patrick
Remembrance of things past: Combray/Proust, Marcel; Heuet, Stephane
Remembrance of things past: within a budding grove/Proust, Marcel; Heuet, Stephane
Sandman companion/Bender, Hy
Sandman mystery theatre: the tarantula/Wagner, Matt; Davis, Guy
Seal of approval: history of the comics code/Nyberg, Amy
Shop talk/Eisner, Will
Spirit archives volume 1/Eisner, Will
Storyteller without words/Ward, Lynd
Tales of terror: the EC companion/von Bernewitz, Fred

Table 1. University of Memphis Libraries Comic Books and Related Acquisitions, 2002–2003 (*Cont.*)

The Comics Journal Library: Jack Kirby/George, Milo
The Comics Journal special edition Summer 2002/Groth, Gary
The Comics Journal special edition Winter 2002/Groth, Gary
The good times are killing me/Barry, Lynda
The great women superheroes/Robbins, Trina
The world encyclopedia of comics/Horn, Maurice
Wonder Woman/Marston, William M.
Your vigor for life appalls me: Robert Crumb letters 1958-1977/Crumb, Robert

Table 2. University of Memphis Libraries Comic Books and Related Acquisitions, 2003–2004

32 stories: the complete Optic Nerve mini/Tomine, Adrian
Adventures of Sock Monkey/Millionaire, Tony
Alan Moore: portrait of an extraordinary gentleman/Millidge, Gary S.
Alan Moore's writing for comics/Moore, Alan
American century: Hollywood Babylon/Chaykin, Howard
American century: scars and stripes/Chaykin, Howard
American Flagg: hard times/Chaykin, Howard
American Flagg: state of the union/Chaykin, Howard
Anarchy for the masses: an underground guide to the Invisibles/Neighly, Patrick
Astro Boy volume 1/Tezuka, Osamu
Astro City: life in the big city/Busiek, Kurt; Anderson, Brent
Batman: the dark knight returns/Miller, Frank
Berlin: city of stones/Lutes, Jason
Black orchid/Gaiman, Neil
Cartoon history of the universe, volumes 1-7/Gonick, Larry
Channel zero/Wood, Brian
Cheap novelties: the pleasures of urban decay/Katchor, Ben
Comics, comix, and graphic novels/Sabin, Roger
Concrete: complete short stories 1986-1989/Chadwick, Paul
Cuckoo/Clell, Madison

David Boring/Clowes, Dan
Elektra lives again/Miller, Frank
Elektra, assassin/Miller, Frank; Sienkiewicz, Bill
Enemy ace: war idyll/Pratt, George
Epileptic 1/David B.
Ghost world/Clowes, Dan
God's bosom/Jackson, Jack
Grasshopper and the ant/Kurtzman, Harvey
Hey wait…/Jason
Iguana/Trillo, Carlos; Mandrafina, Domingo
Invisibles: apocalipstick/Morrison, Grant
Invisibles: bloody hell in America/Morrison, Grant
Invisibles: counting to none/Morrison, Grant
Invisibles: entropy in the UK/Morrison, Grant
Invisibles: kissing Mister Quimper/Morrison, Grant
Invisibles: say you want a revolution/Morrison, Grant
Invisibles: the invisible kingdom/Morrison, Grant
It's a man's world: men's adventure magazines/Parfrey, Adam
Jar of fools/Lutes, Jason
JLA: earth 2/Morrison, Grant; Quitely, Frank
King volume 1-3/Anderson, Ho Che (available in Special Collections)
Kingdom come/Waid, Mark; Ross, Alex
Krazy & Ignatz: 1929-1930/Herriman, George
Like a velvet glove cast in iron/Clowes, Dan
Love and rockets: house of raging women/Los Bros Hernandez
Love and rockets: locas in love/Los Bros Hernandez
Love and rockets: whoa, Nellie!/Los Bros Hernandez
Maakies/Millionaire, Tony
Marvels/Busiek, Kurt; Ross, Alex
Maus I: a survivor's tale: my father bleeds history/Spiegelman, Art
Maus II: a survivor's tale: and here my troubles begin/Spiegelman, Art

Mystery date: a Scary Godmother story/Thompson, Jill
No love lost/Bordeaux, Ariel
Now, Endsville and other stories/Lay, Carol
Our cancer year/Brabner, Joyce; Pekar, Harvey; Stack, Frank
Panel one: comic book scripts by top writers/Gertler, Nat
Panel two: more comic book scripts by top writers/Gertler, Nat
Peculia/Sala, Richard
Promethea volume 1/Moore, Alan; Williams, J.H.
Promethea volume 2/Moore, Alan; Williams, J.H.
Promethea volume 3/Moore, Alan; Williams, J.H.
Road to perdition/Collins, Max A.; Rayner, Richard P.
Sandman volume I/Gaiman, Neil
Sandman volume II/Gaiman, Neil
Sandman volume III/Gaiman, Neil
Sandman volume IX/Gaiman, Neil
Sandman volume V/Gaiman, Neil
Sandman volume VI/Gaiman, Neil
Sandman volume VII/Gaiman, Neil
Sandman volume VIII/Gaiman, Neil
Sandman volume X/Gaiman, Neil
Scene of the crime: a little piece of goodnight/Brubaker, Ed; Lark, Michael
Subway series/Corman, Leela
Summer of love/Drechsler, Debbie
Terminal city/Motter, Dean; Lark, Michael
Tex Avery the MGM years 1942-1955/Canemaker, John
Tintin: the complete companion/Farr, Michael
Torso: a true crime graphic novel/Bendis, Brian M.; Andreyko, Marc
Twentieth century Eightball/Clowes, Dan
Whiteout/Rucka, Greg; Lieber, Steve
World war 3 illustrated/Kuper, Peter; Tobocman, Seth

Bibliography

Atton, Chris. "Beyond the Mainstream: Examining Alternative Literature Sources for Stock Selection." *Alternative Library Literature 1994/95* (1994–1995): 159–66.

Baky, John S. "Truthful Lies: Popular Culture and Special Collections." *Popular Culture in Libraries* 1, no. 1 (1993): 51–66.

Dardess, George. "Bringing Comic Books to Class." *College English* 57, no. 2 (1995): 213–22.

Gardner, Richard K. *Library Collections: Their Origin, Selection, and Development.* New York: McGraw-Hill, 1981.

Griffin, Jane K. "A Brief Glossary of Comic Book Terminology." *Serials Review* 24 (Spring 1998): 71–76.

Highsmith, Doug. "Developing a 'Focused' Comic Book Collection in an Academic Library." In *Popular Culture and Acquisitions.* Edited by Allen Ellis, 59–68. New York: Haworth Press, 1992.

Hoffman, Frank. "Comic Books in Libraries, Archives, and Media Centers." *Serials Librarian* 12, nos. 1/2 (1989): 167–98.

Lavin, Michael R. "Comic Books and Graphic Novels for Libraries: What to Buy." *Serials Review* 24 (Summer 1998): 13–45.

Moran, Barbara B. "Going Against the Grain: A Rationale for the Collection of Popular Culture Materials in Academic Libraries." In *Popular Culture and Acquisitions.* Edited by Allen Ellis, 3–12. New York: Haworth Press, 1992.

Nyberg, Amy. *Seal of Approval: History of the Comics Code.* Jackson: University of Mississippi Press, 1998.

Office for Intellectual Freedom of the American Library Association. *Intellectual Freedom Manual.* Chicago and London: ALA, 1996.

Schenck, William. "An Alternative Way to Acquire New Books." *Library of Congress Information Bulletin* 53 (1994): 473–75.

Scott, Randall W. *Comics Librarianship: A Handbook.* Jefferson, N.C.: McFarland, 1990.

———. "Comics and Libraries and the Scholarly World." *Popular Culture in Libraries* 1, no. 1 (1993): 81–84.

———. "A Practicing Comic Book Librarian Surveys His Collection and His Craft." *Serials Review* 24 (Spring 1998): 49–56.

Witek, Joseph. *Comic Books as History: The Narrative Art of Jack Jackson, Art Spiegelman, and Harvey Pekar.* Jackson: University Press of Mississippi, 1989.

———. "From Genre to Medium: Comics and Contemporary American Culture." In *Rejuvenating the Humanities.* Edited by Ray B. Browne and Marshall W. Fishwick, 71–79. Bowling Green, Ohio: Bowling Green State University Popular Press, 1992.

USING CIRCULATION, ILL, AND COLLECTION CHARACTERISTICS FOR THE DEVELOPMENT OF POLICIES FOR COLLECTIONS AND ILL SERVICES

Heather Wicht, University of Colorado at Boulder
Lynn Silipigni Connaway, OCLC Office of Research

Introduction

This pilot study was initiated to compile statistics for collection development decision making at the University of Colorado at Boulder (CU). Some of the factors in decision making that are of current importance at CU are remote storage and budget cuts. The materials budget has suffered both permanent and one-time cuts that make efficient collection management increasingly important. Like many university libraries, the CU Libraries' shelves have been filled to capacity for some time. In 1998, CU began a remote storage project, and today, approximately 425,000 volumes are stored in a shared remote storage facility in Denver. The CU subject bibliographers have used a variety of methods and tools to select materials for remote storage.

There has also been much interest from OCLC Online Computer Library Center, Inc., members in studies utilizing WorldCat holdings data. Such studies currently in progress at the OCLC Office of Research include library collection comparisons with gap/overlap analyses, identification of unique or last copy, and the determination of intellectual or audience level derived from type of library holdings and a weighted formula.

CU is a Research I, doctoral-granting institution with 25,000 FTEs. The CU Libraries hold approximately three million volumes. They use an Innovative Interfaces integrated library system for circulation and a CLIO database to track interlibrary loan (ILL) data.

The CU Libraries are interested in comparing circulation data and ILL borrowing requests to WorldCat holdings. John Ochola, Ph.D., collection development librarian at Baylor University, published a similar pilot study in *Collection Management*.[1] Ochola's study was one of few to gather and analyze these types of data. Since Baylor University and CU are both ARL libraries and members of the Greater Western Library Alliance (GWLA) and are both participating in remote storage projects, the CU Libraries decided to use aspects of the methodology of the Baylor study for a CU pilot study.

Scope

The pilot study evaluated books owned by CU Libraries, as indicated by WorldCat holdings. The holdings, circulation, and ILL borrowing data from the CU Law Library were excluded, as the Law Library maintains separate integrated library and ILL systems. CU's WorldCat holdings were compared to book circulation data and ILL borrowing requests for books from January 1, 1998, through December 31, 2002. Only circulating titles were included. The ILL borrowing requests were harvested from CLIO database. Canceled ILL borrowing requests were eliminated in cases where the requested item was held by the CU Libraries. Foreign-language books, government documents, dissertations and theses, manuscripts, and music were not included in the data.

Approximately 20% of the ILL borrowing requests were for foreign-language books. Most of these requests lacked sufficient subject classification data, which would have skewed the results of the study. Also, because many of these requests were not filled through OCLC, they did not have associated OCLC numbers, and obtaining subject data from other sources would have been extremely time-consuming. It was decided that a separate investigation was needed to specifically address these requests.

Methodology

The CU Libraries worked with the OCLC Office of Research to determine a definition of the book in order to programmatically identify the CU Libraries' holdings in WorldCat. Based on the MARC record, a book is defined by the following criteria:

1. The bibliographic level is monograph (fixed field code "m") .

2. The record type is language material (fixed field code "a") .

3. No physical description fixed field is present, except for text (007 position 001 is coded "a," "b," or "d") .

4. If defined, the form of item can only be defined as large print or regular print reproduction (if not left blank, 008 position 23 can only be coded "d" or "r") .

5. There is no 245 $h, which is a general materials designation used for nonbook formats.

6. The publisher name and/or ISBN must be present (260 $b and/or 020 must be present).

7. The book must have more than 49 pages; books with less than 49 pages are considered manuscripts (300 $a must include >49 pages).

The WorldCat holdings, circulation data, and ILL borrowing requests were mapped to more than 600 subject categories by Library of Congress Classification (LCC) number. The study incorporated the call number ranges and associated subject categories established by the North American Title Count (NATC). NATC is a statistical collection analysis tool developed by the Association for Library Collections & Technical Services (ALCTS) NATC subcommittee.

For the purposes of analysis, presentation, and discussion, the NATC categories were then consolidated into the 24 conspectus divisions, which were originally developed by the Research Libraries Group (RLG) and later adopted by the Western Library Network (WLN) and OCLC.

The ILL borrowing requests lacked subject data. However, since they were largely processed through OCLC, the researchers were able to map them to WorldCat bibliographic records by OCLC number. Selected fields from the matched WorldCat bibliographic records were then integrated into the existing ILL data.

Because the mappings were based on LCC number, 112,499 records with missing or invalid LCC numbers were excluded from the circulation data in the pilot study. The researchers are exploring automated methods of obtaining LCC numbers for these records.

When the holdings data were initially harvested from WorldCat, the researchers noted a significant discrepancy between the number of CU holdings set in WorldCat and the number of bibliographic records in the CU Libraries' OPAC. They learned that the CU Libraries had recently discovered a problem in the process of setting holdings and were in the process of refreshing CU's holdings. The researchers then harvested a current holdings file for comparison and analysis. As is common in many libraries, CU Libraries do not set holdings on some items; therefore, a discrepancy between CU's local and WorldCat holdings still exists.

ILL requestors' disciplines were normalized by matching requester-provided information to the CU-established academic departments and disciplines. Requesters' statuses—graduate student, undergraduate student, faculty and staff—were also normalized. Because the ILL data were harvested from the CLIO system and not the Libraries' integrated library system, it was impossible to place certain limits on the data that were harvested. As a result, many nonbook materials (audiovisual items, sheet music, manuscripts, theses/dissertations, and foreign-language materials) had to be removed manually.

Because of size limitations in both the Innovative Interfaces review files and Microsoft Excel, records had to be gathered and exported in groups of 50,000 or fewer. This was done by limiting the date of last circulation to specific date ranges. A total of nine files were created in Innovative Interfaces and exported to Microsoft Excel. Because of the way in which the files were divided, duplicate records were found among the files and were programmatically merged together.

Results and Discussion

The pilot study analyzed and compared 1,146,655 records for books with CU holdings set in WorldCat, 343,869 records for books that circulated during the five-year period, and 25,038 ILL borrowing requests for books initiated over the same five-year period.

Within each NATC subject category, a ratio of circulations to holdings was derived by dividing the number of circulations by the number of holdings. The subject areas with the lowest ratios of circulations to holdings were library science (.09), physical education and recreation (.10), and anthropology (.14). The subject areas with the highest ratios of circulations to holdings were engineering and technology (1.27), physical sciences (1.43), and computer science (2.68).

Similarly, a ratio of borrowings to holdings was derived by dividing the number of ILL borrowing requests by the number of holdings within each NATC subject category. The subject areas with the lowest ratios of borrowings to holdings were anthropology (.004), library science (.005), and political science (.006). The subject areas with the highest ratios of borrowings to holdings were agriculture (.047), music (.049), and engineering and technology (.113).

Directions for Future Research

Initial interpretation suggests that the level of circulation and ILL borrowing activity is loosely related to the strength of the curriculum in that subject area. Also, distance education programs in engineering may have elevated the borrowings to holdings ratio in that subject area.

The CU collection development librarians will be examining these numbers more closely to interpret the results and decide on necessary courses of action. Extremes in the circulations to holdings and borrowing to holdings ratios have implications for collection analysis in the context of the curricula.

The researchers will be evaluating both the number of items that circulated and the number of total circulation transactions in order to more accurately identify the circulating subset of the total collection. The researchers will also compare the publication dates and publishers within each NATC subject category among the three datasets. These comparisons will be beneficial in identifying collection use patterns and will provide additional data to support collection development decisions.

The ILL borrowing data will be further examined to analyze the statuses and academic departments/disciplines of the requesters. These data will be correlated to NATC subjects to determine if academic status and discipline correlate to the subject areas of the books that were borrowed.

Notes

1. John N. Ochola, "Use of Circulation Statistics and Interlibrary Loan Data in Collection Management," *Collection Management* 27, no. 1 (2002): 1–13.

The Charleston Conference attempts to provide a balanced overview of collection development and acquisitions issues. Recently that has meant being certain to entertain speaker presentations on electronic as well as print resources. In 2003, we concentrated a significant amount of our program on an exploration of the future of the printed book.

Future of the Book

PLANNING FOR THE FUTURE OF THE BOOK: SOME LONGER-TERM FINANCIAL CONSIDERATIONS IN THE MANAGEMENT OF BOOK STOCK

Patrick Scott, University of South Carolina*

I don't want to comment in this chapter as a rare book specialist but as someone who has over 40 years' experience of academic libraries. My general perspective is that, instead of debating whether the book has a future, we should be planning for the future of our book stock with the same imagination and financial realism that we having been giving to digital resources.

In practical terms, I don't think the apocalypse is coming for the book just yet. People, if not academic libraries, are going to go on buying new books and preserving great ones. The kind of books for which I am currently responsible—the great Nuremberg Chronicle of 1493, the King James Bible of 1611, Audubon's *Birds of America*, first editions in original condition of Darwin, Dickens, Fitzgerald, Hemingway—are going to be preserved by rare book libraries, collectors, dealers, and investors.

What interests me is the impact of library management strategies on the future of more ordinary book stock. Among their goals, almost all libraries inevitably prioritize service to current patrons over the strategic development of long-term assets, and often this means using the book stock in ways that use it up. Unlike corporate balance sheets, few library budgets take account of the capital asset of book stock or make realistic estimates of its depreciation through misuse or its appreciation when properly preserved. Even fewer libraries have financial plans that take account of the long-term financial implications of current management and expenditure choices.

Libraries are indeed going through a major paradigm shift, but from this perspective the shift is not so much from print to digital text as from the unrestricted ownership of resources to their temporary leasing. As we all know, public libraries lease not just databases but also multiple copies of new books. I believe that this pattern will increasingly apply to the circulating collections of academic libraries, where we will see smaller, more intensively managed open-shelf collections, focused on high-demand recent monographs with clear curricular relevance, and with the financial and staffing resources for much higher percentages of acquisition and de-acquisition to and from open-shelf availability. Few academic libraries are currently staffed or funded to do this kind of collection management, but they are going to have to be staffed for this in future, if the match between open-shelf print holdings and student user needs is to be improved. Just as McDonald's knows from its cash registers how many people choose a Big Mac or a salad, we need to know which books on the open shelves and which databases are recurrently interesting to users and which are merely prestige options on the menu.

I can't predict whether academic libraries are going to follow public libraries and lease books as they do databases, but open-shelf circulating, user-oriented book stock is in practice a short-term consumable resource, whether leased or purchased. Unlike databases, the resources if purchased retain at least some market value at the end of the expected user-life, however depreciated. If we put more expertise and steadier cash flow into managing print collections and keep tabs on the numbers and satisfaction of current users of different kinds of resource, even the short-term cost advantage is not always with digital delivery.

But this change is only part of the future we should be planning for. We need to be more realistic about why we are retaining, in the stacks or in closed or off-site storage, book stock that isn't needed on the open shelves by a significant number of current users. The reason is that, in financial as well as intellectual terms, prudent libraries anticipate the patrons of the future as well as serving those of the present.

In academic libraries at least, the license agreements for most digital resources, and the recurrent cost of those agreements, have brought into being two kinds of information access: on the one side expensive annual leasing to provide restricted access for a limited class of patrons to digital resources, and on the other minimal new investment in print materials while encouraging unrestricted access without charge to the aging book stock we already own. On the face of it, there is something off balance in even a state-supported institution charging its own students thousands of dollars in tuition, and then encouraging a student or faculty member from the much less expensive TEC college next door to make equal use of books that other people's tuition has helped purchase. We sign agreements not to give away access to digital resources, and pretty soon we won't be doing it for print.

There are plenty of signs that the paradigm shift from open access to restricted access, to which we have become acculturated from the digital side, is already beginning to affect major libraries in their handling of print materials. Great libraries don't lend their books to other institutions, and great European libraries increasingly charge outsiders for on-site use of their holdings. Even quite ordinary research libraries have become increasingly careful in vetting older books before they are shipped off for consortial or interlibrary lending. The short-term political attractions of free loan have to be balanced against the likelihood of cumulative damage to irreplaceable collections.

If normal library practice begins to treat access to print resources more like access to digital resources, the primary reason will be greater financial realism. We simply can't afford to use up our book stock. Books are potentially a long-term investment, but equally they are a nonrenewable resource. Good books get used, and books that get used get used up. Many books are no longer replaceable, even for ready money. The very books we most need to have available for future users are those most likely to get damaged, destroyed, and then de-acquisitioned through management practices that elide the difference between short-term and long-term book stock.

Not only space, but prudence, will lead most major libraries to move an increasing percentage of their stock from circulating collections to closed-stack storage, on- or off-site, and make it available for use under much more stringent controls than in the past. It costs a lot, in expert staff time, to make decisions on the replacement of damaged or outworn book stock, and replacement will not always be possible. A lot of libraries now outsource their acquisition selection; diminished professional staffing and squeezed monograph budgets mean that libraries that miss titles on first publication are unlikely to acquire them later. The Wal-Martification of library operations is clearly cutting costs and professional staff in the short run, but most shortcuts in tech services cede a long-term advantage to those libraries that balance them with in-house expertise. The long-term advantage will lie with the libraries that keep the staff and budget to identify and buy the books other libraries aren't getting sent and to buy or accept as gift duplicate archival copies of in-print books for which damagingly heavy use can be predicted.

We already have a two-tier library system for print resources: serious libraries and the rest, the freeloaders. It's not a division by size but by the depth and individuality of the book stock and its adequacy for the future needs of the library's future users. Libraries that own, acquire, or build strong book collections and unique research collections have a responsibility and a duty to manage those collections as a capital resource for the long-term benefit of their own institutions.

As the book stock of weaker libraries ages and their inadequacies become more apparent, stronger, better-managed libraries will increasingly expect a modest income stream from fees for allowing outsiders on-site access, from occasional loans under stringent conditions to responsible institutions, and from the provision of digital or hard copies from the print originals they have had the foresight to acquire and preserve. Indeed, I expect that good libraries will over the next decade begin to share or reallocate the space and staff they now dedicate to free-access digitization initiatives (money out, even if it's often grant money) to set up on-demand hard-copy book production technology, capitalizing on older materials they own that other people need or prefer in book format (money in or at least costs covered).

By contrast, libraries that do not maintain and preserve adequate print collections now will very soon need to budget annual funding for borrowing or other access to print materials, just as they currently allocate funding each year for access to digital resources. I anticipate that ambitious academic departments at institutions with inadequate libraries and neglected print collections will increasingly recognize the benefit in funding access for their faculty and advanced students to better libraries at other institutions, just as traditionally departments and colleges set aside travel support for researchers. In time, central administrations will find that they must fund such access to other libraries through reallocation of funding from the home library.

For over a century now, libraries have been managed as if books would last forever, and as if any individual book would always be freely available somewhere. These have always been false assumptions, but their falsity is now more obvious than it was. You can't borrow books that no one owns, that no one has preserved, or that no one is willing to lend. You have no reason to loan a book to an institution that has long been freeloading, and lots of good reasons for not doing so. Even now, many libraries provide through their catalogs access to print resources that are not on the shelves, not on-site, not under their own management, and not consistently available—resources that users can get hold of, not "just in time" but just in theory.

The future of the book depends on changed management strategies for the book collections. Our future patrons need to be assured of stable, ongoing, predictable access, not to information or to books in general, but to particular editions of particular books. The book stock of major libraries is a nonrenewable resource. Book collections, even journal backruns, are an asset, like any other expensive long-term asset. If mismanaged, the asset is wasted. If wisely handled, book stock is a steadily appreciating investment. Canny library managers now, as in the past, should be balancing short-term and longer-term expenditures and considering a significantly increased proportion of their budget for this kind of long-term investment.

Notes

* Rare Books & Special Collections, Thomas Cooper Library, University of South Carolina, Columbia, SC 29208 (scottp@gwm.sc.edu). The views expressed in this chapter are personal, not official, and should not be taken as in any way reflecting the official position of the University of South Carolina or its libraries.

THE FUTURE OF THE BOOK: ROBUST OR ON LIFE SUPPORT?

Mark Herring, Winthrop University

You've heard this story, surely:

While we were doing all this, Circe said, "So far so good, and now pay attention to what I am about to tell you—heaven itself, indeed, will recall it to your recollection. First you will come to the Cyber-Sirens who enchant all who come near them." If any one unwarily draws in too close and hears the singing of the Cyber-Sirens, his library will never be the same, and his patrons will never welcome him again. For the Cyber- Sirens sit in a green background and warble him to digitization with the sweetness of their promises. There is a great heap of dead books lying all around, with the words still rotting off them. Therefore pass these Cyber-Sirens by, and stop your faculty and staff ears with wax that none of them may hear; but if you like you can listen yourself, for you may get your faculty and staff to bind you as you stand upright on a cross-piece half way up the Reference Desk, and they must lash the rope's ends to the Desk itself, that you may have the pleasure of listening. If you beg and pray them to un-loose you, then they must bind you faster.

I had hardly finished telling everything to the men before we reached the island of the two Sirens, for the wind had been very favorable. Then all of a sudden it fell dead calm; there was not a breath of wind nor a ripple upon the water, so the men furled the sails and stowed them; then taking to their oars they whitened the water with the foam they raised in rowing. Meanwhile I look a large wheel of wax and cut it up small with my sword. Then I kneaded the wax in my strong hands till it became soft, which it soon did between the kneading and the rays of the sun-god son of the Sonny Bono Copyright Extension Act. Then I stopped the ears of all my men, and they bound me hands and feet to the mast as I stood upright on the Desk; but they went buying printed materials. When we had got within earshot of the land, and the orders were coming in at a good rate, the Cyber-Sirens saw that we were getting in shore and began with their singing. "Come here," they sang, "renowned Bookman and listen to our voices. No one ever sailed past us without staying to hear the enchanting sweetness of our song-and he who listens will go on his way not only charmed, but wiser, for we know all the ills that publishers lay upon [you] by spontaneity, brevity and cumulative effect , and can tell you everything that is going to happen under the rubric of Fair Use. Don't let it get you down. It's only paper turning. Just buy some CDs for burning and you'll be on your way." They sang these words most musically, and as I longed to hear them further I made by frowning to my faculty and staff that they should set me free so I could sign up immediately: open access, all day, all the time, 24/7 is what those cyber-wenches whined ; but they quickened their stroke, and bound me with still stronger bonds till we had got out of hearing of the Cyber-Sirens' voices.

Isn't it interesting that after this moment, Ulysses falls into the hands of Scylla and Charybdis, otherwise known as Digital Millennium Copyright Act and the Tasini Decision?

Seriously, where are we vis-à-vis the future of the book? Is it as robust as ever, or are we entering the final stages, its veritable life support. Will we usher in, as one state leader has said, the era in which libraries are no longer useful but are obsolete, and soon we'll just buy one book and zap it all over the place?

Helping us examine these issues are five gods and one goddess who have deigned to attend our court. They are, in alphabetical order:

- **Matthew Bruccoli,** the Emily Brown Jefferies Professor of English at the University of South Carolina, and is the leading authority on the House of Scribner and its authors. He is the author of *Some Sort of Epic Grandeur: The Life of F. Scott Fitzgerald* and the editorial director of the *Dictionary of Literary Biography*. He is curator of the Bruccoli Collection of F. Scott Fitzgerald at the Thomas Cooper Library, University of South Carolina.

- **Wayne Chapman,** professor of modern British and American literature at Clemson University and specializes in textual, bibliographic, and genetic approaches to literature from the evidences of manuscript and book production. He is the author of books on W. B. Yeats and Virginia Woolf and the editor of two volumes for the Cornell Yeats in Manuscript Series, *The Countess Cathleen* (1999) and *The Dreaming of the Bones* and *Calvary* (two one-act plays in a single volume, 2003). He coedited a special number of *Yeats Annual*, entitled *Yeat's Collaborations*, for Palgrave Macmillan (2003), and is at work on several projects, including a book called *Yeat's Poetry in the Making: Dream Whatever IS Well Made."* He has been the editor of *The South Carolina Review* since 1996, and is the founding editor of Clemson University Digital Press as well as the director of the Center for Electronic and Digital Publishing, College of Architecture, Arts and Humanities, Clemson University—offices he has held since August 2000, when the center first came into being.

- **Walt Crawford,** a senior analyst at RLG in Mountain View, California. Crawford has been a full-time professional in library automation since 1968, at RLG since 1979. He is currently lead designer for Eureka, RLG's end-user search service, and in that process has now used roughly 70 different OpenURL resolvers. (But that's a different session.) Crawford started speaking and writing about the future of books in 1992, after seeing a few dozen too many dogmatic predictions of the inevitable triumph of e-books and the death of print. Two relevant books, an award-winning article ("Paper Persists" in *Online*), and dozens of other columns, speeches, and articles later, he keeps on because the silly predictions keep coming. Crawford clearly believes in books, with 14 published to date, but also believes in digital communication. That's how he makes his living, and his oddball Web 'zine is the equivalent of four short books a year. He also appears in print magazines and journals about 30 times a year.

- **Steven McKinzie,** currently the social science librarian at Dickinson College in Carlisle Pennsylvania. Originally from Texas, Steve did graduate work in history both at East Carolina and Vanderbilt, where he also received his MLS. He went to Dickinson in 1988 laboring respectively as the documents librarian, head of serials, and chair or director of the library, and now is the liaison to the social sciences. Steve's current publishing and research interests include virtual reference, information literacy, collection development, and the library as a profession. He has written numerous reviews for *JAI* and other library publications.

- **Allene Stuart Phy-Olsen,** a professor at Austin-Peay State University in Clarksville, Tennessee. She graduated from Stephens College (A.A) and the University of Kentucky and holds three degrees (M.A., Ed.S., Ph.D.) from Peabody College and Vanderbilt

University. Professor Phy-Olsen has Taught in Lycee Mohammad V in Rabat, Morocco; at the U.S. Naval Intelligence School, Anacostia, Maryland; at Kansas City Kansas Junior College; at George Peabody College (15 years, including 4 years while finishing graduate school); and at Alabama State University, Montgomery. She is in her thirteenth year at Austin-Peay State University. She has done postgraduate work at a number of U.S. and foreign universities in Canada, France, Switzerland, and Italy. She has traveled the world over on all continents except Australia. Professor Phy-Olsen developed Peace Corps programs in language and literature for Zaire, Kenya, and Liberia and trained Peace Corps volunteers. She is the author of three books, literally thousands of reviews, and scores of articles.

(Mr. Bruccoli and Mr. Crawford did not submit chapters for these proceedings.)

THE FUTURE OF THE BOOK: THE CLEMSON EXPERIENCE

Wayne K. Chapman, Clemson University

First, let me thank Mark Herring for inviting me to speak at the conference and my thanks, too, to the conference organizers, especially Yvonne Lev, Katina Strauch, and Regina Semko. The subject of the panel involved two topics, really: "the Future" and "the Book." Since I'm not a clairvoyant, I'm going to stay on message about the book in the present—that is, on how it is defined and doing in practice at my little publishing house during a historically bad moment for universities and their presses. Also, since I'm neither an economist nor a pessimist, I assume the future will not look like the last three years at all times. Nevertheless, unless you haven't noticed, there *is* a revolution going on in the production and use of academic books by universities both as makers and consumers of books. An editor is obliged to see the course of change and, in a sense, to help chart it for the sake of literature broadly defined.

Three years ago, we wrote an institutional charter at Clemson University for the Center for Electronic and Digital Publishing (CEDP), laying the foundations for a digital press but acknowledging that profound disagreements were being voiced in the public debate on new media. For Winthrop University Libraries, Dean Herring was part of that debate. I asserted that three variables in criticism (text, author, and context) are affected by the technological revolution and that all approaches to the study of literature so far devised are salient in some way and yet betray an interest in one or two of the three variables to the exclusion of one or both of the others. What has happened to the notion of the "definitive text?" Does criticism have the stuff to deal with global, not merely corporate, authority for texts produced collaboratively and read on the World Wide Web? Can texts be gendered if constructed globally and in more than one dimension? Literature, finally, *does* have something to do with texts and people who make them. So what will the future hold for students who experience their popular culture on the Internet? Texts, authors, contexts—energy, mass, the speed of light.

Trying to imagine what life will be like in the profession of literature in a few years and, consequently, in the classroom and the world of the publishing scholar/critic, I tell my students that we need a general theory of criticism like the general theory of relativity—a unified theory. I give them a humble kind of relativity, one not yet unified theoretically because of the need to work out how the fundamentals are changing.

Reading is a different experience for us all today depending on the medium used, just as the writing process profoundly changed for my generation in the mid-1980s when word processors replaced typewriters almost overnight. What is happening to the dissemination of the knowledge university's produce in the book industry? It probably never occurred to Dr. Johnson that printed books, the great technological advance of the late Middle Ages as literacy increased with the rise of university education, might one day seem doomed. This perception is everyone's problem in academia right now, not just those of us in the humanities. But solutions have been suggested. In the April 2001 issue of *Harper's Magazine*, Michael Korda put it bluntly: "The larger and more disturbing question is whether the book itself has a future"[1]; envisioning ironic "salvation" in the technology that is threatening all but a few of the largest publishing syndicates, Korda thinks there is an "awesome potential" in electronic publishing to do "the whole business of scholarly publishing, and of publishing first novels, poetry, and essays" that tend to sell in small numbers. This was good to read after Clemson had already set its course as a publishing house.

As editor of *The South Carolina Review*, one of the top collegiate literary journals in the country, I believe universities have prestigious traditions that they should and will maintain in spite of increasingly challenging times and the hard reality of the fiscal "bottom line." As executive editor of Clemson University Digital Press, I direct a small, self-supporting academic press for the twenty-first century. There's such a thing as being too small, I imagine, but I assure you that being self-supporting on grants, private gifts, subscriptions, sales, copyright fees, and such is a virtue difficult to overestimate when virtually everything else in the academy is being cut. The University of Massachusetts Press, for example, might not have felt the ax come down so heavily this past summer if it were not so conventional in this regard. Endurance, in the long run, will be for publishers who change their tactics to ensure the viability of their product in a "niche market."

I like to say that we are prepared to follow the example of the smart mouse that survived the dinosaurs because we, too, are small and adaptive. We aim to meet high editorial standards commensurate with those of the Association of American University Presses (AAUP), and we are committed to a strategic plan that would obtain affiliate membership in that organization after publishing three monographs in each of three years. That is in addition to our journals, *The South Carolina Review* and *The Upstart Crow: A Shakespeare Journal*. Our mission statement stipulates that as a trademark Clemson University Digital Press shall stand for "the best that has been built, created, performed, and written" in the "spirit and context of the university's Guiding Principles," on which we are annually assessed. "As a platform for collaboration with community outreach and educational goals inherent in its Mission Statement, CUDP satisfies the injunction of the definition to disseminate the fruits of research by invoking AAUP's educational objective in a fundamentally practical way. Traditional and nontraditional modes of publication (including, especially, electronic and digital publication of refereed scholarship) [. . .] involve[s] the editorial and technical abilities of faculty and students in various graduate and undergraduate programs." I should add that for every book we print it is our general policy to publish an e-book, a free edition on the Internet (in PDF or HTML format and with appropriate links to sponsors, associated organizations, collections, and related works).

As a venture in public service publishing, the point is not business and profit but the serendipitous and synergetic agency of individuals who collectively negotiate and, consequently, *make* books together. Technology is serving, not driving, it. The medium is *not* the message, primarily. And teaching is as consequential as learning is to the process. Our students learn the drill and discipline texts and editors demand because an audience expects it; they also learn to apply in the lab computer skills that they learn in the classroom as graduate students in one of two programs. As a member of the literature faculty and a hands-on editor, I teach modern literature and writing in the core curriculum and then give this kind of instruction in the direction of our publication program. I work with four part-time editorial assistants on our journals (two from the literature and two from the professional communication graduate programs), and I direct two MAPC graduate assistants employed by CEDP. In English the "tech line" is not the Maginot line. The CEDP and digital press are on it, the "new territory" of which our president speaks, and it is becoming more and more imperative for faculty, in general, to get on that line and to work both sides of it. In English, a territory where the arts and humanities regularly coalesce and synthesize, it's not about writing (or communication) *and* literature, but about *writing literature*.

I love books—as they *have been*; as they *are*, evolving in new media; and as they *shall be* in the future, in forms not mutually exclusive of one another but coexistential. My house looks like my office—I live with books. I love reading them, writing them, and making them. I can't imagine living in a world without them, but an awful lot depends on how one defines the concept "book" and allows for it to take the form of the digital beside its familiar material manifestation. Directed at a niche market, one's objective might sometimes be *the book as we know it*, but increasingly the imperative is for Web-based book productions, to the good effect of keeping alive as an option the old book as well as the one that is emerging in digital editions and miniscule print runs on a demand basis. Thus, "the Book" is very much alive although the book trade in academia is not at all well.

Now that you've shaken hands with CEDP and the digital press, consider some of the shock waves that information technology has been making in academia these days. I give you a sampling of headlines from *The Chronicle of Higher Education* in the last couple of years:

- "Professors Should Embrace Technology in Courses" (D. Lynch). Sometimes professors don't; this is an article about intellectual property.

- "Does Technology Fit in the Tenure File?" (J. Young). On whether creation of scholarly Web sites and electronic teaching tools should be counted in evaluation of faculty.

- "The Deserted Library" (Carlson). On students abandoning reading rooms to research online or study at Starbucks.

- "An Online Library Struggles to Survive" (Foster). Questia's great expectations in for-profit services "hasn't won over college librarians or scholars."

- "Are University Presses Producing Too Many Series for Their Own Good?" (Waters). That is, niches are nice but narrower can be a nuisance.

- "Academic Press Gives Away Its Secret of Success" (Jensen). Or the logic of free online access to books to reduce the cost of marketing them.

- "Staying in Print: The Romance of the Literary Magazine" (Goldstein), by the editor of *Michigan Quarterly Review,* about preserving the "totems" of our cultural "zeitgeist, and I'd be a fool not to acknowledge a bias in favor of any English professor who doubles as editor of a literary journal.

- (not least) "Understanding the Economic Burden of Scholarly Publishing," subtitled "The bottom line is that scholarly publishing isn't financially feasible as a business model—never was, never was intended to be, and should not be" (Davidson).

That's a lot to think about. And I've given it to you in no particular order. Business and finance issues are there. Teaching and research issues are there for the faculty as well as for students. And service is there for the institution and for the editor who thinks "audience, audience, audience."[2] For a university press, like a faculty, the challenge that technology offers is demanding and essential, galvanizing and liberating, as Clemson President James Barker affirmed when he said: "We realize that we are in some new territory here and we like it. We like being in the new territory even though it's confusing and we don't have all the answers yet." When AOL Time Warner decides to sell its problematic book division to settle debts,[3] one might wonder why a university should wish to join in such "confusion." The answer is that major research institutions shoulder a mission they cannot shirk. For that reason, production of printed books in academic fields will be continued, primarily by universities themselves, for the sake of the dissemination of knowledge that the academy produces. Clemson University has developed a new academic plan with intentions to invest substantially in information and communication technology as a focus area as soon as we come out of the negative growth pattern of the last three years and, as expected by public universities in South Carolina, possibly not before another disappointing fiscal cycle in 2004–2005. To that extent, the dissemination of knowledge by a declining institutional subsidy—or "life support"—is a condition evident to us regionally, nationally, and globally. Still, I wager that the situation will change before too long. The history of the book, after all, is measured in centuries and millennia.

Notes

1. Michael Korda, "Out of Print: Publishing's Future, Seen from the Inside," *Harper's Magazine* (April 2001): 84.
2. Susan Rabiner and Alfred Fortunato, "Thinking Like a Book Editor: Audience, Audience, Audience," *The Chronicle of Higher Education* (February 22, 2002): B16+.
3. Verlyn Klinkenborg, "Nothing but Troubling News from the World of Publishing," *New York Times*, January 27, 2003 [Online], available: nytimes.com. 27 Jan.2003.www.nytimes.com/2003/...27MON3.html (accessed June 21, 2004).

Bibliography

Carlson, Scott. "The Deserted Library." *The Chronicle of Higher Education* (November 16, 2001): A353–38.

Davidson, Cathy N. "Understanding the Economic Burden of Scholarly Publishing." *The Chronicle of Higher Education* (October 3, 2003): B7–10.

Foster, Andrea L. "An Online Library Struggles to Survive." *The Chronicle of Higher Education* (September 12, 2003): A27–28.

Goldstein, Laurence. "Staying in Print: The Romance of the Literary Magazine." *The Chronicle of Higher Education* (January 10, 2003): B14–15.

Jensen, Michael. "Academic Press Gives Away Its Secret of Success." *The Chronicle of Higher Education* (September 14, 2001): B24.

Lynch, Diane. "Professors Should Embrace Technology in Courses." *The Chronicle of Higher Education* (January 18, 2002): B15–16.

Waters, Lindsay. "Are University Presses Producing Too Many Series for Their Own Good?" *The Chronicle of Higher Education* (October 27, 2000): B7–8.

Young, Jeffrey R. "Does Technology Fit in the Tenure File?" *The Chronicle of Higher Education* (February 22, 2002): A25–27.

THE FUTURE OF THE BOOK: BRIGHTER THAN YOU MIGHT EXPECT

Steven McKinzie, Dickinson College

When I was growing up, I liked to rummage around my grandparents' farm in rural east Texas. One of my favorite spots was a storage shed, filled with old furniture, discarded equipment, assorted farm implements, and in one corner an old framed photograph of my great uncle, attending a harness-makers' convention in Fort Worth, Texas, in 1911.

The picture of an important family member standing amid a distinguished company of posed harness makers sparked the imagination. One could easily envision the convention with its session presentations and panel discussions, entertaining topics such as "new developments in harness design," "international leather prices," "prospects of overseas markets," or "the challenge of large draft animals harnessing."

What is unlikely, however—in fact, what is almost impossible to imagine—is a session on what would have been arguably the most relevant topic of all:—a presentation on the development of the internal combustion engine, automobile manufacturing, and the probable devastating effects of both on the future of the indigenous harness-making trade.

The picture of my great uncle, the tradesman, and the imaginary scenario invites comparison and prompts questions. Are we librarians, traditional print publishers, and those who seem to appreciate the unique characteristics of the book, the purveyors of an outmoded and perhaps dying trade? Like the harness makers of the last century, are we simply artisans of a new century, clinging to a way of life, to a trade, to an approach that is doomed to be discarded? It is a question worth asking.

The photograph that I've asked you to imagine of my great uncle at the harness-makers' convention also illustrates the kinds of technical changes that we have seen over the last hundred years—especially in the area of transportation. When librarians, futurists, publishers, and information specialists talk of technical change in printing and information science, they often insist that the changes we have seen in information technology mirror the extraordinary changes in the technology of transportation. That and the media drive the conversation about changes wrought by technology.

And the changes have been extraordinary. There can be no question about that. Let me give you some examples. In the early part of the nineteenth century, barges and riverboats dominated American transportation culture, just as did railroads in the later nineteenth and early twentieth centuries. Samuel Clemens took his pen name, Mark Twain, from his days as a riverboat pilot, and his *Life on the Mississippi* became an American classic. In fact, this major waterway was so important that news of the fall of Vicksburg, the Confederate fortress on the banks of the Mississippi, in July 1863 significantly overshadowed Lee's defeat at Gettysburg. From a practical angle, one of the northern economic arguments for preserving the Union was that the Midwest states could never tolerate the notion of a foreign power controlling the mouth of the Mississippi.

As we all know, the dominance of this Mississippi riverboat culture largely gave way to railroads in the hundred years following the Civil War. Railroads, steel, coal and iron—robber barons, industrial tycoons—were all part of a matrix centered on rail transportation. In the latter part of the last century, the story changed yet again. Railroads gave way to automobiles, trucking, and an interstate system of highways.

It has been often claimed that railroads themselves were to blame for this transition. Like my great uncle the harness maker, the argument goes, they became the victims of changes that they failed to understand and developments that they were incapable of handling. One hears the refrain from library circles even today. Look what happened to the railroads! A favorite metaphor of the print/digital debate has been the seeming decline and increasing irrelevance of railroads. Virginia Massey-Burzio, in an article in *The Journal of Academic Librarianship*, quotes James Rettig and Constance Miller, who suggest that if "librarians choose not to change, they had best contemplate the fate of the railroads."[1]

Briefly summarized, this argument contends that railroads lost out because they forgot what they were about. They weren't in the railroad business; they were in the transportation business. Similarly, librarians aren't in the book business. We are in the information business. The sooner we realize that, the sooner we can abandon our outmoded fascination with the printed page. We are about information—not about books.

The problem with the transportation example or metaphor in our discussions of technology is that it is based on the kind of slipshod historical analysis that doesn't bear close scrutiny. In fact, a careful analysis of American transportation history argues the very opposite of what some of the all-digital futurists are claiming. Let me explain.

As we all know, river traffic no longer dominates American transportation. Few of us travel by riverboats. Nor do railroads have the place in our economy they did in the nineteenth century. But here is the point: Both are still enormously important.

River traffic, far from being obsolete, as many of might expect, is still the chief means of transferring much of the nation's grain. Currently about 85% of the grain grown in the Midwest travels by barge down the Mississippi. River traffic is a thriving trade and a major dimension of our economy.

But what about railroads, you ask? In preparation for the conference, I performed a classic undergraduate library assignment. I perused the ProQuest trade journals and discovered some very interesting things.

To begin with, railroad management knows very well its limitations and mistakes. Second, railroads are far from technically backward. The United States has arguably the best, most modernized rail system in the world. Railroads have also become savvy managers and risk takers. A number of the articles that my undergraduate research uncovered revealed a management and an industry that is amazingly innovative in its use of automation, robotics, and satellite tracking systems.

In addition, almost every major city in the country is now courting railroads with grants and enticements for computer rails. There is even a burgeoning interest in and development of smaller railroads in some parts of the country. All of these factors combine to give railroads a surprisingly large chunk of the American transportation market share: 41% according to the latest figures. No, railroads have not undergone some sort of "fate" as James Rettig and Constance Miller suggest. They are an aggressive and vital part of the U.S. economy.

Most of us are old enough to remember experiencing some of the horror that greeted the ubiquitous VHS format. Futurists claimed that it would put movie houses out of business. They said the same thing about radio. Television would render radio irrelevant and obsolete. Of course, nothing of the kind has happened. Movie box office sales are skyrocketing, just as VHS and DVD sales and rentals are booming. And radio has taken off in the last two decades in ways that no one would have envisioned, National Public Radio and talk radio being two of the more unexpected successes.

We don't think about or view movies in the same way that we did 40 years ago.

We don't gather around a home radio to listen to episodes of *The Shadow* and presidential addresses. We don't cruise the Mississippi in riverboats, although riverboat gaming is making an unexpected comeback. Certainly few of us travel the rails as much as our ancestors did.

Nor should we insist that books retain the position of cultural relevance that they did in past generations. Historians tell us that when Thomas Paine wrote *Common Sense,* almost everyone in the North American colonies read it. I don't see individual books having that sort of cultural and psychological influence today. But the traditional printed book—novels, biographies, scholarly monographs—does exert an extraordinary level of cultural influence.

Several months ago, I finished reading David McCullough's *John Adams,* a Pulitzer prize–winning biography that was something of an overnight classic. The traditionally bound hardback copy of the book affected me profoundly. It altered the way that I thought of the early Republic, changed the way that I viewed Adams, and gave me an entirely different view of Adams's friend and sometimes political enemy, Thomas Jefferson.

The biography produced that effect because it was masterfully written and richly detailed, rife with careful analysis and balanced judgment. Few things but an extremely well written book and extremely popular monograph like McCullough's have the ability to do that. Why could a mere book accomplish so much? Part of it may have something to do with Michael Gorman's notion of sustained reading having a certain value and intellectual potency in and of itself.[2]

The rest may have something to do with the advantages the book has as a medium—all very obvious to anyone. Books have convenience. They have amazing durability. (If they don't have permanence, they are still enormously durable.) They are relative inexpensive, and they have amazing portability.

In this sense of enjoying certain advantages over their rivals, books resemble railroads and radio broadcasting. Railroads offer economy of scale: the hauling of large quantities of heavy material with relative ease, such as coal and chemicals. Railroads, by the way, dominate coal shipping, which will become increasingly lucrative as our country turns away from hydroelectric and nuclear electrical plants.

In a similar way radio, offers inexpensive, nearly ubiquitous audio broadcasting—audio without the distraction of video. It is an extraordinary phenomenon.

No, in the final analysis, books, libraries, and the publishing industry aren't like my uncle the harness maker. They're rather more like movie houses, Mississippi barges, railroads, and radio broadcasting. We think of them differently than we did, and so we should. But they remain amazingly important. And like railroads and radio broadcasting in particular, because of the unique advantages they enjoy, books have a very bright future.

Notes

1. Virginia Massey-Burzio, "From the Other Side of the Reference Desk: A Focus Group Study," *The Journal of Academic Librarianship* 24, no3 (May 1998): 208–15.

2. Michael Gorman, *The Enduring Library: Technology, Tradition, and the Quest for Balance* (Chicago: American Library Association, 2002).

TRADITIONAL BOOKS AND E-BOOKS

Allene S. Phy-Olsen, Austin-Peay State University, Texas

What is the future of the traditional book? Predictions are always hazardous, but observations of the current scene may have value. Traditional books admittedly present problems. Right now, at considerable expense, I am building a cottage behind my home that will shelter the overflow of my library. The house I share with my husband and three cats is itself a library. Books are in double rows on shelves of every room, and we advance cautiously lest we start an avalanche with the books that spill out of our shelves and off our tables into stacks on the floor.

These are the books that have survived all their enemies. They may not be those treasures susceptible to moth and rust, and thieves may not break in to steal them. Fortunately the low-class burglars in our neighborhood do not like books. Yet other perils constantly threaten: wood-eating insects, mold, fires, and floods. And we all know how books published during the last hundred years are susceptible to disintegration. There is the all-too-familiar experience with a paperback book that self-destructs as we read it.

So, do electronic books arrive to solve our problems? Since I grew up in rural Kentucky before electricity and running water and am conservative by temperament, I thought I might get a clearer answer to this question from my students, who were born into a digital world. Yet e-books, they tell me, are only good for reference work. Over any extended period of time, they cause eye strain. They require equipment that frequently crashes, especially close to the time when reports are due, or quickly becomes obsolete. But their prime objection is this: e-books cannot be read in bed. They are unpleasant to touch, look at, or even smell. They are not yet compatible with the human body.

Only one student I questioned said she really liked e-books: They cost her nothing (she used school library resources) and they vanished as soon as she was through with them.

This response does not persuade me. I do not want my books to disappear. I want them in the real world where I and my most prized possessions may be found, not in some virtual world. If I should ever achieve notoriety and someone should decide to write my biography, it could easily be reconstructed from my library. The books of childhood are there, as are those I taught from last semester. My books are filled with marginal notes, where I have argued with their authors, sometimes cursed them, and occasionally written love notes to them. I keep all my books, in near pristine condition, despite the marginal notations. I do not like to lend them out. Wherever I go, I always carry one as a security blanket.

Judging from the responses of my students and my own impulses, I feel it will be a long time before electronic books, or whatever comes along to surpass them, will attain the popularity of the books we know. While I understand fully why books exert a fascination on individuals, I have never fully grasped the reasons why in several times and places they have actually become objects of worship. And I ask myself if e-books can ever serve this function.

Consider how the scrolls of the Torah are revered in Jewish worship services. From scrolls to the codex this mystique has indeed proved transferable. Think of the wonderfully illuminated pages of the Holy Koran, or how verses from the Koran, in Arabic calligraphy, have become a sole and adequate form of artistic decoration in some cultures. Why are books so basic that Moslems have divided all humanity into two groups: people of the book and pagans without a holy book or without hope?

Consider also how family Bibles have been revered in Christian households, not only as the Word of God but as a repository of family records. When I was a child, I sometimes had occasion to attend the inauguration of governors in Nashville and Frankfort. I was intrigued by the oaths of office, always taken on a family Bible held by the official's spouse. At the end of the ceremony, the official would kiss the Bible and then kiss the spouse.

After college I worked briefly as secretary for a company that sent young men about the countryside selling Bibles. Hard-working salesmen had no trouble placing these books, even in homes that already owned several Bibles. From the files of the company, I learned how decades earlier, when substantial parts of the American South were illiterate, Bibles still sold well, as holy objects that blessed any house. In homes where the book could actually be read, it held an honored place beside the home medical encyclopedia. Now I ask myself, will the e-book ever occupy this place in parlors?

Possibly the ultimate veneration of the book may be observed in the Sikh religion of India. At the Golden Temple at Amritsar, the sacred Adi Granth is awakened each morning with songs of praise by the temple attendants, and each evening it is put to rest with lulling prayers. Marriage vows are made in its presence, and it presides over the naming of children.

When will electronic books take on such numinous qualities? Will electronic books ever attain the beauty of our finely illustrated traditional books? When will e-books become pleasing to the touch? When will palm readers be built into teddy bears so that even children will want to take them to bed?

After all objections and reservations have been heard, I freely acknowledge the merit of e-books as they currently exist or potentially exist with present technology. Since religion is much on my mind—I am teaching two online comparative religion courses next semester—I will concentrate on electronic resources that can facilitate my task. Some excellent ones are available. Abington Press's *New Interpreter's Bible* may be had on CD-ROM, its entire 12 volumes condensed into a concise package, along with two translations of the Bible and critical commentary. As a bonus, additional reflections on faith and life by prominent religious leaders are included. Even better is *The Maxima Bible Library* on CD-ROM, providing all of 24 Bible translations, complete with commentaries and dictionaries, as well as links to Josephus. The bonus here is a virtual multimedia tour of the Holy Land.

Resources now exist that can more easily than in the print medium link Bible translations with Greek and Hebrew editions. It is even possible to have voice readings in the original languages as well as in our own dear tongue. When James Earl Jones reads from the King James Version of the Bible, we feel as if God Himself is speaking to us!

The works of the Greek and Latin Church Fathers, of St. Thomas Aquinas, Martin Luther, and John Calvin are also available, with most helpful concordances and other aids. I am delighted to have this material in convenient electronic form, because I use it only for study and cross-referencing. Since I never take Calvin to bed, my usual problems with e-books do not really matter here. The encyclopedic nature of the digital environments for these studies is indeed awesome.

Now I see yet another wonderful use for e-books. A few years ago, in the bargain bin of a computer store, I found a game for $1.00. I thought I would try it since there seemed little to lose. It was a second-generation Sierra narrative game by Jane Jansen with the provocative title *Gabriel Knight, Sins of the Father*. From the moment I installed the game on my computer, I was captivated. It was brilliantly interactive, moody, and atmospheric. It translated me into familiar, loved scenes of New Orleans, immersing me in a milieu of jazz and voodoo. At one point in the game I even found myself in a confession box within the cathedral of St. Louis. The game enthralled me for several days, until I finally solved all its problems and got through it, not without some help from an Internet site where sub-teens were playing the game and sharing their skills. They did not know that I was a grandmother; they simply accepted me as one of their own. My regret is that the computer on which I played *Gabriel Knight* long ago gave up the ghost and the program will not install on my more up-to-date machines. So this classic game, which I would love to replay, is now useless to me.

But my dream e-book was generated from this experience, along with a telephone conversation with a Sierra technician who listened patiently and sympathetically as I outlined my concept. He only lamented that the market now demanded games of speed and violence rather than the interactive narrative ones on which Sierra had earned its reputation.

But I still hope someday to be able to make a grand virtual tour through Dante's Inferno, Purgatorio, and Paradiso. This tour will be a collaboration among the best translators, illustrators, animators, game makers, a few superb dramatic readers, and myself. I envision a *Divine Comedy* accessible in my choice of late medieval Tuscan dialect, in modern Italian, or in a good English translation, whichever I may choose (much as DVDs today usually offer a choice of language tracts). Since leading illustrators from Michelangelo to Leonard Baskin have been inspired by Dante, the artwork should present no problem. I will, taking the role of Dante, travel through his netherworld at my own pace, guided by Virgil. I will speak to all the popes, princes, and doomed lovers I find there, and they will reply to me in the noble words of Dante. It is possible that I may be unable to advance to higher circles of the Inferno, or later even get out of Purgatory, until I have performed certain feats. These can be made gamelike and instructional, while still within the style and spirit of Dante. When e-books give us adventures and pleasures—and educational experiences—on this order, then they can exist without apology, in their full glory, beside our most cherished traditional books.

Technology is the backbone of book and serials acquisitions. At the conference we heard a presentation on the tools that we employ in technical services with a glimpse of what this foretells about our future. Other presentations focused on how to design effective acquisitions Web sites, how to integrate vendor-based products, and how to incorporate electronic reserves into university portal products.

PORTALS, COURSEWARE, AND MORE: WHERE DOES THE LIBRARY FIT IN?

J. Christopher Holobar, The Pennsylvania State University

> *For libraries, this means asking how they can differentiate themselves from their competitors even while adopting and sharing many of their competitor's practices.*—Anna Keller Gold, Multilateral Digital Library Partnerships for Sharing and Preserving Instructional Content and Context

Although "competitors" might seem a strong word, libraries are increasingly in competition with a dizzying array of online information resources and services. At Penn State, several of the many units operating under the banner of information technology were working in 2001 to develop and enhance two separate products: the Penn State Portal and Angel Courseware.

The Portal Project, essentially a new initiative modeled after such commercial portals as My Netscape and My Yahoo, was intended to integrate a number of university services into a single, customizable point of access for students and faculty. Angel is a courseware package developed at Indiana University/Purdue University, and it was chosen to replace our in-house course content delivery systems. At the same time, the University Libraries had formed a group to redesign our Web site to allow users to more easily access our resources and services.

We examined information about the Portal and Angel projects with the following goals in mind:

- How do we take advantage of these new technologies?

- How can we use these technologies to promote our unique resources and services?

- How can we maximize the ability of users to easily customize library resources and services?

On the basis of these observations, we put together two groups, working in collaboration with the ITS Portal and Angel teams. As our group discussions developed, we quickly realized that while the overall goal was integration, we first needed to step back and examine all of our resources and services *individually* to determine which would work best with these two very different products. The results are discussed in the following sections.

Penn State Portal

The Portal allows users to construct a page that displays information, everything from course registration to personalized Web space to local weather, through "channels" that can be added, deleted, and arranged in any order on the page by the user. The Portal group identified a wide variety of library resources, services, and locations, and organized this information into five library channels that users can add, delete, and arrange in any order on their portal home page. Users can select from among any of more than 350 online databases to include in their Library Resources channel, and select any subject or campus library home page. Other channels link to user Library Accounts; Virtual Reference, including e-mail and online chat; and a direct keyword search from the portal into the catalog.

ANGEL Courseware

Use of the Angel Courseware package has exploded since its introduction in 2001. There are currently more than 3,800 courses using Angel throughout the PSU system, with more than 2,600 faculty and 55,000 students registered. While Portal authentication is by PSU ID only, Angel interfaces with the Registrar's systems so that authentication is also limited by course enrollment.

Because Angel has a more specific function as courseware than the university portal, the Libraries initially identified two representative services that seemed to fit best with the purpose of the courseware: Course Reserves and Library subject guides (a third tool, linking to library virtual reference, was added to Angel in spring 2004).

The Reserve Reading tool, which is currently used by over 350 courses, allows faculty to activate a direct link to an existing list in the course reserves module of our online catalog. Access from the student interface is through the same tool. The tool allows instructors to integrate all reserve readings, print and electronic, into a single list. Because student ID and course information is passed automatically from Angel to the Cat, students do not need to authenticate again to access their lists.

The Library Subject guide tool helped us not only to promote library resources arranged by discipline but also to better organize a number of existing guides and develop a common template that the libraries systemwide can use when creating new guides. Faculty in Angel view a list of guides related to their course discipline and have the option to make any of these guides, created by more than 50 librarians throughout the Penn State Library system. Faculty may also request, via email link, new guides related to specific courses. Guides include research tips, links to relevant resources, and contact information that helps students identify librarians with particular subject expertise.

Although not without its challenges, the collaboration between the Libraries and ITS through the Portal and Angel projects proved fruitful and set the stage for collaboration on future enhancements and services. It has allowed the Libraries to tailor content and services to specific applications, and within contexts other than the Libraries' Web pages. Through the customized portal channels and subject research guides, collection development specialists are able to target appropriate resources to specific disciplines and promote the wealth of licensed full text content available.

> *As geography loses its primary basis for organizing libraries and as the phenomenal growth of digital content continues, libraries are challenged to identify ways to make their virtual roles visible and tangible to their campus communities.*—Wendy Pradt Lougee, Diffuse Libraries: Emergent Roles for the Research Library in the Digital Age

The library offers users an increasing array of carefully chosen content, yet with the increasing amount of information available online, simply making this content available is not enough. The library must actively engage and collaborate with other online information services, interpreted broadly, in ways that support both diversification and integration, to ensure that, wherever our users may access information in the course of their academic activities, they will also have immediate access to the most relevant library resources and services.

INTEGRATING VENDOR-BASED SYSTEMS INTO TECHNICAL SERVICES OPERATIONS

Rebecca L. Mugridge, Penn State University Libraries
Nancy Markle Stanley, Penn State University Libraries

Introduction

In this chapter we discuss Penn State's experiences integrating Web-based vendor ordering systems with the Libraries' integrated library system (ILS). We start with some background information about the Penn State University (PSU) Libraries that will provide some context for why we were interested in implementing such a process. Although we discuss why our ILS was not meeting our needs, this isn't intended to be a criticism of our ILS; rather, it will be clear that the PSU Libraries' organizational structure presents some challenges that required us to think about options other than our ILS for achieving the efficiencies we desired in our ordering processes. We discuss which features of the vendor systems appealed to us and follow that with a discussion of the steps that we took to implement these projects, including the decisions that we needed to make, testing, and training. We conclude with a brief discussion of what we've learned and some advice for vendors.

Disclaimer

Although we refer to three library materials vendors and one ILS vendor in this paper, we want to make it clear that we are not endorsing or criticizing them. They are part of *our* experiences with these projects, and are used for illustrative purposes only. We believe that the planning and implementation of these projects can be applied in projects at other institutions and with other vendors.

Background

Penn State is a land grant university with 24 campuses spread across the state. Only a few of those campuses have technical services units; primarily, technical services operations are centralized at the University Park Campus, in the acquisitions, cataloging, and serials departments. However, in some cases the campuses have been authorized and trained to initiate orders for some materials (primarily monographs) and to add them to the catalog (if they are added copies or locations). This workflow has eased some of the workload at University Park and resulted in greater autonomy and satisfaction at the campuses (and sometimes a quicker turnaround time). In 2001, the PSU Libraries migrated from a home-developed, nonintegrated library system to SIRSI Unicorn's integrated library system. This created many changes for us and caused us to rethink many of our processes and workflows. The ordering features of Unicorn are some of the factors that caused us to be interested in exploring other options. One of the biggest challenges for us has been the use of Unicorn's Z39.50 search and import program, SmartPORT. Finding a way to avoid the need to train and retrain staff in the use of SmartPORT was a significant incentive.

This chapter covers aspects of three projects. In 2002 we implemented the use of Academic Book Center's Bookbag, primarily for our non-University Park campuses. It involved ordering materials on the Bookbag Web order form, retrieving a file of records supplied by Academic according to our agreed-upon specifications, and loading them into Unicorn. This process, which took over six months to develop, test, and implement, was a positive experience and led to our investigating similar processes with other vendors with whom we do a significant amount of business.

In fall 2002 we began exploring the use of Yankee's GOBI 2 for many of our University Park firm orders. We anticipated implementing a similar workflow as with Bookbag but expanded the scope of this project to obtain PromptCat records and shelf-ready processing. We are still in the process of developing the specifications for this project, and it has been delayed slightly while we convert our Bookbag system to Blackwell's Collection Manager.

In September 2003 we received notification that Bookbag would not be supported past 60 days after the notice. We would have to convert our Bookbag ordering processes to Blackwell's Collection Manager, a similar Web-based ordering service. Because of the tight deadline, all work stopped on the GOBI 2 implementation, and we spent an intensive period of time modifying our Bookbag specifications to work with Collection Manager. We achieved our (imposed) goal of implementing Collection Manager by mid-November 2003.

Why Not Use the ILS System for Order Placement?

One might ask, and rightly so, why a library would not use its expensive integrated library system for placing orders. ILSs are designed to address a wide range of services across the entire library; therefore, it is intentionally very complex. In addition, when libraries purchase such systems, they customize them to meet a wide array of local needs by establishing policies. For example, at Penn State each location was set up as a separate library for many reasons, for example, to prevent inadvertent use of another library's fund. The complex bells and whistles that are part of ILSs are needed for many functions but perhaps not for order placement.

To place an order in our current system, one must click on several screens and complete many fields. While macro software packages help us to make the process more efficient in utilizing the ILS, frequent upgrades to the system require that macros also be updated as well. It also represents an additional software expense for every workstation. Another cost stems from the required retraining and rewriting of procedures. With more than 20 libraries, located across a wide geographic area, and more than 60 staff affected, training is a very costly endeavor in both staff time and dollar output for travel for either the trainers or trainees.

The advantage of the ILS for order placement is that it can be customized to download multiple records from another system, while doing record checking against funds, ISBNs, etc. Reports can be developed and generated for predefined errors in the download, such as "fund over expended."

Screens, Clicks, Tabs, and Scrolling in the ILS

To demonstrate the above assertions in greater detail, we have included sample screens. To place an order in Unicorn's Acquisitions WorkFlows module, one must access three or more screens and touch over a dozen fields. The completion of even a simple, straightforward order requires about 50 seconds (Figure 1).

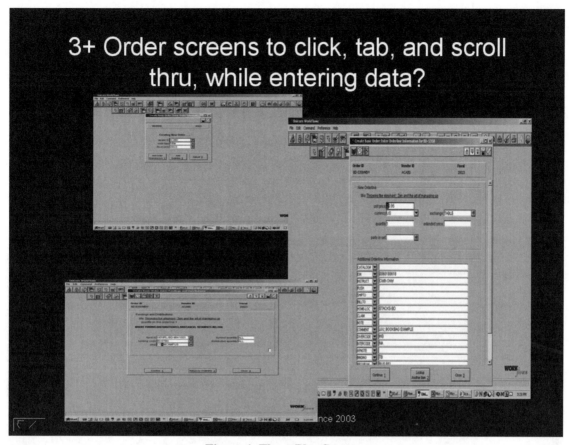

Figure 1. Three Plus Screens.

So Why Choose the Library Materials Vendors' Systems?

Library materials vendors' ordering systems and screens are often greatly simplified, utilizing a single screen and a few fields to place the order. Keep in mind, such systems do not need to accommodate a wide range of library services but instead are focused on the acquisitions process for acceptance and fulfillment of orders.

The materials vendors' systems that we have been working with have allowed us to establish defaults by login, automatically supplying constant data across order records as each new order is created, for example, location code and related fund. Such systems also contain fairly extensive order histories and status, alerting staff to potential problems, primarily with duplication. Simplicity also eases training (but more about that later in the chapter).

The materials vendors' database also helps selectors and bibliographers. They can view their considerations, possibly consult tables of contents and reviews, and establish order requests to be sent to acquisitions for placement. The order histories, which include status information such as not-yet-published and out-of-print notifications, should diminish needless duplication and requests for unavailable items. At Penn State, 25% of submitted order requests are currently returned to requesters because they are duplicates. Once selectors begin to select in the database, we hope to see this figure change. In addition, it should reduce turnaround times for ordering. Downloaded records generally include brief bibliographic and order records. The orders are created as they are downloaded. Upon item receipt brief bibliographic records can be overlaid with full-level records. Libraries can negotiate whether to use the vendors' bibliographic records or engage OCLC's PromptCat service through the materials vendor.

Sample Screens from Materials Vendors' Databases

The features of the sample screens that we point out are not unique to a particular vendor. Similar features are often available from multiple vendor databases. On the next screen from Bookbag (Figure 2), there are five basic fields to be completed. All other fields are completed based on defaults. Generally, it requires about 20 seconds to place this order.

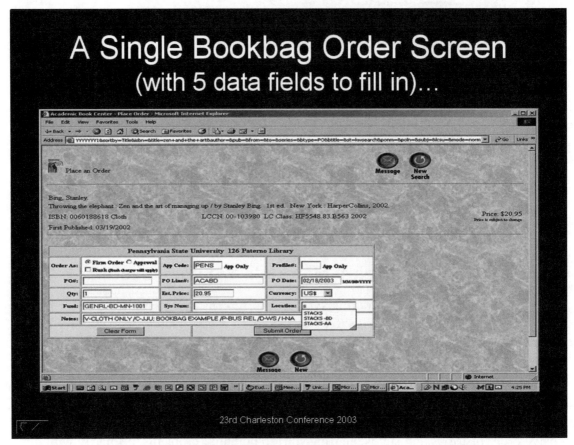

Figure 2. Single Bookbag Order Screen.

In Blackwell's Collection Manager (Figure 3), one can input a single order or simply click on a number of items in a list, placing a number of orders simultaneously. To complete the order or orders, a single screen with a few fields, some of which the content is established by predefined defaults, needs to be completed.

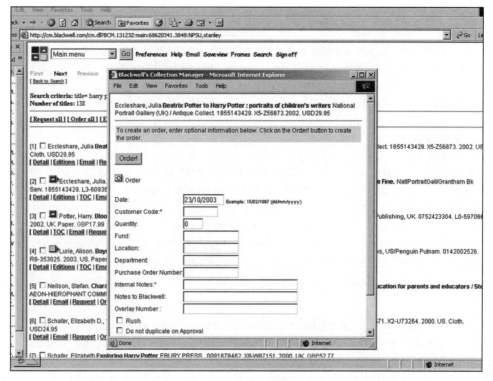

Figure 3. Blackwell's Collection Manager Order Screen.

The vendors' databases also provide the mechanism for customizing fields for local usage. Again, they are established by individual logon. In YBP's GOBI 2 (Figure 4), up to a hundred orders can be placed simply by typing in the ISBNs. We also are now in the implementation phase for utilizing this tool.

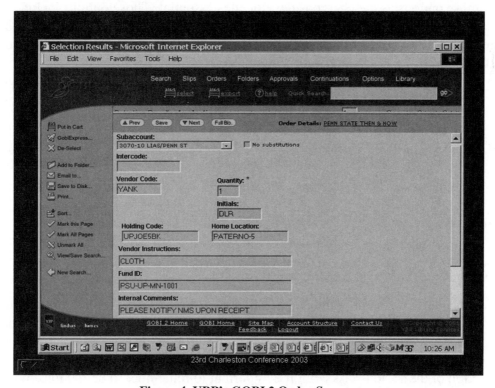

Figure 4. YBP's GOBI 2 Order Screen.

One of the most challenging parts of this process has been the assignment of purchase order numbers. By accepting the idea that the algorithm of the numbers do not need to be consistent across all orders in WorkFlows, we have been creative in producing them on the fly as the orders load, using the location codes and vendor title numbers. In fact, the type of number utilized often indicates the source of the order.

Implementation

One of the most important tasks that needs to be done at the beginning of a project is to ensure that there is administrative support. If one is planning to invest significant time and energy in a project, it is essential to have the Libraries' support. This includes having an estimated budget of the costs of the implementation and getting the administration to approve it. One way to propose a project like this is to break it down into its component parts. In our case, we estimated the costs for each of the following situations: How much will it cost to implement ordering only? How much to get cataloging records? How much to get shelf-ready processing?

Following on the heels of securing administrative support is determining who would work on the project. It is critical to identify stakeholders and include them in the process. Stakeholders include any party that will be affected by the changes under consideration. They included, in our case, four library departments: acquisitions, cataloging, systems, and collection development. Other stakeholders are the vendors, including both the materials vendors and the ILS vendor. To have a successful project, it is critical to have the right people at the table, and it is essential to have representatives from each of the stakeholder groups involved.

As the charge for the implementation group is developed, it is useful to have a clear idea of what the desired end result should be. Materials vendors offer many different options, and a review of those options as the charge is developed is essential. Those options include, in addition to placing orders, EDI, delivery of cataloging records, shelf-ready processing, and more. Finally, when the implementation group has gathered together, it is good planning to develop a strategy to address the issues and outline the project. Part of this process is determining project tasks and assigning responsibilities. For example, at Penn State, some of the assignments included

- developing an estimated cost for the delivery of cataloging records and shelf-ready materials for the items we would be ordering,

- reviewing the quality of order records delivered by the vendor,

- developing a flowchart of current workflow and a flowchart of the anticipated workflow,

- developing specifications, and

- developing and offering training sessions.

Project planning software or the creation of a Gantt chart might be helpful to monitor the progress of the implementation. We've found it to be useful to have a visual way to monitor progress in a project; it allowed us to easily report our progress to our administrators and share it with the department and others who might be interested. It is essential to determine goals for the completion of the various tasks, but it's important to remember to be flexible. What we've discovered is that everything takes longer than expected, and there are a lot of unknown variables. Some of the issues we faced during the implementation were

- a re-evaluation of the budgetary support,

- a reorganization of our systems office, and

- projects that drew away from the time systems office staff had to devote to the project. An example of the latter is that our implementation of GOBI 2 has been delayed because of the switch from Bookbag to Collection Manager.

Know What You Want

To ready the project for developers at Penn State, we really need to know, in the final analysis, exactly what we want and to communicate our needs by creating a detailed specification report. All decisions must be made firm at this point. Such decisions include who will place the orders in the vendors' databases, whether to download or export the items as requests or orders, and what the match points will be for loading the records and later for overlaying the bibliographic records at the receiving stage. One needs a clear understanding of the type of bibliographic records to be loaded at the order stage—brief or full—and whether the final records will be purchased from the vendor or PromptCat.

If the project includes receiving shelf-ready books, then separate profiles must be developed for each location or library. Ongoing budgetary needs must be provided for the cost of MARC records and shelf-ready services. Some materials vendors charge an annual subscription price for using their database. Costs must be weighed, of course, against local savings.

Testing and Evaluation

In any project of this type it is important to give testing and evaluation plenty of time and attention, enough so that everyone involved feels confident in the process and workflows. Testing and evaluation might include

- reviewing the order records to be sure that they are adequate to enter into the online catalog for however long it takes for the item and its accompanying cataloging record to arrive;

- reviewing the order records to ensure that what was asked for has been delivered by the vendor;

- reviewing the load of the order records to make sure that the load specifications developed by systems office staff are working correctly;

- reviewing the quality of the cataloging records that are received;

- reviewing the quality of the shelf-ready processing that is received;

- making sure that the cataloging records are accurately overlaying the order records (i.e., the match and replace load specifications are working as intended); and

- making sure that the load reports are accurate, for example, reporting errors accurately, etc.

Training

As we've mentioned, one of the benefits of moving to a vendor-based ordering system is that the training is often easier, especially when those being trained are at dispersed locations. In our case, having over 20 campuses, each of which needed training in how to order materials, it would have been prohibitively expensive to travel to each campus or even to have regional training. Similarly, it would have been quite expensive to bring all of those persons who need training to our University Park campus, where the trainers reside. With the much simplified ordering screen offered by Academic's Bookbag, and now Collection Manager, it was possible for us to simply create written documentation and distribute it through e-mail. Another option is to take advantage of training offered by the vendor. In our experience, we were able to use YBP's training in a "train the trainer" capacity. We had a certain number of selectors who have been enthusiastic about using GOBI 2, and we invited them to a training session, along with the implementation group. Those trainers offered to continue training other selectors. In addition, more detailed training that includes local procedures will need to be developed and presented. Online Web-based training software can be utilized; we've had some good experiences with NetMeeting and WebEx, both on the receiving and providing ends.

What We've Learned

There are always questions of whether we need to touch the records and books upon receipt. Local practices may dictate additional work. For example, in our Libraries, if an item is funded by an endowment, we add a searchable notes field to the bibliographic record, acknowledging the donor. A book plate is inserted in the item.

We have learned that we must employ our ILS system for order placement of certain items, for example, bibliographic records with multiple ISBNs, which create problems with match points and rush orders, which we treat uniquely in order to monitor them. Not-yet-published items are not placed, for the most part, until the item is published, and therefore they need special monitoring as well.

Conclusion

In closing, we would like to provide advice to materials vendors. Once libraries become dependent on your system, early notifications of changes that will affect them must be communicated (six months' notice is suggested), especially if those changes are significant. If budgets would be affected, libraries need a year before substantial changes can take place. It is important to maintain close and frequent communication with such customers.

Our advice to ILS vendors is to look at the model created by materials vendors and simplify your screen, wherever possible, for input of orders. Clear diagnostic messages are also very important to include in your product.

Finally, our advice to libraries is to focus such projects with only major vendors. It is a lot of work to implement such a process, and it's important that it be worthwhile. It may not be worthwhile for a small number of orders. However, we've found that collaboration within the library, involving acquisitions, cataloging, systems, and collection development staff, and outside the library, involving materials vendors and others, may help libraries gain productivity and increase efficiencies.

BUGGY WHIPS AND PLASMA SCREENS: TECHNICAL SERVICES—THE NEXT GENERATION

Michael P. Pelikan, The Pennsylvania State University

This chapter examines the interrelation of work that needs to be done, the tools we use to do it, the workflow imposed upon us by those tools, and how all of these interact as things evolve over time. To do this, I'm going to take us through the introduction and evolution of a few groundbreaking technologies of the previous century, to see if the patterns that emerge might provide us with any clues to our future.

Technological inventions give us new and, often, improved means to accomplish tasks we want accomplished. By its nature, each example of technology requires that we follow a particular workflow to achieve the desired result. At its simplest, this might mean that, for a knife to cut a potato, we'd best use the sharp side of the blade. As the technology becomes more advanced, however, the workflow often becomes more specific to the tool: To slice potatoes with a food processor, first we must slice them with a knife to a size that will fit into the food processor's feed tube. Next, after filling the feed tube, we employ a plunger or similar device to push the potatoes down through the food processor's spinning blades. Next year's model, although it will likely work upon a similar principle, will undoubtedly introduce some new wrinkles to the procedure we follow to achieve the desired end.

And so it is with software—take, for example, word processors. These sophisticated tools exemplify the idea that we must align our workflow to that demanded by the tool. I'm sure that we've all had the experience of moving from an old familiar word processor into a brand new, "improved" one. Such transitions can be very painful—indeed, one might come away concluding that word processors are so-named for their grim ability to process our carefully chosen words much as a food processor handles our carefully chosen potatoes!

Now we'll turn to the tasks we employ our technology to perform. I have the recurring impression that it becomes very easy to perceive the tasks we're trying to accomplish and the workflow our tools require us to use as very nearly the same thing. Put another way, it becomes very easy to let the distinction between the tasks we're trying to accomplish on the one hand, and the workflow our tools require us to use on the other, to become blurred. In other words, many of the things we actually spend our time doing are, indeed, things that we would have to do regardless of the technology we employ—but there are many things we do that are, in fact, the result of the tools we employ, rather than a natural characteristic of the essential tasks we work to accomplish.

In addition, as our tools evolve (which they seem ever to do), the steps we are required to take to accomplish our tasks change also. Often, things that we had to do to accomplish something no longer are necessary, or in fact are replaced by strange, new things we must do to achieve the same desired end result.

What's more, if we draw the idea of what we might term "user interface as metaphor for workflow" into the scene, the picture can become downright complex and, I hope you'll agree, worthy of examination.

To clarify the distinctions between these interrelated concepts, let's use the cellular telephone as an example. The rapidity with which these extremely advanced-technology devices have swept into the marketplace, becoming commodity items, has been breathtaking, vastly outpacing, for example, even the rate at which personal computers took over the workplace.

Their underlying technology is of little or no concern to the users. I believe what has made the rate of ascendancy of the cell phone so swift is that its user interface (for which, read "workflow") is completely intuitive, completely transparent, to anyone who's ever used an old fashioned home telephone. The form factor of the cellular devices is an easy conceptual step from the cordless phones at home that connect to the landline telephone network through a wireless base station. The designers of cell phones have done this intentionally—to make them as easy to use as a phone at home.

Let's not forget, however, that the underlying technology that enables me to place a call on my cell phone from Fort Sumter in Charleston Harbor to a person in State College, Pennsylvania, or Valdez, Alaska, or Rome, Italy, is entirely, radically different from what was used to accomplish voice communications just a few years ago. The user interface has been preserved not because the technology demanded it but because it eased the path of transition for the user. Now, having made the conceptual leap from placing a call from the telephone in our kitchen to placing a call from anywhere we happen to be, we are ready for the complete transformation in available user interfaces that, I'm sure, the product designers have in store for us. It has become almost natural to see someone walking down the street with a tiny phone clamped to one ear, speaking as if the party on the other end of the line was hard of hearing. More jarring, perhaps, has been the recent emergence of people using hands-free headsets plugged into the phones clipped to their belts. These worthy characters appear to be walking down the street carrying on a loud conversation with nobody—a sight to which I'm sure we will eventually become accustomed.

We might extract several observations from all this. For now, let's just say that it is the form factor or user interface given the technology by its designers that plays a large part in the degree and rate of acceptance the technology gains—perhaps in proportionate measure to the functionality of the technology itself. How proportionate? That depends upon how important the functionality itself is. If a new technology provides a radical leap forward in functionality, early adopters have proven that they'll put up with some terrible user interfaces, as long as they gain access to that new functionality—as our next case will illustrate.

The other point to keep in mind as we move into this next case is the distinction between the workflow elements that are a result of the user interface and those aspects of a system's functionality that would remain the same regardless of the design decisions made along the way (but more about that a little later).

For our next case, we turn to the horse-drawn carriage. This form of conveyance was ubiquitous up through the end of the nineteenth century and into the early part of the twentieth century.

Let's talk about form factor as it relates to the horse-drawn carriage. Its highlights included the use of four wheels (typically), a seat permitting the driver to face in the direction of travel, reins of sufficient length to permit the driver to give directional commands to the horse, etc. One small but important feature of the user interface was the buggy whip. This comprised a handle on a stiff, somewhat springy shaft of wood or metal with a length of leather whip at the end. A driver could use this tool to augment the level of communications with the horse permitted by the reins and/or voice.

It proved desirable, eventually, to provide a convenient place to store the buggy whip when not in use—one that would keep it out of the way yet permit ready access to it if needed. This device was the buggy whip holder. A minor but measurable industry grew up to manufacture these buggy whips and buggy whip holders. A search of online antique dealers (or even eBay) will quickly turn up surviving examples. The buggy whip and its use, the holder, the knack of grabbing it quickly and using it when needed, all were central aspects of the user interface, and the workflow, of the horse-drawn carriage. These, in part, shaped how a person perceived and understood the technology involved in personal conveyance. The industries that built them lasted for a while but ultimately folded when the metaphor, the user interface, underwent a dramatic change.

The source of this change was a new machine—one that took the basic form factor of the horse-drawn carriage and added to it a mechanical source of motive power to replace the horse. The early examples of this new machine looked for all the world like a horse-drawn carriage without the horse. Because it is a prevailing rule that people encountering something new will explain it to themselves in terms of something they already know, the first widespread name for the new machine was the "horseless carriage."

At first the numbers of the new machines were few; they were really the playthings of the rich enthusiast. The manufacturers and purveyors of horse-drawn carriages were sanguine, their futures unthreatened. The buggy whip holder makers kept making buggy whip holders. All was well until Henry Ford said, "I'm going to build a motorcar for the great multitude," and then did so.

This, of course was the Ford Model T. You could say that the Model T was the Apple II of the automotive world—just as it was said that the Apple II was the Model T of the personal computer world.

Here at last was an "Auto-Mobile"[1] for the common person. Here, also, we find a stunning example of the lengths to which people are willing to go with a nightmarish user interface on a piece of technology if the functional payoff is great enough.

The Model T has survived to this day in sufficient numbers that there are Web sites devoted to helping the modern enthusiast adjust to the demands it places upon a would-be driver's dexterity and kinesthetic logic. From one such site we find the following description of the array of pedals and levers confronting the owner-operator of a Model T:

> There are three pedals on the floor, two levers on the steering column, and one floor lever to the left of the driver. The floor lever is neutral while in the upright position, second gear when in the forward position while the leftmost pedal is not depressed, and emergency brake when all the way back.
>
> The leftmost pedal is first gear while depressed, second gear if the floor lever is forward when released. The middle pedal is reverse gear and the rightmost pedal is the brake. The right lever on the steering column is the gas, and the other lever is the spark advance.
>
> The brakes function using bands which constrict the transmission, unlike a modern car which uses brake calipers attached directly to the wheels.[2]

All of this would be very useful, if you could get the machine started. If there was a single aspect to the Model T's design that prevented it from truly becoming a machine that could be used by practically anyone, it was this one inescapable fact: To start the engine you had to use a hand-crank. This required strength, dexterity, and practice. Once again, the steps involved have been painstakingly enumerated on the World Wide Web, and a quick search or two will provide you with a detailed description of the process. Suffice it to say that the proper procedures had to be followed at all times. One false move and the crank could kick back and break your thumb, if not your arm. This was more than enough to ensure that even if many families bought a Model T, not many members of the family got to operate it!

It wasn't until 1912 that the technical breakthrough that was needed was finally introduced. Here again the tale is recounted in a modern retelling on an antique automobile enthusiast's site:

> Henry Leland, the head of General Motors' Cadillac division learned of the death of an associate that had resulted from an accident involving the hand-cranked starting of an automobile. The associate been driving and had stopped to help a woman whose car had stalled. Her car backfired as he was trying to start it, breaking his arm in two places. While recuperating in the hospital he developed pneumonia and died.
>
> Leland assigned two engineers, Charles Kettering and William Chryst, to tackle once and for all the problem having to hand-crank engines to start them. Kettering and Chryst had come to GM along with its recent acquisition of the Dayton Engineering Laboratories Company (DELCO) who had developed a small high-torque electric motor, originally with the idea of replacing the hand crank common on the cash registers of the day.
>
> Two months later, Kettering and Chryst demonstrated their system to Cadillac. More than just an electric motor to replace the crank, the system included a battery to power the starter motor, a generator to charge the battery, and an electrical ignition system for the engine to replace the magneto system relied on up to now. Even in light of modern improvements, what Kettering and Chryst had designed for the 1912 Cadillac was essentially the prototype for the electrical system of every modern automobile that followed, right up to the present day.[3]

The point to take away from this example is this: While the basic functionality of a radically new device may be sufficient to initiate user adoption of the technology, it is often a second-generation or later improvement addressing some fundamental flaw in the system or providing a needed refinement that enables the technology finally to achieve widespread acceptance.

Over time, the user interface of the automobile has become, to a large extent, standardized. In addition, while the superficial form of the controls may differ, the underlying functions they perform are now widely enough understood that most people who are familiar with one automobile are able to operate another without too much difficulty. One knows that there has to be a way to turn on the headlights, or lower the windows, or operate the windshield wipers. The process of acclimating oneself to a new car is to look for the means to perform the functions that we know must be there.

Let us turn next to one more prevalent technology that attained maturity in the twentieth century: the technology for the recording and reproducing of sound.

An 1878 *Harper's Magazine* carried a full-page illustration of Thomas Edison's amazing new invention. It shows him operating the device (by turning a hand-crank, a fact upon which we probably needn't dwell) and speaking into it, then depicts its reproduction of the words he had just spoken—perhaps his rendition of "Mary had a little lamb," which, most agree, were the first words ever recorded and reproduced.

Edison knew he had a potential winner in this new system and turned his attention immediately to patenting it and marketing it. An early printed advertisement shows Edison looking out of the page, making eye contact with you, the reader. His expression is one of confidence, his message, above his signature, reads, "I want to see a phonograph in every American home."

The user interface of the early phonographs was fundamentally different from those we may remember growing up with. The main differences all result from the fact that the early units employed no electrical amplification of the sound. Instead, there was a horn, often very ornate, working along the same principle as a megaphone to make the sound audible. For those who wished to listen in private, the horn could be removed and in its place an India rubber tube could be fitted. The photographic archives at Menlo Park as well as the Library of Congress and the Smithsonian contain many examples of these early units, including some wonderful shots of dignified folks listening gravely to a musical performance or stirring oration, holding India rubber tubes to their ears.

The acoustic, nonelectrical nature of the early phonographic technology extended into the recording studio as well. Here, enormous horns, often several of them, sometimes many feet in diameter and extending in length across the room, took up positions later to be occupied by microphones. The singers or instrumentalists had to project their performance directly into these horns and give it everything they had, since the physical power needed to vibrate the needle that cut the groove in the record had to come solely from their own sheer loudness.

There was another aspect to these early recordings, one that might warm the heart of today's recording company executives. At least at the start, there was no technology to enable the large-scale reproduction of a cylinder. This meant that there was no master cylinder from which all others were copied; indeed, there was essentially no way to produce a copy of a recording. The modern observer wonders, how did they produce recorded cylinders in sufficient numbers to make a go of this as a business? The answer lay in more mechanical ingenuity. The recording studios developed elaborate machines that essentially ganged a number of cylinder mechanisms together. Each cylinder required its own network of acoustic horns to feed in the sound. In the photo archives mentioned above there are examples of arrays of 13 horns arranged together, virtually a wall of horns, to feed 13 cylinders. Standing directly opposite the wall of horns there could be a brass band made up of musicians who were employees of the studio. The recording technicians would get the machines rolling and the band would perform a march—just two or three minutes' worth, for that was all the cylinders could hold. Then the technicians would exchange the recorded cylinders for fresh, uncut cylinders and the band would play the march once again, producing 13 recordings for each playing of the march. It could take days to repeat this process enough times to fulfill demand.

Now we're back to workflow—for notice, please, how different the working processes in the recording studio of 1910 were from those of the later years of electrical, stereophonic, high fidelity recording studios. And yet, you see, some processes were nearly the same: Even to the present day, some aspects of the recording process have gone fundamentally unchanged. For example, then as now, the musicians have to be arranged physically and oriented in relation to the sound pickups such as to achieve a natural, well-balanced sound. The moment of hush before the technicians start the recording, the cue to the musicians to begin, the intense concentration of the all involved during the "take," the silence that follows as the recording is checked—all of these are much the same today as they were then.

This illustrates how there are aspects of any working process that remain the same, that are unaffected by the evolutions and upheavals in the technology employed to achieve results. Many aspects of workflow are the product of the technology, but some are inherent in the process, lasting and independent of the technology employed.

By way of transition to our next example, a well-known leader of a major modern technology firm recently made the following comment during a luncheon address in Detroit, Michigan: "My daughter and I were walking down the street and I said, 'Let's go over to the record store.' And she said, 'What's a record?' " The speaker was Bill Gates, chairman of Microsoft, which leads us neatly into the last segment of this discussion.

The vast majority of recordings produced today are born-digital; that is, the recorded content is sampled from analog to digital almost as soon as it can be captured from the microphone. From that stage in the process forward, the recording, editing, storage, access, reproduction, and manufacturing all employ digital systems built upon common root technologies, platforms, and operating systems. The same born-digital revolution extends to the words we write into journal articles and books, to the still images captured by professional and amateur photographers alike, increasingly to the motion picture and television we see, and to a large and growing extent to the conversations we carry on over the telephone.

In 1975, within the first year of founding Microsoft, and in words strikingly reminiscent of both Ford and Edison, Bill Gates called for "a computer on every desk and in every home." In an impressively compressed span of time we've seen computers evolve from room-filling, task-built number crunchers to small, commodity-priced, general-purpose machines that can readily be configured to different purposes with the addition of specialized software and peripherals.

The machines we use have undergone a similar path of evolution as the early automobiles in many respects. The early models were crude, hand assembled, and needful of a determined, dedicated enthusiast for use. Their form factors and user interfaces varied widely, some of which were frankly awful.

Evolution has been swift. Look at portable computers, for instance. From the 30-pound "luggable" systems we've progressed to 3-pound laptops with more than 100 times the processor speed, over 1,000 times more random access memory (RAM), and 10,000 times the hard disk capacity. Today's handheld computers carry more computing power than we sent the Apollo astronauts to the moon with.

In 1993, now more than 10 years ago, Gates said in a *Boston Globe* interview: "Specifically, when the company was founded we said a computer on every desktop, and in every home. If we made a mistake in that vision, it was that we forgot to say and in every pocket and in every car and a bunch of other places as well. So we would amend it to make it more outrageous—18 years after it was first uttered and viewed with some derision by at least the broad computer industry."[4]

Gradually, conventions have developed in computer software user interfaces; voluntary, nonbinding expectations of predictable response to commonly used command forms: F1 for the help system, Esc to back out of a menu or dialog box, etc. In addition, users have become familiar with what kinds of functionality to expect in commonly used applications. Much as a driver in a new car knows that there has to be a way to adjust the seat, a word processor user knows that there has to be a way to set margins, apply paragraph formatting, set up automatic save intervals, etc.

It seems likely that the form factors will continue to undergo perpetual upheaval over time. Let's return briefly to the cell phone analogy spun earlier. The cell phone appears as a familiar form factor that disguises a massive, underlying, and completely radical transformation in the way content (in this case, chiefly two-way voice communications) is exchanged. In much the same way, the Internet, and especially the World Wide Web, have fundamentally overthrown what even a few years ago we thought was possible for the personal computer hardware that, by outward appearances, appears largely unchanged. The increased speed and computing power we now have enable us to deal with the content we gobble up from the Internet, but it is the Internet itself that has given content providers the means to feed us (for which, read "sell us") not just written and printed text but audio and video on demand. The sheer scope of this change is only beginning to emerge.

In the most important respects, the last remaining obstacle to the anticipated explosion in the pervasiveness of this content distribution model is found in the still-emerging systems needed to handle the management of digital assets; the arbitration of digital rights; and the transactions of access requests, fulfillment, royalties distributions, copyright protections, etc. The present situation is in every way analogous to the pre-1912 days when we had the basic platforms worked out, but the lack of an alternative to the physical demands of the starter crank held back universal access to the power of the automobile.

All locked together under a growing pile of acronyms we find the beginnings of systems to address this. A television producer will want a world in which the use of even a single frame of copyrighted video will be controlled by underlying systems that can interpret content ownership expressed in machine-readable terms, to set constraints upon acceptable use, to grant conditional permissions, and to initiate the all-important automated micro payments representing the appropriate royalty.

So it is with the published content moving from the printed page to the Web. Bibliographic, technical, and administrative metadata must take the place of Byzantine, cumbersome licensing language, difficult enough to interpret in human-readable form, and instead find expression in machine-readable code. Once achieved, this will make electronic content essentially self-describing and self-reporting, able to "phone home" to report routine access, usage, and citations. We clearly need to move beyond IP range licensing and toward user-group licensing, requiring breakthroughs not only in *authentication* (knowing who someone is) but also in *authorization* (what they're permitted to do) as well as *certification* (your system can believe my system when it says that Michael Pelikan is a Penn State eduperson faculty librarian home-based at University Park).

It's all very complex. To say blithely, "Well, we'll do it with metadata" would be like a team of NASA designers reducing the tasks that faced them after John Kennedy's 1961 challenge to reach the moon by the decade's end by saying, "No problem, we'll do it with titanium."

And make no mistake—the whole panoply of competing concepts and interests collected into the humble phrase "Digital Rights Management (DRM)" *is our moon shot!*

Ultimately, the technical systems that handle all of this will have to recede from the desktops and into the networks themselves—perhaps down to ownership signatures at the packet level of network transport—analogous to becoming part of the OSI model itself.[5]

We've gone through this entire discussion without using the term that has come into common use to describe this new library we're hoping to build. Recall our discussion about the transition from horse-drawn carriage to automobile. In terms of terminology, there was a stop along the way between those two labels. People who saw the first mechanical attempt at self-propelled transportation named what they saw on the basis of what they knew—they called it a horseless carriage. As has been observed by others in recent years, we seem to be following in the same pattern in our use of the term *digital library*.

The term *horseless carriage* was coined to describe in terms that folks of the time could understand something that was new and not yet fully evolved. *Digital library* is a term that is, in every respect, analogous to *horseless carriage*. We don't know what this thing we're now calling the digital library is really going to be like—what it will evolve into in 25 or 50 years.

I want here to assert that what we have in the digital library today is, in terms of technological advancement, somewhere between the horseless carriage and the Model T. Standing between us and the 1912 version of the digital library are all of the factors we have yet to bring together to address DRM, copyright, cross-institutional authentication, and access privileges. In other words, making the user experience seamless, achieving functional standardization of the interchange of administrative, technical, bibliographic, and transactional data needed to pull all of this off—these are entirely analogous to achieving what Kettering and Chryst accomplished in 1912 with the introduction of an electric starter and unified electrical system for the automobile.

We have some idea of what we have to do to build it. We know that the resulting product is not necessarily going to look entirely like what we think of as a library today. Inescapably, along with the underlying technologies, our workflows will continue to undergo change.

And yet, those eternal issues of librarianship, all of the arts and sciences captured in the phrase "the organization of information for purposes of retrieval," that have endured already, ever the same regardless of workflow or interface, seem likely to remain at the center of our profession.

My point here is that by the time today's toddlers are meeting in Charleston, it would be my guess that solutions to the thorny issues we now address as obstacles to the achievement of what we call today the "digital library" will not only have been solved, but those solutions will have been implemented on a level as fundamental to our basic network architecture as those issues addressed in the OSI Reference Model: They will have receded "into the wall" and become part of the basic infrastructure.

Notes

1. The American public eventually settled upon the word "auto-mobile," which in turn devolved to the nonhyphenated form. Here I must credit my sister Miriam Ruth Pelikan-Pittenger, a classicist, for pointing out to me that this compound word combines Greek and Latin roots; were the word to have come strictly from the Latin the machine would have been called the "ipsimobile," whereas from the Greek it would have been the "autokineticon."

2. http://www.modelt.ca/background-fs.html.

3. The source for the description paraphrased here is a narrative on the history of General Motors found on the Antique Auto Club of America's site at http://www.aaca.org/autohistory/05.html. One inevitable outcome of this was that the manufacturing of hand-cranks ultimately went the way of the buggy whip holder. Perhaps a few of the more resilient entrepreneurs survived by changing with the times, making and marketing new accessories over the years: first the clear plastic seat covers, then perhaps the nodding, winking cat for the rear shelf, then retooling to make storage units for eight-track tape cartridges, then cassettes, then CDs, and now finally graduating to cup holders in the iced latte era.

4. "Bill Gates, Evangelist Microsoft Chairman Preaches the Gospel of the Information Highway," *Boston Globe*, City Edition, October 20, 1993.

5. A Google search on the term "OSI Reference Model" will fetch the casual reader more than he or she may wish to know in detail about the underlying architecture of the networks we use every day. About as good a layperson's introduction as any can be found at http://computer.howstuffworks.com/osi.htm/printable.

LIBRARY ACQUISITIONS WEB SITES MADE FEASIBLE: GOALS, DESIGN, SOFTWARE, TECH SUPPORT, AND WORKFLOW

John Riley, Eastern Books
Antje Mays, Winthrop University

Program Summary

Library acquisitions Web sites are a growing presence among publicity methods geared at user communities. Who uses such Web portals? For whom should they be designed? How complicated it is to design a good Web site? Is professional-quality design important? Why/why not? What should be included on a Web portal? How should a Web site be designed to best represent the content with the intended degree of effectiveness? Who should be responsible for this site? What do small libraries not blessed with large IT pools do? How do large libraries keep the design process from being compartmentalized into too many IT hands?

Elements of Good Web Design: Dos and Don'ts—Issues

- **Style sheets/design conformity:** Depending on your organization's Web design and media relations policy, a library acquisitions Web site can experience huge variations of stylistic freedom. Be sure to check for any style compliance issues before investing much effort and time in your site.

- **Staff pictures**: Personable or capricious? Fun? Or personal safety risk for victims of abuse and/or stalking?

- **Group photos:** Staff changes make initial group photos obsolete.

- **Organization and design**: Does the site's organization visually represent the information presented? Keep the design clean. Minimize clutter by resisting the temptation to pack maximum information on one page.

- **Content:** What should be included? Let ongoing projects and acquisition staff's information needs be your guide, especially in the beginning.

Technical Aspects

- **Scripts:** Are they universally supported? If not, they will generate unwelcome script errors on viewers' screens.

- **Software:** To start, see what software is available to choose from your university's or parent organization's licenses. There is no "right" or "wrong" software. Choose the software that best supports your workflow. If several people with differing levels of technical skill share site maintenance, choose a user-friendly "what you see is what you get" editor such as Netscape Composer or Frontpage.

- **Technical support:** How much technical support can you expect from library systems and/or organizationwide computing? Acquisitions teams with more technical expertise can fill the knowledge gap when computer departments do not offer much support. However, in the absence of a readily available local pool of technological sophistication, delays and disappointments can be minimized by keeping the Web site simple.

- **New acquisitions data and book lists:** Be careful with vendor-specific performance data, to avoid negative reactions. For new acquisitions lists with live links to the actual catalog record, Excel/Access programming and Expect Script take much of the "manual labor" out of generating the live Web lists. Information on Expect Script (and the downloadable script itself) is available at http://expect.nist.gov/.

- **Linkages:** Is the acquisitions site easy to find from the library's main page, or is it "buried?"

Workflow Issues

- **How much work is involved?** Initial setup and design groundwork are time-consuming, and planning stages can take several months. However, maintenance and content update is low—one hour per week or less on average.

- **Workflow:** Start small, begin with an electronic file already on hand, use software that is easy to use, and tap IT for specific knowledge. Some libraries start with a committee but disband the committee after the design work is done, and site maintenance goes to the department.

Point of Interest—Other Than Staff, Who Else Is Looking at the Site?

- **Acquisitions sites as recruiting tool:** Thoroughly minded candidates look at the Web site of their target library to get a feel for workflow, procedures, "who does what," and the collection development philosophy.

- **Helpful hints for acquisitions practitioners at other institutions:** Links to currency converters, vendors for materials by format and/or geographic regions, and acquisitions and gift policies often provide inspiration and how-to-do-it examples to outside libraries seeking to improve their own processes.

- **Vendors:** Identify the most fruitful library contact information by gleaning an idea of workflow and processes.

Webography

- MTSU Acquisitions—http://www.mtsu.edu/~vvesper/acq.html

- Technical Services Unlimited (Virginia Beach Public Library; cosponsored by UCSD)—http://tpot.ucsd.edu/TSU/. Good example of collaborative effort.

- Trinity College, Library Technical Services—http://www.trincoll.edu/depts/libtech/

- University of Florida—http://www.clas.ufl.edu/CLAS/american-universities.html. Links for American universities

- University of Northern Iowa, Rod Library Acquisitions—http://www.library.uni.edu/acq/.

- University of Virginia, Acquisitions Department—http://www.lib.virginia.edu/acquisitions/.

- Winthrop University Library Acquisitions Portal—http://faculty.winthrop.edu/maysa/AcqTools/AcqDept_VerifyTitles.html.

U sers are why our libraries exist, and why publishers publish. Products are designed based on user behavior. The impact of user behavior based on subject discipline informs the market and provides sound implications for electronic resources and print preferences.

NOT ALL USERS ARE ALIKE: HOW DO AGE AND PRODUCTIVITY AFFECT USER BEHAVIOR?

Peter B. Boyce, Maria Mitchell Association and American Astronomical Society
Carol Tenopir, University of Tennessee
Donald W. King, University of Pittsburgh

Abstract

A survey of the usage patterns of astronomers shows large differences in behavior between the productive and not-so-productive cohorts. The productive half of the user community accounts for 80% of the publications, exhibits no dependence of usage upon the age of the user, and is willing to master difficult procedures to use online services. The less productive set of users show usage decreasing with age. The entire cohort overwhelmingly prefers the journals over the e-print servers as a source of definitive information. Within the astronomical community the e-print servers are used as a tool for keeping aware of recent developments but not as a substitute for the journals.

In 2002 the authors conducted a survey of the membership of the American Astronomical Society (AAS) to assess the usage patterns of astronomers with regard to the electronic information services available to the astronomical community.[1]

Astronomy makes a perfect test bed for studies of this sort because it is a small discipline with a limited number of core journals. Gomez shows that 90% of the cited articles are published in 11 journals.[2] In addition, astronomers have had electronic journals since 1995[3] and a well-linked electronic information system since 1997.

The astronomical community has a well-established and comprehensive set of information resources consisting of feature-rich electronic journals, a searchable abstract database, an archive of full text backfiles for all the core astronomical journals, and several international databases holding tabular data and catalogs of information. All the services are interlinked and interoperable, providing an integrated resource for most of the usual information needs of the users. This system has been available in its current form since 1997.

The Astrophysics Data System (ADS) is a NASA-supported service set up for the astronomical community (http://adswww.harvard.edu).[4] The central component of the ADS is a searchable database of abstracts of the astronomical literature deep linked (one click) to full text of the articles. The coverage is virtually complete for the core literature in astronomy. The second component of the ADS is a store of full text, page-image scans of nearly all the important astronomical literature, complete from page 1 of volume 1. As well as being linked to the full text, the ADS abstracts are linked to data tables, reference lists, future citations back to the article, abstracts of similar articles, etc. As will be seen, this is a powerful system for the users.

This chapter focuses on the behavior patterns of the more productive users. We measure productivity by the number of papers submitted to refereed journals. In our survey, we asked how many papers they had submitted to a peer-reviewed journal during the previous two years. According to our survey, the average astronomer submits 2.8 articles per year. This is not a true measure, since many of these articles have multiple authors. Abt has done several analyses of published astronomical literature.[5] Making appropriate corrections for multiple authors, percentage of astronomers in graduate school, etc., our results are consistent with Abt's earlier results—a publication rate of somewhat more than one-half refereed paper per year per astronomer.

We divided our survey responses into three productivity classes, as shown in Table 1. The characteristics of these three productivity classes are shown in Figure 1. The productive astronomers make up 46% of our sample but produce 78% of the published literature and account for 61% of the reading. The productive astronomers read twice as many articles per month as the cohort of astronomers we have labeled nonproductive.

Table 1. Definition of Productivity Classes.

Label	Definition
Non-Productive	< 1 refereed articles per year
Average	1–2 refereed articles per year
Productive	>2 refereed articles per year

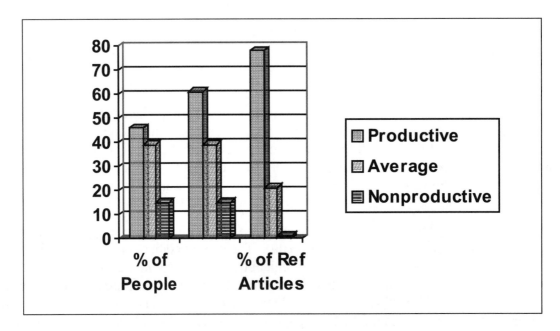

Figure 1. Characteristics of Productivity Classes Showing the Percent of the Population, the Percent of the Total Usage of the ADS, and the Percent of Refereed Articles Contributed by Each Class.

In the AAS survey we asked about awareness and usage of various electronic information services. The central role played by the ADS's abstract database is apparent from Figure 2. Every productive user knows about and uses the ADS, the searchable abstract database. One of the surprising results of our survey was the high use of electronic resources by older astronomers. Figure 2 demonstrates this for usage of the ADS. In particular, productive astronomers of all ages use the online abstract database. Even for the less productive (and less active) users there is very little falloff of usage with age. The left-hand set of bars shows the percentage of respondents who are aware of the service, and the middle set shows the percentage of respondents who use the service. The right-hand set of bars in Figures 2a and 2bshows the percentage of those astronomers aware of the service who actually use it.

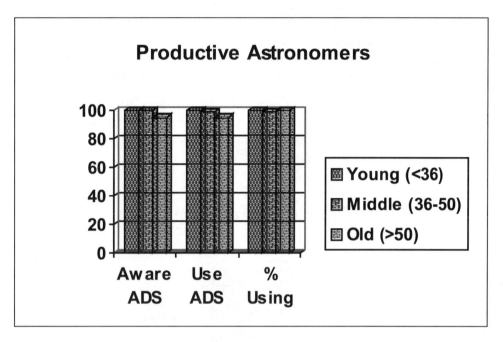

Figure 2a. Percent of Productive Astronomers Aware of and Using the ADS. The right-hand set of bars shows the percentage of astronomers aware of the ADS who actually use it.

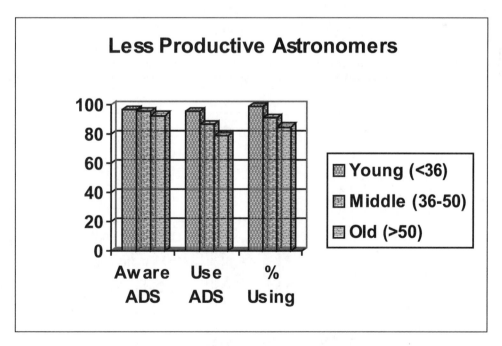

Figure 2b. Nonproductive and Average Astronomers Aware of and Using the ADS. Note the small decline in awareness and usage with age among the less productive astronomers.

Note that all the productive users both know about and use the ADS regardless of the age of the user. Among the less productive astronomers, the older users are slightly less likely than their younger colleagues to use the ADS. However, the fact that 80% of the oldest and least productive astronomers use the ADS confirms the importance of the ADS to the astronomical community.

The astronomical community has a long tradition of using paper abstracts, and in today's electronic environment, much of the community has turned to using the ArXiV e-print server (http://arxiv.org). Since the manuscripts remain on the ArXiV server after they are published, we adopt the term *e-print* to refer to the electronic manuscript both before and after publication. Figure 3 shows the percentage of astronomers who have used the ArXiV in the past year.

While there are other e-print services available, astronomers almost exclusively use the ArXiV server. Other services used in astronomy tend to be selective services limited to small subspecialties. Non-ArXiV usage is less than a few percent, so we take the ArXiV usage as representative of astronomers' work patterns.

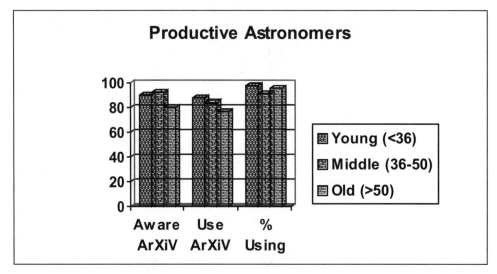

Figure 3a. Percent of Productive Astronomers Aware of and Reading E-prints on the ArXiV Server. The right-hand set of bars refers to the percent aware of the service who actually use it.

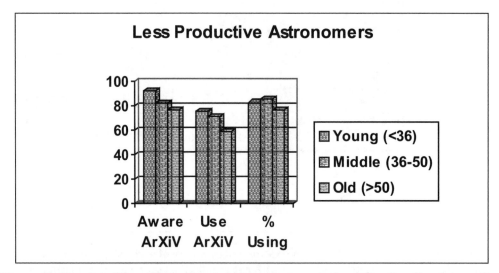

Figure 3b. Percent of Less Productive Astronomers Aware of and Reading E-prints on the ArXiV Server. The decline in usage with age is larger than it is for the ADS service.

The awareness of the ArXiV e-print server among the productive astronomers is marginally smaller than awareness of the ADS, but among the people who are aware of it, the percent reading from the ArXiV server is very high and independent of age. However, among the nonproductive users, the usage does fall off with age.

If we now consider the submission of articles to the ArXiV server, we see a more pronounced version of the same pattern. Figure 4 shows that productive astronomers are somewhat less likely to submit an article than to read from the ArXiV server. However, there is still very little dependence of usage upon the age of the user.

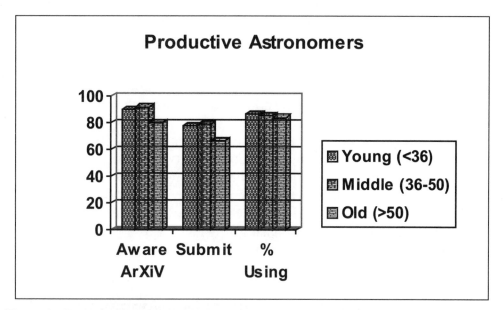

Figure 4a. Percent of Productive Astronomers Aware of the ArXiV E-print Service, Who Have Submitted an Article to It in the Previous Two Years, and of Those Aware of the Service Who Have Actually Submitted an Article in the Previous Two Years.

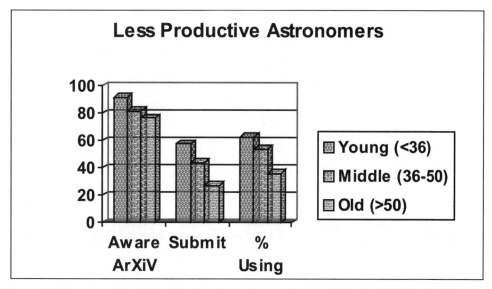

Figure 4b. Percent of Less Productive Astronomers Aware of the ArXiV E-print Service, Who Have Submitted an Article to It in the Previous Two Years, and of Those Aware of the Service Who Have Actually Submitted an Article in the Previous Two Years.

On the other hand, the less productive users are much less likely to have submitted an article to the ArXiV server, and there is a strong dependence upon the age of the user. Only one-third of the nonproductive users over age 50 have submitted an article within the previous two years. In part this result may be due to the difficulty of submitting articles. The ArXiV is not known as being a user-friendly service, particularly for the new user. Within the astronomical community it has been referred to as a "user-belligerent" service. From our results, it seems clear that the productive user will do whatever is necessary to use the service, regardless of age. The less productive users, even the younger ones, do not feel as motivated to learn how to use a difficult service.

Ease of use is not the only factor governing usage. The perceived value of a resource will also affect the usage patterns. Our survey asked about the value of both the peer-reviewed journals and the non-reviewed e-print servers.

We gave the respondents five categories, ranging from worthless to critical to their work. Figure 5 shows the percentage of respondents who found the journals and the e-print servers either "Very Useful" or "Critical" to their work. Figure 5a shows the responses for the purpose of keeping up with recent developments. Here the journals are preferred slightly over the e-print server even though there is a time lag of several months between when the manuscript is submitted and when it is published. As a side note, over two-thirds of the respondents wait until an article is accepted by a peer-reviewed journal before they post it on an e-print server. This significantly reduces the time between when an article is posted to the ArXiV e-print server and when it appears in the journal and reduces somewhat the value of the e-print server as a means of keeping up with new developments.

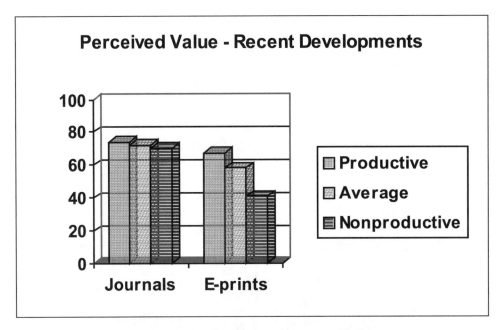

Figure 5a. Perceived Value of Information Resource. Percent of respondents rating resource as "Critical" or "Very Useful" for keeping up with recent developments.

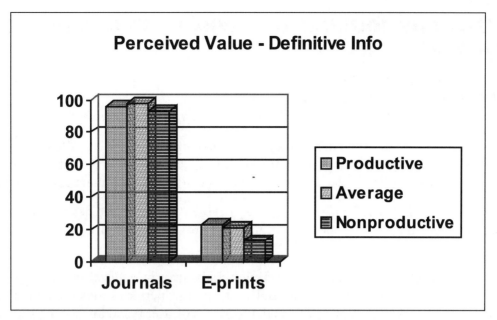

Figure 5b. Percent of Respondents Rating Resource as "Critical" or "Very Useful" for Obtaining Definitive Information. Note that astronomers prefer the journal for definitive information by an overwhelming factor. The use of e-prints seems to be reserved for rapid communication.

Figure 5b shows the responses for users seeking definitive information. It is immediately obvious that the peer-reviewed journals are the service of choice for finding definitive information—which we defined as information older than two years.

We believe that the usefulness of the journals as exhibited in Figure 5 is the result of the journals being part of a complete information system that exists for astronomy. The combination of the journals, the searchable abstract database, the complete full text backfiles, and the online astronomical data centers provides an integrated, interoperable online resource that serves the user community better than any of the components taken alone.

Notes

1. Carol Tenopir, Donald W. King, Peter Boyce, Matt Grayson, and Keri-Lynn Paulson, Keri-Lynn. "Relying on Electronic Journals: Reading Patterns of Astronomers," *Journal of the American Society for Information Science and Technology* (in press).

2. M. Gomez, "A Bibliometric Study to Manage a Journal Collection in an Astronomy Library," in *Library and Information Services in Astronomy IV*, ed. B. Corbin, L. Bryson, and M. Wolf (Washington, D.C.: U.S. Naval Observatory, 2003), 214.

3. Peter B. Boyce, and Heather Dalterio, "Electronic Publishing of Scientific Journals," *Physics Today* 49 (1996): 42; Peter B. Boyce, "Building a Peer-Reviewed Scientific Journal on the Internet," *Computers in Physics* 10 (1996): 216.

4. Michael J. Kurtz, Guenther Eichhorn, Alberto Accomazzi, Carolyn S. Grant, Stephen S. Murray, and Joyce M Watson, "The NASA Astrophysics Data System: Overview," *Astronomy and Astrophysics Supplement* 143 (2000): 41.

5. Helmut A. Abt, "Publication Characteristics of Members of the AAS," *Publications of the Astronomical Society of the Pacific* 102 (1990): 1161; Helmut A. Abt, "Is the Astronomical Literature Still Expanding Exponentially?" *Publications of the Astronomical Society of the Pacific* 110 (1998): 210.

PATTERNS OF JOURNAL USE: WHAT ARE OUR USERS TELLING US?

Carol Tenopir, University of Tennessee
Donald W. King, University of Pittsburgh
Peter B. Boyce, Maria Mitchell Association and American Astronomical Society

There is, of course, no such thing as a monolithic "information user." We have typical groups and subgroups of users and select or design products and services that best meet these typical needs of major groups. Certain caveats underlie all of our comments and conclusions:

- *There is no one "user," only indicative user types or groups.* We design products and services for a majority of our user group or the groups and subgroups that are most readily identified.

- *User behavior is like evolution.* Sometimes it advances in a steady progression, but at other times it may be subject to fits and starts or slow periods followed by quantum leaps. Another way to express this is that patterns of user behavior may be subject to disruption temporarily or permanently by unforeseen technological innovations (for example, the Web in the mid-1990s) or world events (for example, 9/11). In most cases users' expectations build as they use and experience new things.

- And finally, whenever we talk about human behavior *we are by necessity talking about averages of groups or subsets—typical behaviors,* not every single thing every individual will ever do. The unexpected individualistic behavior is interesting but not always helpful for product design.

In spite of these caveats, we actually now know quite a bit about average and typical behaviors of our major groups through hundreds of studies conducted over the last decade. Tenopir's recent report for the Council on Library and Information Resources (CLIR) summarizes these studies and provides further details.[1]

This chapter concentrates on subject expert users: faculty and other researchers who know about their subject and about quality of sources. Clearly there are many subgroups within this main group, including different branches of science and different workplaces. For a further discussion of the differences between engineers, chemists, and others, see Tenopir et al. and King et al.[2] Boyce describes one user group, astronomers, in detail (see also previous chapter).[3] In this chapter we concentrate more on what we have learned in general about science faculty during three recent surveys. The surveys were conducted between 2000 and 2003 at the University of Tennessee, University of Pittsburgh, and Drexel University. For more details on these surveys see King.[4]

University scientists read more than almost any group except graduate students. As shown in Figure 1, on average the number of articles read by university science faculty has increased from approximately 150 articles per year in surveys done by Donald W. King in1977 to more than 216 articles per year in our 2000–2003 surveys.[5] Because scientists are reading more, they value system features and services that help them read more in not much more time. They tell us loud and clear that desktop delivery, no waiting, and no direct charges to them are important factors in e-journal use.

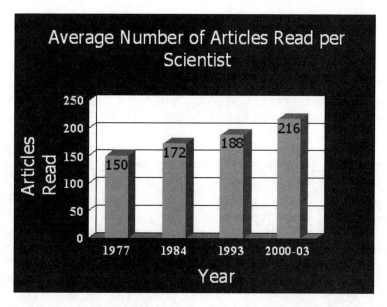

Figure 1. Average Number of Articles Read per Scientist.

There is still considerable variation among subject disciplines, with engineers reading the fewest articles per year (on average 72 articles per year), and university medical faculty the most. Total time spent reading varies as well, because engineers spend the most time per article (81 minutes per article on average), and university medical faculty read the greatest number of articles (322 articles per year on average) but in rapid fashion (spending on average 22 minutes per article).[6] Medical faculty need portable, well-organized articles for the large amount of current awareness reading they do on the run; engineers like to sit down and get their teeth into an article they choose for reading.

The number of personal subscriptions has gone down steadily for most researchers, from nearly six several decades ago to under two currently.[7] (See Figure 2.) Medical faculty still subscribe to over six paper journals, however, university faculty subscribe to more than other researchers.[8] In conjunction with the decline in number of personal subscriptions, the importance of library-provided journal articles has grown.

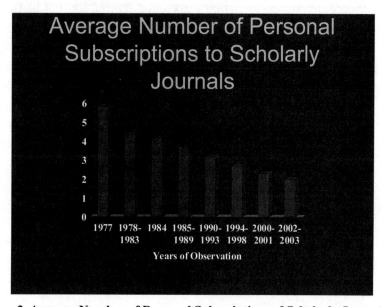

Figure 2. Average Number of Personal Subscriptions of Scholarly Journals.

Readings from library-provided articles vary from 34 to 48% in the surveys conducted at the University of Tennessee, University of Pittsburgh, and Drexel University and actually are probably much higher as faculty are often not aware of the origins of something they get on their desktop (see Figure 3). The University of Tennessee libraries, for example, did not do much branding of their electronic journal collections at the time of this survey, so faculty did not realize the role the library played in their journal access.

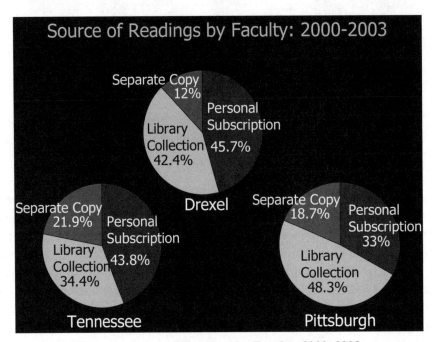

Figure 3. Source of Readings by Faculty, 2000–2003.

The number of sources for articles has increased for most scientists, so that most now rely on a variety of sources for journal articles. Most readings come from library-provided print and electronic subscriptions, from aggregator databases provided by the library, or from personal print subscriptions, but anywhere from 12 to 22% of faculty readings come from separate copy sources. Separate copies are articles divorced from a journal or from a fee-based aggregated database, including e-prints, pre-prints, reprints, articles sent by colleagues, and articles found at author Web sites or other free Web aggregators.

Personal subscription readings are still almost all in print journals; at the University of Pittsburgh and Drexel University the library readings are mostly electronic. The policy of the library can have a big impact: Drexel University implemented a policy several years ago to almost totally rely on electronic journals.[9] Pittsburgh and Tennessee have extensive print and electronic collections, but Tennessee was in transition at the time their survey was conducted in 2000–2001.

There is an even bigger variation by subject discipline, however. As can be seen in Figure 4, scientists and social scientists read much more in electronic sources for journal articles. Humanists (nonscientists) still rely print for three-quarters of their readings. It is difficult to say whether this reflects merely availability of electronic resources or preferences.

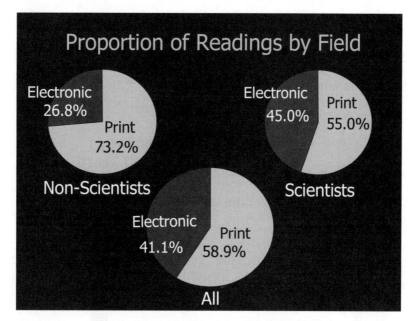

Figure 4. Proportion of Readings by Field.

About one-quarter to one-third of readings is of articles older than a year old, and these are reported to be of high value for the purpose of reading. Over time, we have found these proportions to hold true: The same percentage of older materials is read as was true in the 1970s through 1990s.[10] As shown in Figure 5, for older articles, scientists rely heavily on the library-provided sources.

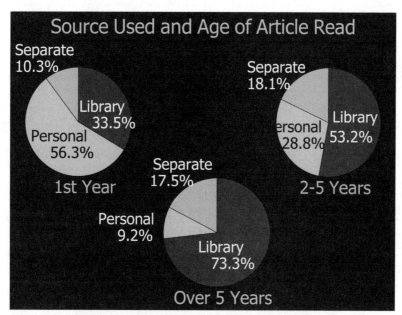

Figure 5. Source Used and Age of Article Read.

In summary, recent research reports show many things that faculty are telling us about their use of journals and e-journal alternatives.[11] We can say with confidence from the results of many research reports that:

- Faculty adopt e-resources if they are convenient, relevant, and time-saving.

- There is no one right solution for every subject discipline.

- Print is still used at times in every discipline.

- Print is still most popular for books.

- Two-thirds of readings are in the first year of publication.

- Most e-journal users print out relevant articles.

- Browsing in core journals is important, especially for current awareness.

- Searching is important for new topics, research, and writing.

- E-journal readers read in more titles than print readers, but an 80-20 rule applies.

- Reading from library-provided electronic materials is increasing (although readers may not be aware of where their electronic resources are coming from).

Notes

1. Carol Tenopir, "Use and Users of Electronic Library Resources: An Overview and Analysis of Recent Research Studies," *Council on Library and Information Resources* (August 2003) [Online], available: http://www.clir.org/pubs/abstract/pub120abst.html (accessed June 21, 2004).

2. Carol Tenopir, Donald W. King, Peter Boyce, M. Grayson, Y. Zhang, and M. Ebuen, "*Patterns of Journal Use by Scientists Through Three Evolutionary Phases,*" *D-Lib* 9, no. 5 (May 2003) [Online], available: http://www.dlib.org/dlib/may03/king/05king.html (accessed June 21, 2004); Donald W. King, Carol Tenopir, Carol H. Montgomery, and Sarah E. Aerni, "Patterns of Journal Use by Faculty at Three Diverse Universities," *D-Lib* 9, no. 10 (October 2003) [Online, available: http://www.dlib.org/dlib/october03/10contents.html (accessed June 21, 2004).

3. Carol Tenopir, Donald W. King, Peter Boyce, Matt Grayson, and Keri-Lynn Paulson, "Relying on Electronic Journals: Reading Patterns of Astronomers," *Journal of the American Society for Information Science and Technology* (in press).

4. King et al., "Patterns of Journal Use by Faculty at Three Diverse Universities."

5. Carol Tenopir and Donald W. King, *Towards Electronic Journals: Realities for Scientists, Librarians, and Publishers* (Washington, D.C.: Special Libraries Association, 2000).

6. King et al., "Patterns of Journal Use by Faculty at Three Diverse Universities."

7. Tenopir and King, *Towards Electronic Journals;* Tenopir et al., "Patterns of Journal Use by Scientists Through Three Evolutionary Phases."

8. Carol Tenopir, Donald W. King, and Amy Bush, "Medical Faculty's Use of Print and Electronic Journals: Changes Over Time and Comparison with Other Scientists," *Journal of the Medical Library Association* (April 2004).

9. Donald W. King and Carol H. Montgomery, "After Migration to an Electronic Journal Collection: Impact on Faculty and Doctoral Students," *D-Lib* 8, no. 12 (December 2002) [Online], available: http://www.dlib.org/dlib/december02/king/12king.html (accessed June 21, 2004); Carol H. Montgomery and Donald W. King, "Comparing Library and User Related Costs of Print and Electronic Journal Collections: A First Step Towards a Comprehensive Analysis," *D-Lib* 8, no. 10 (October 2002): 10. Available at http://www.dlib.org/dlib/october02/montgomery/10montgomery.html (accessed June 21, 2004).

10. Tenopir et al., "Patterns of Journal Use by Scientists Through Three Evolutionary Phases."

11. Tenopir, "Use and Users of Electronic Library Resources."

Index